IMAGES
of America

LEMOORE

On the Cover: Lemoore men show off a sign at the corner of Fox and D Streets in downtown Lemoore. Probably part of a civic promotion, the big arrow says, "On direct route to Sequoia Nat'l Park, Gen. Grant Nat'l Park, Stratford, Hanford, Fresno, Porterville, Visalia and Tulare." (Courtesy of the Sarah A. Mooney Museum.)

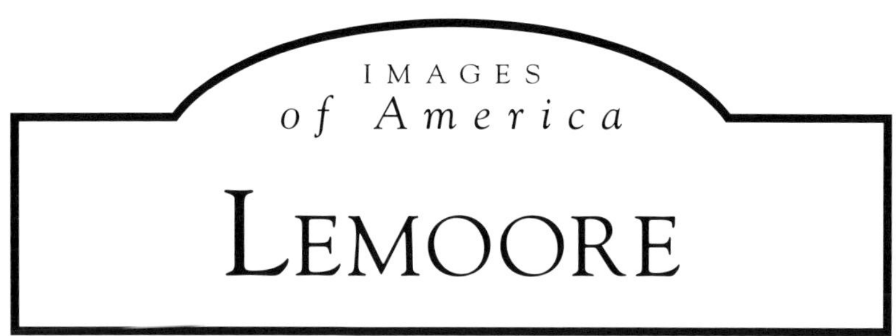

Cynthia J. Wright and
Judy Cox-Finney

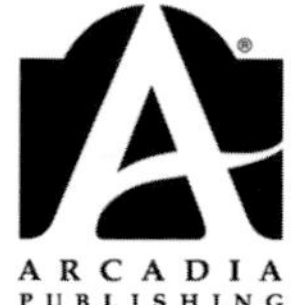

ISBN 978-0-7385-8154-5

Published by Arcadia Publishing
Charleston, South Carolina

Printed in the United States of America

Library of Congress Control Number: 2010928638

For all general information, please contact Arcadia Publishing:
Telephone 843-853-2070
Fax 843-853-0044
E-mail sales@arcadiapublishing.com
For customer service and orders:
Toll-Free 1-888-313-2665

Visit us on the Internet at www.arcadiapublishing.com

To my husband, Joe Wayne, who offered support and extreme patience when this book consumed large pieces of my time and effort over an extended period. And to my daughter, Kelly, for constant comic relief, and my son, Matt, and his new bride, Chelsea, for being impressed by my effort.

—Cynthia J. Wright

My part of this book is dedicated to my family, who helped me finish by showing respect for my work and the patience of Job, and to Cynthia for her work with the photographs. Steve Emanuels was of great help to me, and without him I would not have even attempted this project.

—Judy Cox-Finney

Contents

Foreword

I relocated to Lemoore 23 years ago, and the first thing I did was subscribe to the weekly newspaper. It had been a lifelong habit. I can remember the editor of our own weekly newspaper in Concord, California, composing an article for the next day's paper right there on his Linotype machine. I was paid 5¢ per each column inch for whatever news or gossip I could bring in. And it was in his shop where we would gather every week to put out our high school newspaper. Thus began a love of the weekly newspaper and a 25-year career in agricultural journalism.

When I began reading the *Lemoore Advance* back then, I quickly realized that someone named Judy Finney was doing most of the reporting. When I dived into learning about local history, another habit, Judy quickly became a great source of information, and we collaborated on many stories though the next score of years. We even served together on the board of the Lower Kings River Historical Society.

Editors and publishers came and went over the next few years, but the one constant was Judy. When the *Lemoore Advance* was discontinued in 2009, she hopped over to the *Hanford Sentinel* and is still reporting on Lemoore as best she can under limiting conditions.

The coauthor of this book, Cynthia J. Wright, has the distinction of being the *Lemoore Advance's* final editor—caught in the crosshairs of a communications revolution, which, sadly, includes the demise of thousands of weeklies. Her legacy may well be the publication of this book.

It is a legacy in which I gladly share. Judy's depth of knowledge of people and events combined with Cynthia's perseverance in collecting the photographs and then putting it all together has produced a photographic history and narrative of Lemoore that no other duo in town could or would have achieved.

This book brings together the largest number of photographs of the history of Lemoore ever put between two covers. And it contains the most complete outline of the town's history ever written. I say outline because nobody has ever done the complete job, and there is plenty of research out there for somebody to do. One can only hope.

That old Linotype machine I used to watch, and the ones used at the *Lemoore Advance*, are long gone. But the computers of people like Judy Cox-Finney and Cynthia J. Wright have replaced them and have served to record and preserve a terrific piece of California history.

—Steve Emanuels

ACKNOWLEDGMENTS

This book would not have been possible without the generous help of many people and organizations. We especially want to thank Steve Emanuels, a local historian, who helped us by reading through the text of the book, proofreading, and checking for accuracy. His advice and help with some rewrites were invaluable.

Sarah A. Mooney Museum volunteers, especially Steve and Lynda Emanuels, were instrumental in making this book possible. This group gave us unlimited access to the museum, allowing us free use of their historical photographs, publications, relics, and archives.

The Kings County Museum members made their historical displays available, especially of Tachi-Yokuts, which added to our knowledge of this Native American tribe. The Kings County Library has an invaluable collection of history books on Lemoore and Kings County and a Web site with historical photographs.

The area's schools have been well documented in Harold "Hoot" Gibson's *History of Kings County Public Schools, California*. The staff at the Lemoore High School District was always willing to lend us a hand tracking down the district's history and photographs.

The City of Lemoore's office staff and planning department, especially Holly Smyth, took personal time to help locate photographs of historical buildings and find historical records not easily available.

Lemoore's first responders, the Lemoore Volunteer Fire Department and the Lemoore Police Department, jumped on board and were more than eager to help with memories, photographs, and rare historical records. Special thanks to John Plourde and Ted Schlosser.

The public relations staff at Naval Air Station Lemoore, especially Melinda Larson, made it possible to find great photographs representing the station's first years. They provided materials from the base's dedication, resulting in a better understanding of the partnership between Lemoore and the U.S. Navy.

St. Peter's Catholic Church provided not only the history of their church, but also photographs of the Tachi-Yokuts and early military images. Staff and members of Lemoore Presbyterian and First United Methodist Church gave us a firm base to write about the area's churches as well as historical photographs.

Jack Stone provided photographs and information on the growth of agriculture around Lemoore. Salli Day's memories of growing up in Lemoore gave ample leads, photographs, and a better understanding of what Lemoore was like for children growing up here in the 1930s and 1940s. Eleanor Terra-Finney helped with stories about early Portuguese families living in Lemoore and what the downtown of Lemoore looked like in the 1930s and 1940s. Without the Orsaba family, much of the business history of individual stores outside of the downtown area would have been a lot harder to find. Virginia Lee gave her time and the use of family photographs, allowing a firsthand account of Lemoore's Chinatown and Asian immigrants.

It was wonderful working with area families and associations. Many residents came to us and provided leads, or maybe just a bit of Lemoore trivia. Sitting around the kitchen table and just talking about Lemoore was one of the highlights of our historical research.

The publisher, John Poultney, along with Arcadia Publishing's other staff, were professional and patient with two people who thought they knew what they were doing when they set out on this project, but found things a little more complicated than they expected.

Writing this book has been demanding, at times stressful, but always exciting. Thank you to everyone who helped and contributed.

Introduction

It was land that could be both hospitable and tough. Though it was desert most of the year, there were rivers and sloughs crisscrossing the land. Artesian wells also bubbled up at various points in the area. A large, shallow lake—the largest lake west of the Mississippi, if measured by surface area—provided food and shelter. The lake would be named Tulare Lake by early Spanish visitors, after the tule reeds (bulrushes) that flourished in its warm, shallow waters. It was located at the base of California's Coastal Mountains and in the southwestern part of what would become Kings County. In 1862, it was described as extending for 60 miles north and south and 36 miles at its widest point.

Several Native American groups lived along Tulare Lake. Before the current Native Americans lived along the shores, Paleo-Indians lived on the bounty of the lake and the surrounding land up until 8,000 years ago, disappearing for some reason 1,000 to 2,000 years before the next group of people came to live there.

Long before Spanish clerics and soldiers crossed the rolling foothills from their missions near the Pacific Ocean, groups of Native Americans, Yokuts, were making their living following herds of tule elk and some deer. They subsisted on many small animals and harvested acorns, berries, and other vegetation. The group in Kings County near what is now Lemoore was the Tachi-Yokuts.

Archeologists working for the University of California have found evidence of this group dating back at least 1,000 to 2,000 years. Never large in numbers, the Tachi-Yokuts lived along the western edge of the valley and even called parts of the Kettlemen Hills home when the heat of the valley forced them to seek cooler climes during the summer months. Although they had no written language, they left amazing baskets, stone artifacts, and rock art in the Kettlemen Hills to remind later generations of their life as hunter-gatherers.

Native Americans were giving way in the Central Valley, as in other parts of America, to the rapid expansion of European and American settlers. American settlers followed the lure of gold and later moved south into the great grazing and farming area known as California's Central Valley. Near the western edge of the valley these settlers established a small town. It would later become one of the top agricultural areas in the world and be the home of the U.S. Navy's largest inland air base. That little town is Lemoore, California, established in 1871.

Lemoore, arriving relatively late on the frontier scene, is a microcosm of the American experience. The same elements can be seen in its history that drove almost all western, and American, expansion. They include the need and desire for land, the removal of the Native American population, the introduction of rapid transport in the form of railroads, the growth of population along with the railroad, the development of roads with the introduction of Ford's automobile, and the small towns' involvement in the great wars of the 20th century. Lemoore's support of American domestic and foreign policy throughout its existence—some by sacrifice, some forced—has been a committed effort by the area's people. Much has been given by the area's military men and women to help preserve our freedoms.

Today Lemoore continues to grow and expand and help meet America's needs through vast farming, industrial, and military support. It is now a small city of 23,000 people. Lemoore provides a small-town environment with an urbanity only found in areas where longtime residents interact with a large influx of diverse people.

Descendants from the original American settlers still live in the town, some still on the farmlands their ancestors first developed for grazing and then farming. Into the mix come people who serve their country through the navy and the air station just a few miles west of Lemoore.

What follows in this book is the photographic history of a unique, but purely American, community. There are differences between Lemoore's history and the histories of other towns. This is largely because of the changes in agricultural practices and the influence of the American military complex upon the area. But it is still the history of all Americans, whether they are the native peoples, those who settled early in the west, or those who came later to add to the vast base of prosperity that became known as California's Great Central Valley. This is the history of Lemoore, California, "small-town U.S.A."

One

The Tachi-Yokuts

The Yokuts Indians were not the first group of Native Americans who inhabited the greater Lemoore area. Paleo-Indians were the first known peoples to have lived in the Tulare Lake Basin. Tulare Lake came to the margins of Lemoore in a particularly wet year.

Their serrated rock tools found on the edges of these lakes in recent years, along with other clues, told scientists these Paleo-Indians were not unlike others around the United States, all of whom disappeared for unknown reasons about 8,000 or 10,000 years ago.

After a hiatus of some 2,000 or 3,000 years, another group of distinct and separate peoples appeared in California. These were the Yokuts Indians. With several semipermanent villages, the Tachi-Yokuts lived on the northern shores of Tulare Lake.

Their earliest interactions with another culture were with the Spanish soldiers and clerics who roamed across the foothills from their Catholic missions near the Pacific Coast. Native Americans, and especially their children, were often enticed and forced to live at one of the missions. Some would escape and return to their valley homes, bringing along some horses taken from a mission. Decades of troubles would follow, not only with the Spanish, but also with the newly arrived Americans. Finally in 1858, a party headed by Justin Esrey forcibly guided about 200 Native Americans, not all Tachis, to a government reservation above Fresno at Fort Miller. They were poorly cared for there. Many of the Tachis eventually found their way back to the lake, but lived in abject poverty, bereft of their foods, culture, and traditions. In 1921, the federal government purchased 40 acres near the old Native American village of Wiu and named it the Santa Rosa Rancheria. It remains today, 7 miles south of Lemoore, and is an important feature of the town's past and present.

When gaming centers were allowed on reservations, the Tachis built the Southgate Bingo Palace in 1983. It has evolved into today's thriving Tachi Palace Hotel and Casino. Proceeds from the Palace have paid for a medical center, a school, and senior and youth centers on the Rancheria.

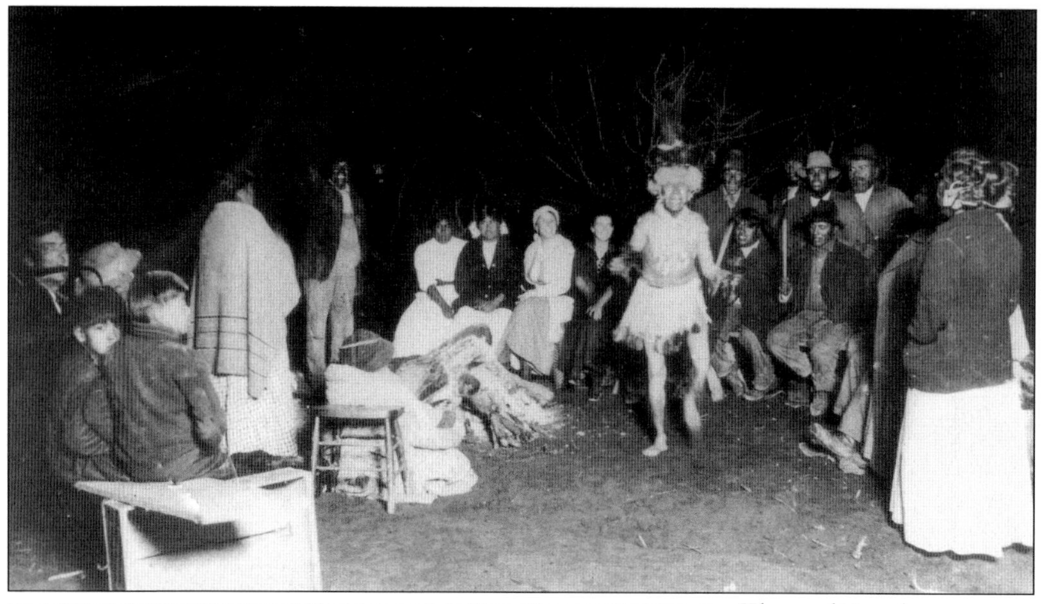

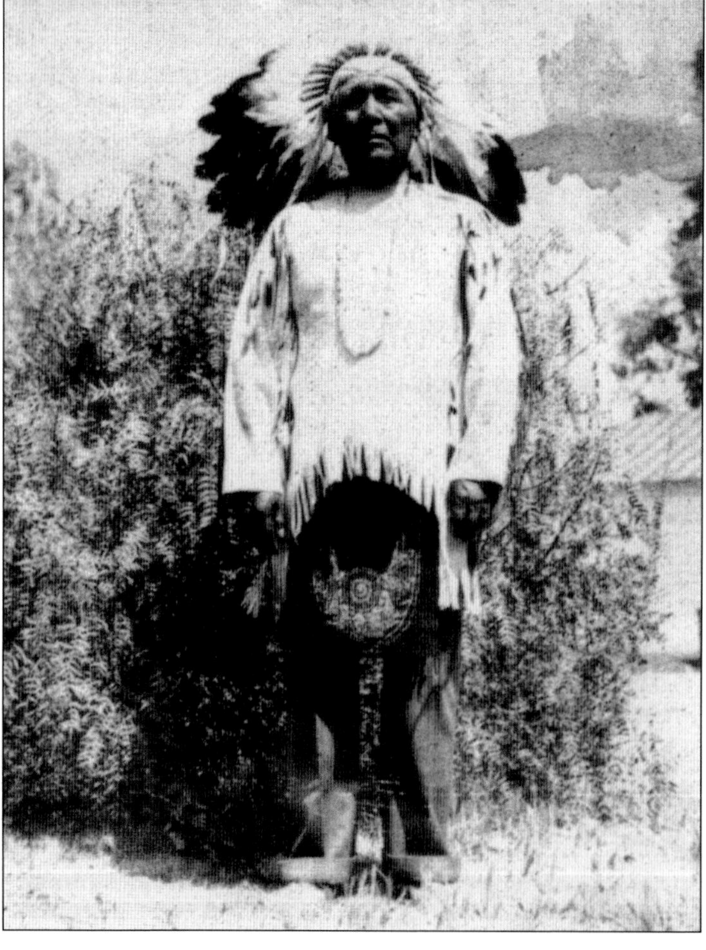

The traditional Tachi spring dance is demonstrated by "Old Bob" on March 1, 1916. Bob died in 1923, and Clarence Atwell brought the dance back in 1940. (Courtesy of Steve Emanuels.)

Jim Sando Burnell is dressed in traditional tribal garments around 1950. (Courtesy of the *Lemoore Centennial Book*.)

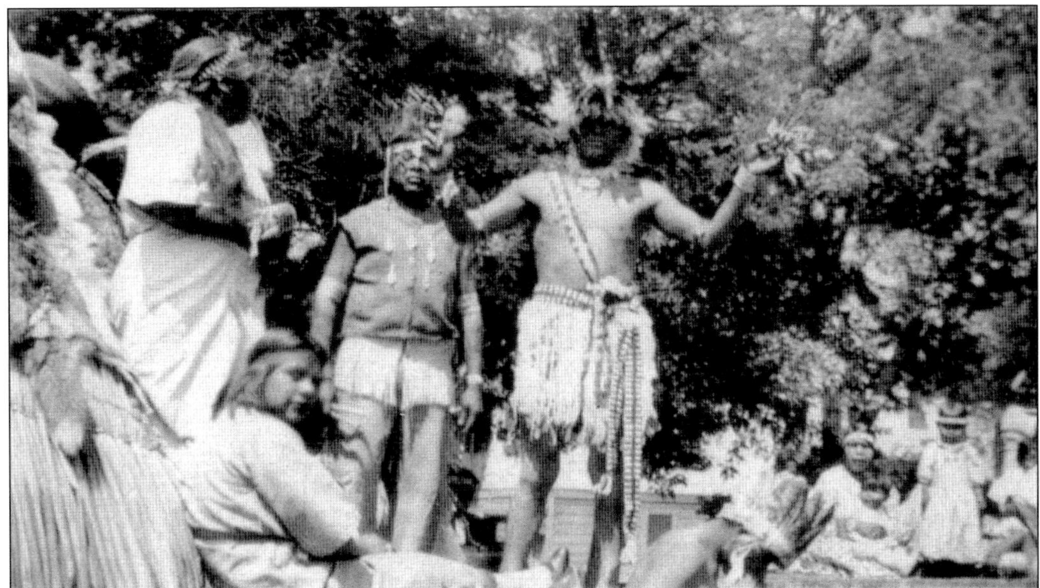

Clarence Atwell was the tribe's medicine man in 1937 at the Santa Rosa Rancheria. He later became the chief. (Courtesy of the *Lemoore Centennial Book*.)

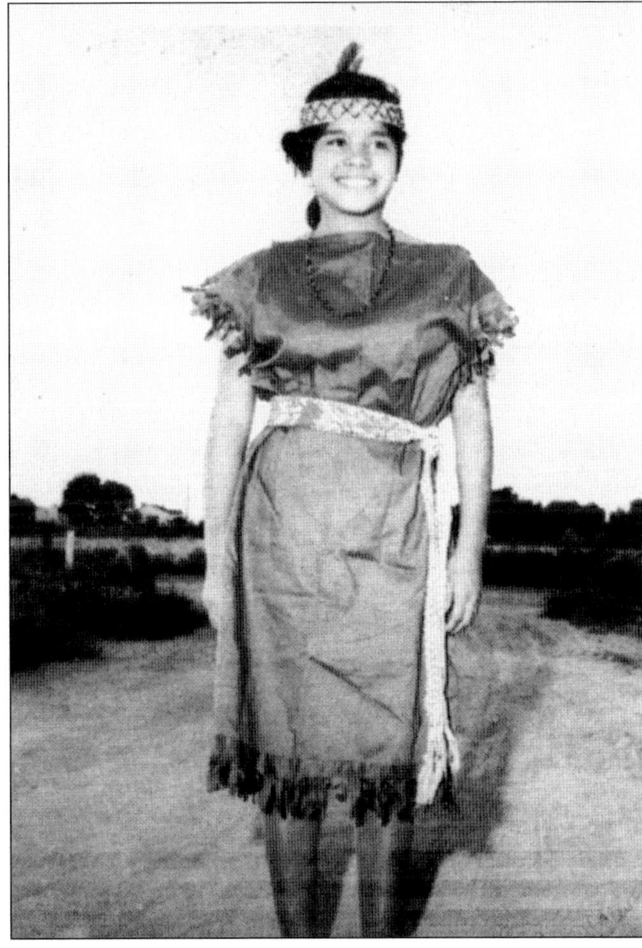

Donna Sisco was the Indian Princess of the Santa Rosa Rancheria in 1963. She is the granddaughter of Nick Sisco, who was the chief of the Rancheria in about 1940. (Courtesy of the *Lemoore Centennial Book*.)

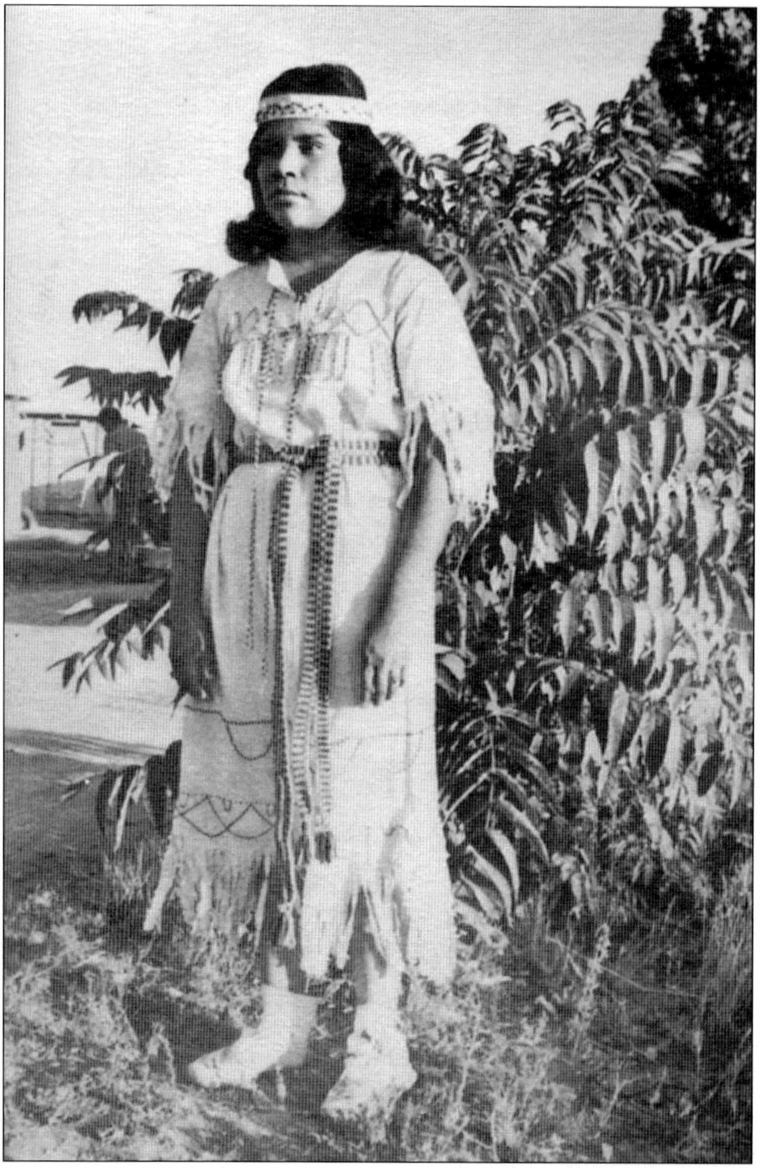

Marie Sisco was the Indian Princess at the Santa Rosa Rancheria in about 1950. (Courtesy of St. Peter's Catholic Church.)

This photograph of Cornelia Jeff's family was taken in 1945. (Courtesy of the *Lemoore Centennial Book*.)

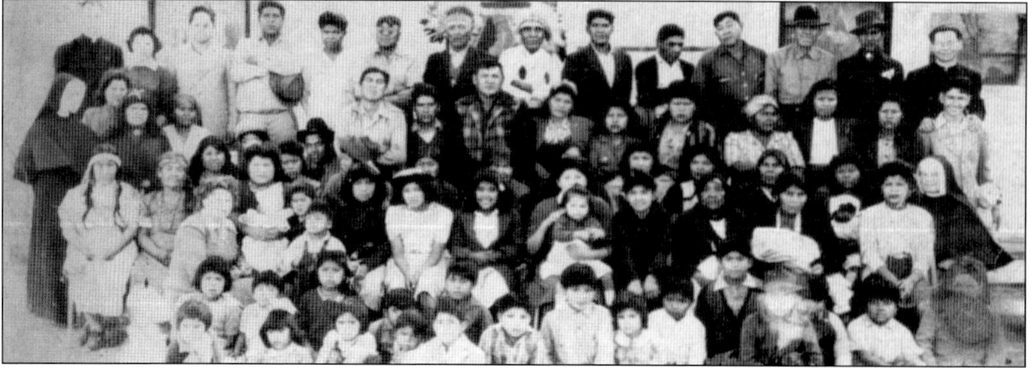

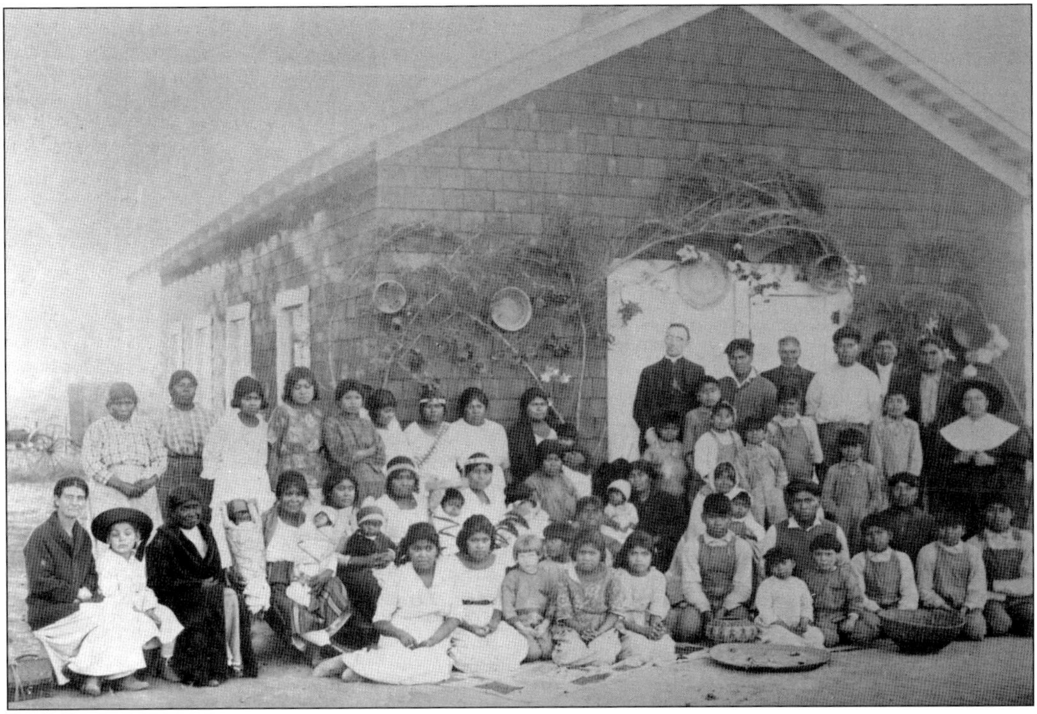

A group of Tachis gathered at the Catholic church on the Santa Rosa Rancheria around 1921. (Courtesy of St. Peter's Catholic Church.)

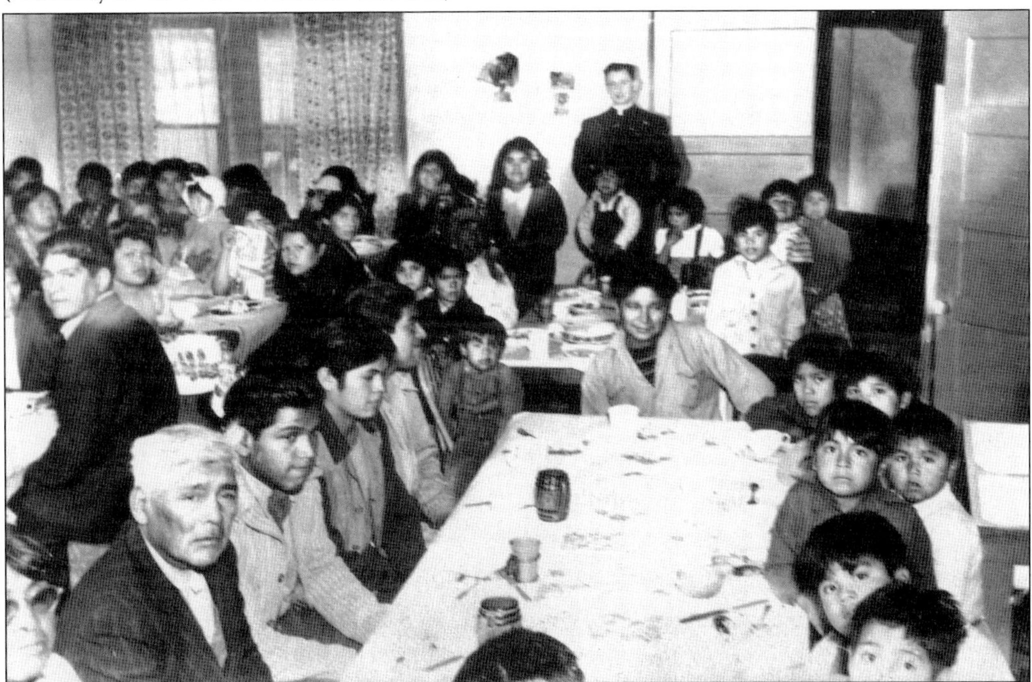

Tachis enjoy Christmas dinner at the Native American schoolhouse in 1943. The priest in the photograph is Fr. James Bennis, who died in 1984 at the Nazareth House in Fresno. (Courtesy of St. Peter's Catholic Church.)

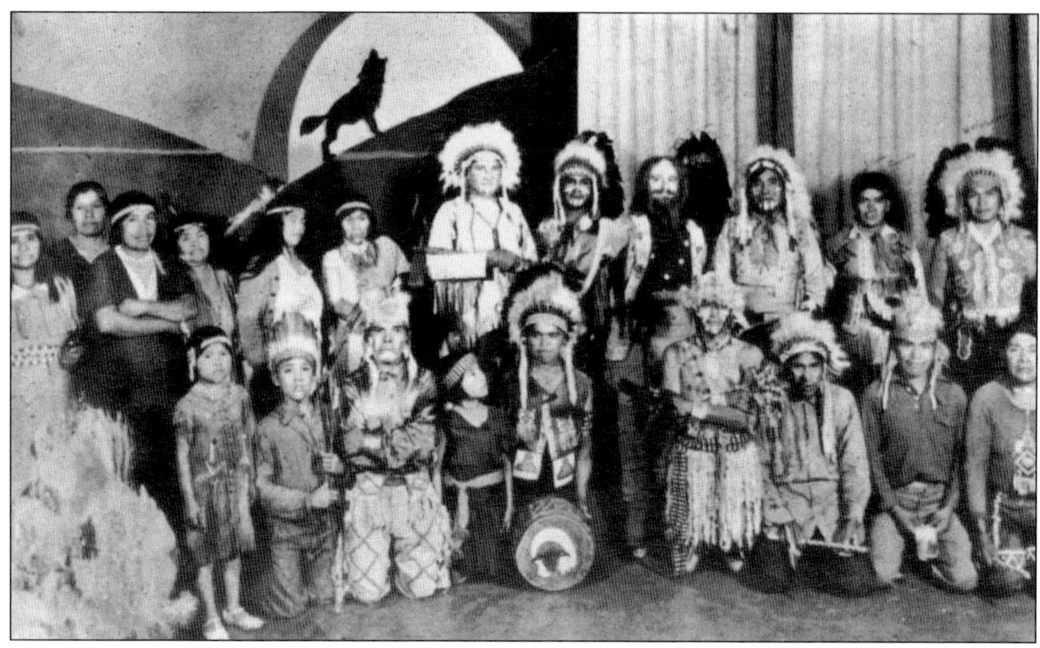

Native Americans from the Santa Rosa Rancheria in Lemoore pose for a picture after they performed a dance in Coalinga in 1942. (Courtesy of St. Peter's Catholic Church.)

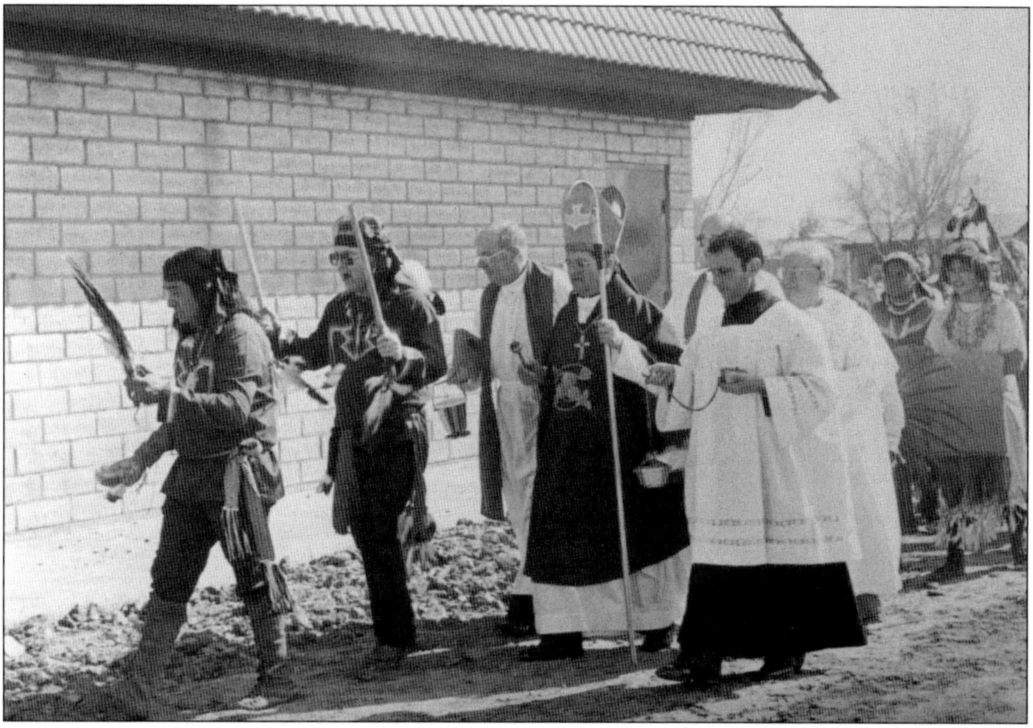

The Santa Rosa Indian Chapel was dedicated on February 22, 1987. The procession is led by Chief Clarence Atwell, followed by Michael Raymond; Bishop Madera; Anthony Nunes; Father O'Friel; Father Wall, O.P.; Father Kareta, O.F.M.; and Native American maidens. (Courtesy of St. Peter's Catholic Church.)

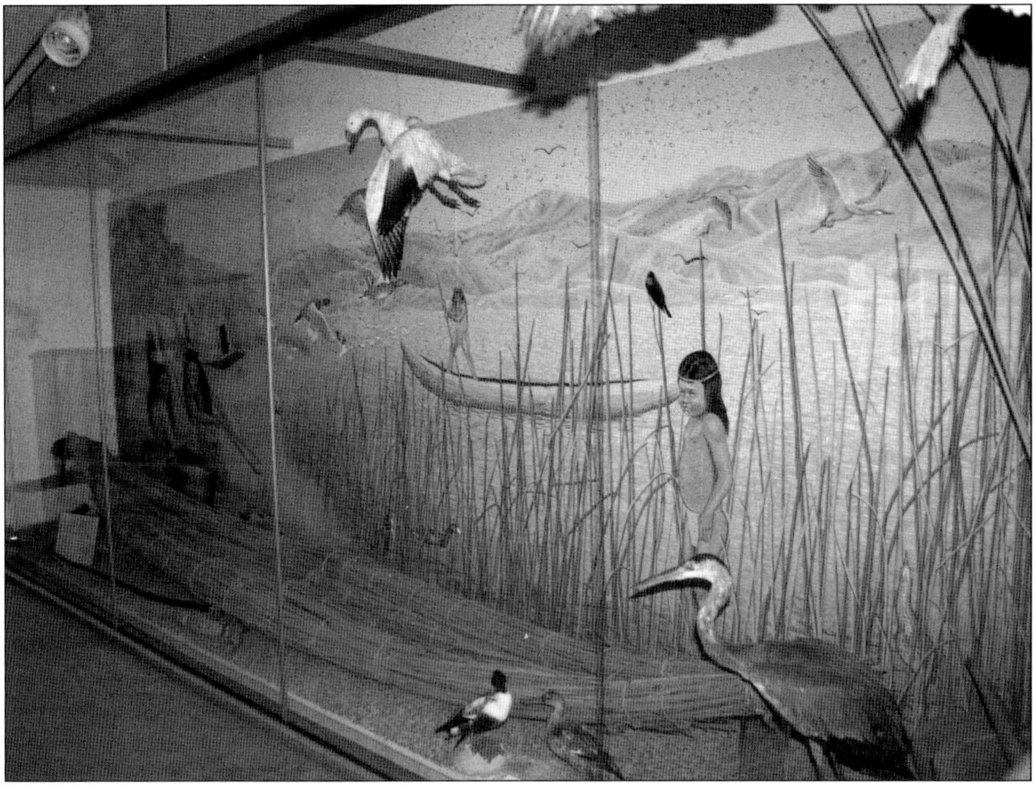

An exhibit at the Kings County Museum near Hanford depicts a scene that might have typically been seen in the early days of what is now Kings County. The tribe lived near Tulare Lake, the largest lake west of the Mississippi at the time. The Tachi-Yokuts had free reign of the land. They used the fruits of the land and the lake to survive. (Photograph by Cynthia J. Wright.)

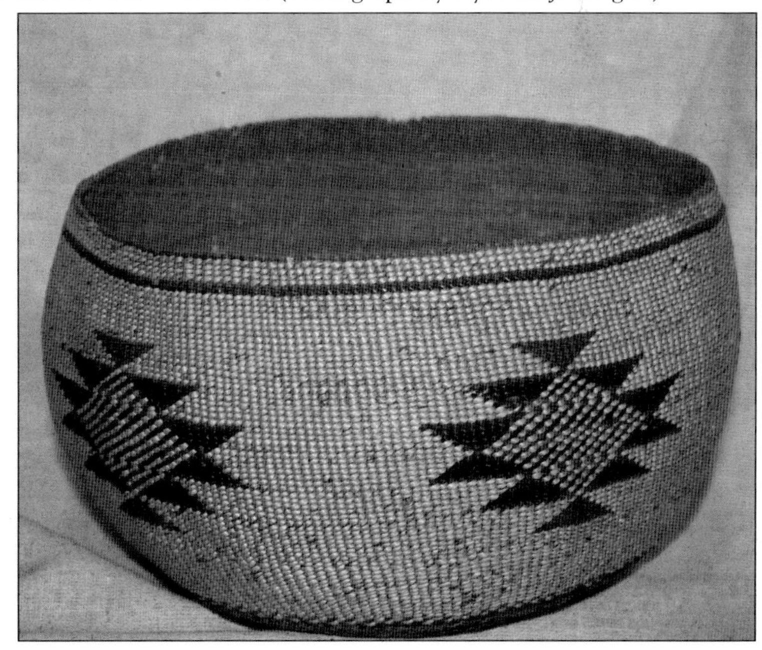

A selection of baskets woven and used by the early Tachi-Yokuts is on display in the Kings County Museum outside of Burris Park near Hanford. The baskets were made of tules from the shores of Tulare Lake. Tules were a variety of bulrushes that grew in the marshy lowlands around the lake. (Photograph by Cynthia J. Wright.)

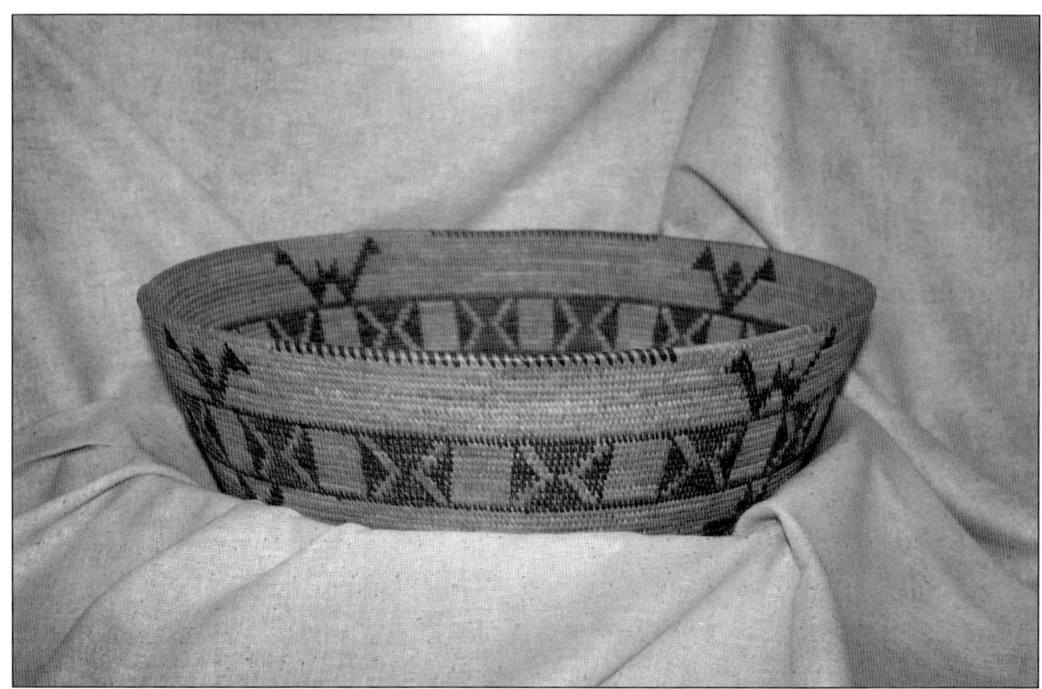

The Yokuts excelled in the art of basket-making. The baskets were made from the roots and stems of the tules. (Photograph by Cynthia J. Wright.)

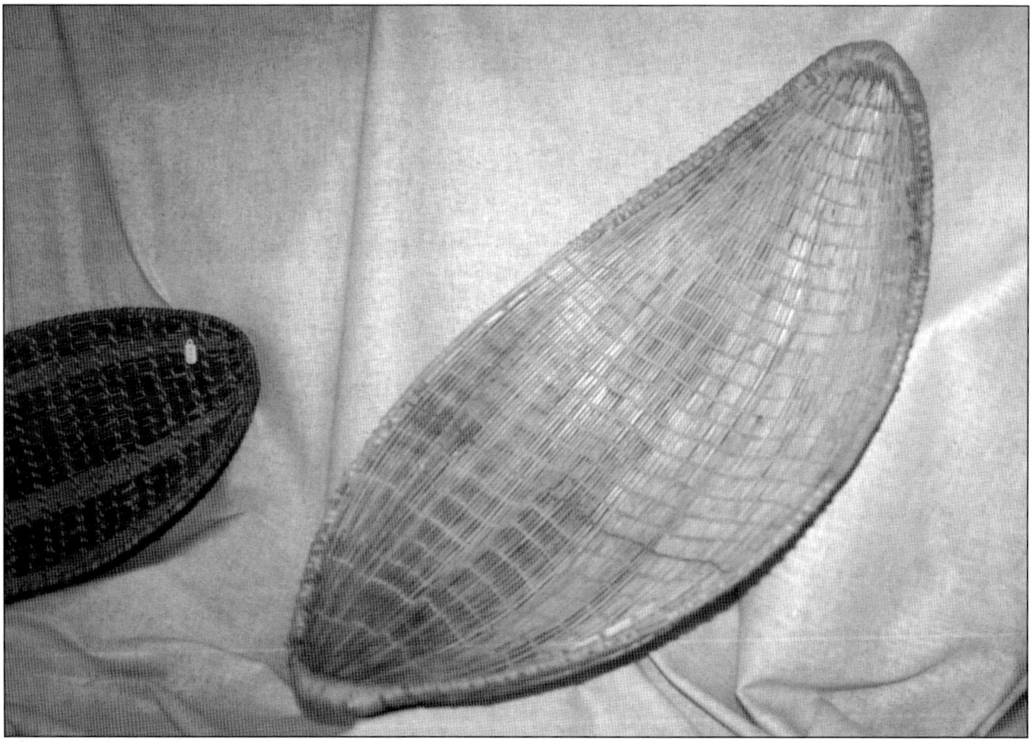

The baskets were made so well that they could hold water. They could be used for cooking by putting hot rocks in the water with raw foods. (Photograph by Cynthia J. Wright.)

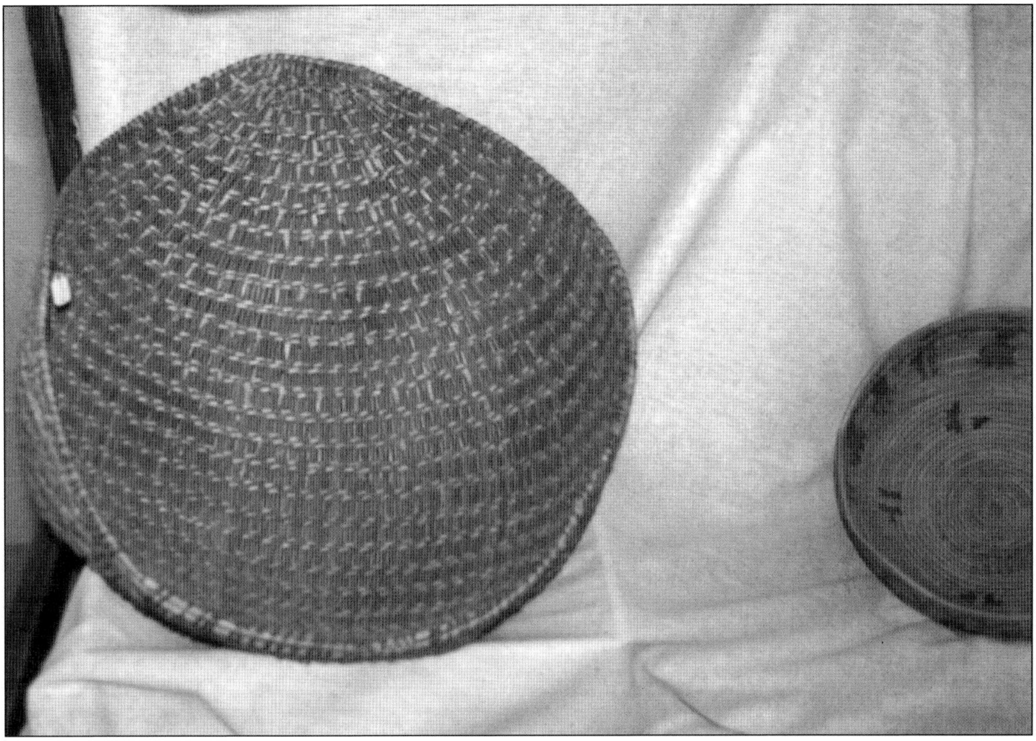

Bunchgrass, which grew along the streams and sloughs, was used as filler or coiling material for the baskets. The roots of swamp grass were scraped clean and split in half to make long sewing strands. The awl used in stitching was made from the split leg bone of a deer. (Photograph by Cynthia J. Wright.)

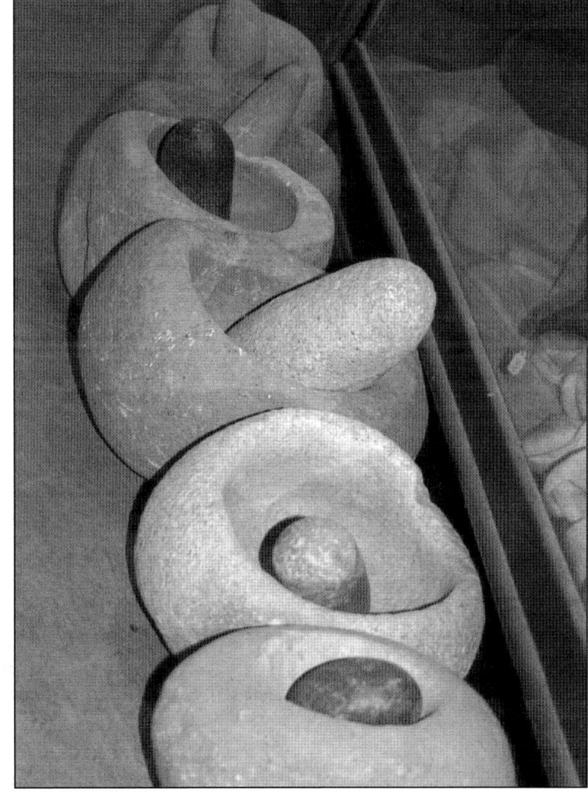

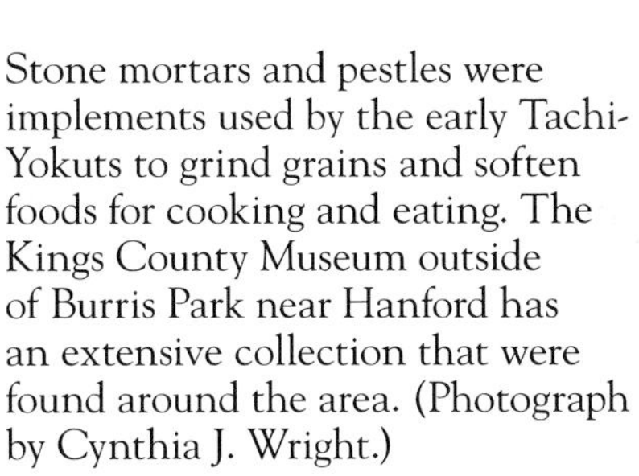

Stone mortars and pestles were implements used by the early Tachi-Yokuts to grind grains and soften foods for cooking and eating. The Kings County Museum outside of Burris Park near Hanford has an extensive collection that were found around the area. (Photograph by Cynthia J. Wright.)

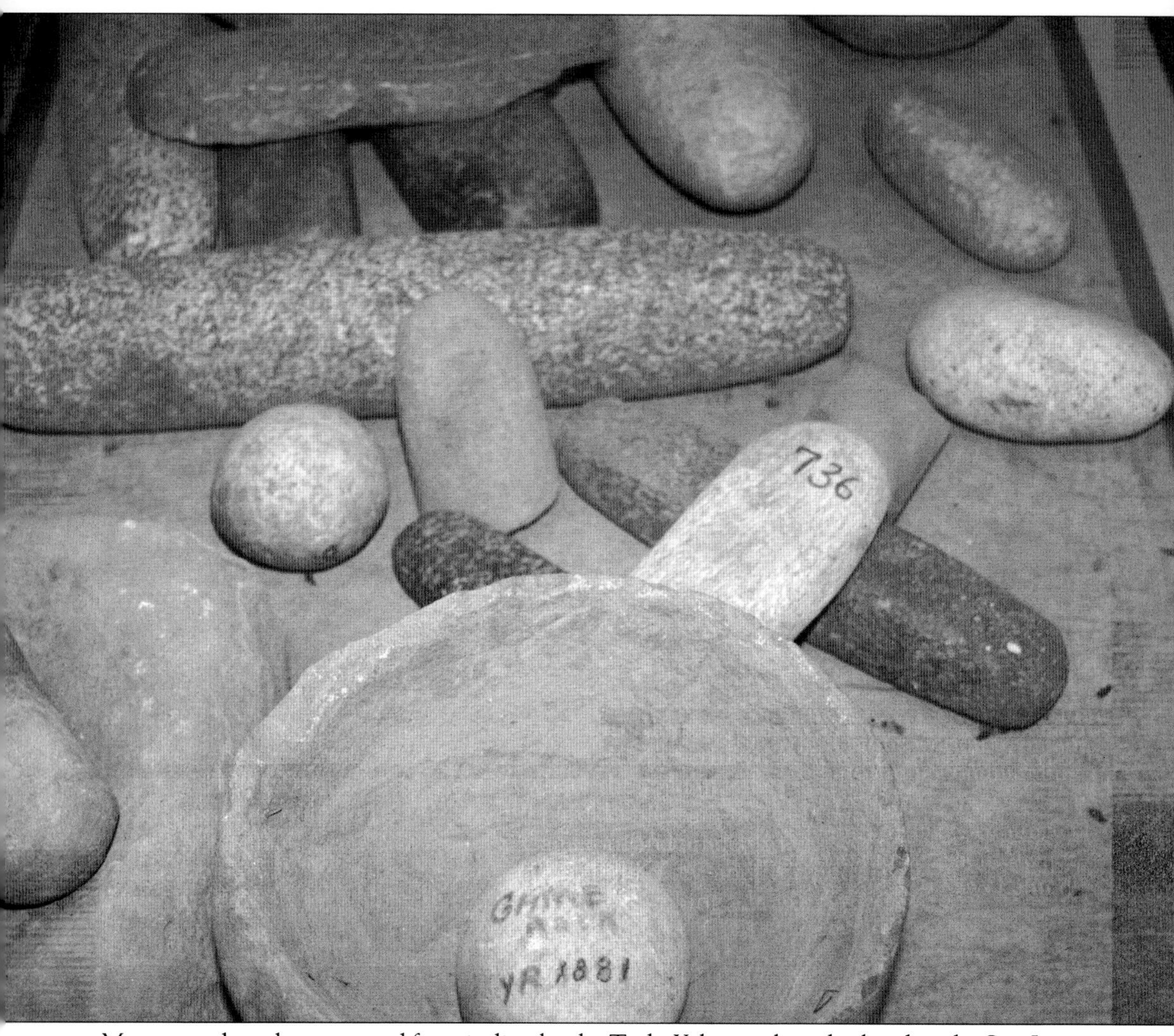

Mortars and pestles were used for grinding by the Tachi-Yokuts tribe, who lived in the San Joaquin Valley and the surrounding foothills. The tribe still resides near Lemoore on the Santa Rosa Rancheria. (Photograph by Cynthia J. Wright.)

Two

Early Lemoore

Nearly 20 years before the town of Lemoore would even be dreamed of, brothers Justin and Jonathan Esrey arrived from Illinois amid the oak trees and swamplands on the south side of the Kings River, where they bred and fattened cattle. They were about 7 miles west of Kingston, the closest place to buy groceries and supplies. They urged their sister, Amanda Rhoads, and her husband, Daniel, who had settled near Gilroy, to join them. After a dry spell in Gilroy, they too came to the relative lushness of the Kings River. Before Amanda would stay, however, Daniel had to promise to build a house. Their adobe house still stands today near the intersection of Highway 41 and Lacey Boulevard.

In 1856, few settlers were in the vicinity, but the lure of land, including state-owned swamp and overflow land, kept more stockmen coming. Within a few years, there was a thriving economy of cattle being raised on grass, hogs being fattened on acorns, and wheat being planted on the moisture-laden shores of Tulare Lake. By 1870, a number of landowners began to think farming might be lucrative. Twenty-three of them filed a "Claim for Water" with the state on October 15 and began to form the Lower Kings River Ditch Company. This effort would spur great changes in the area and spawn a new town much closer to their needs.

The trip to Kingston for supplies had become tedious, so farmers watched with interest when Dr. Lovern Lee Moore bought 160 acres in 1871. A year later, he carved out 10 acres and filed a plat map for a new town. It was rumored a railroad would be built west from Goshen to Coalinga and would run right through Moore's subdivision. He called the new town La Tache, but federal post officials named it after the applicant—thus Lemoore. Moore auctioned off lots on the 10-acre site in 1872. They sold for between $75 and $150 each. The town started across from today's Lemoore High School.

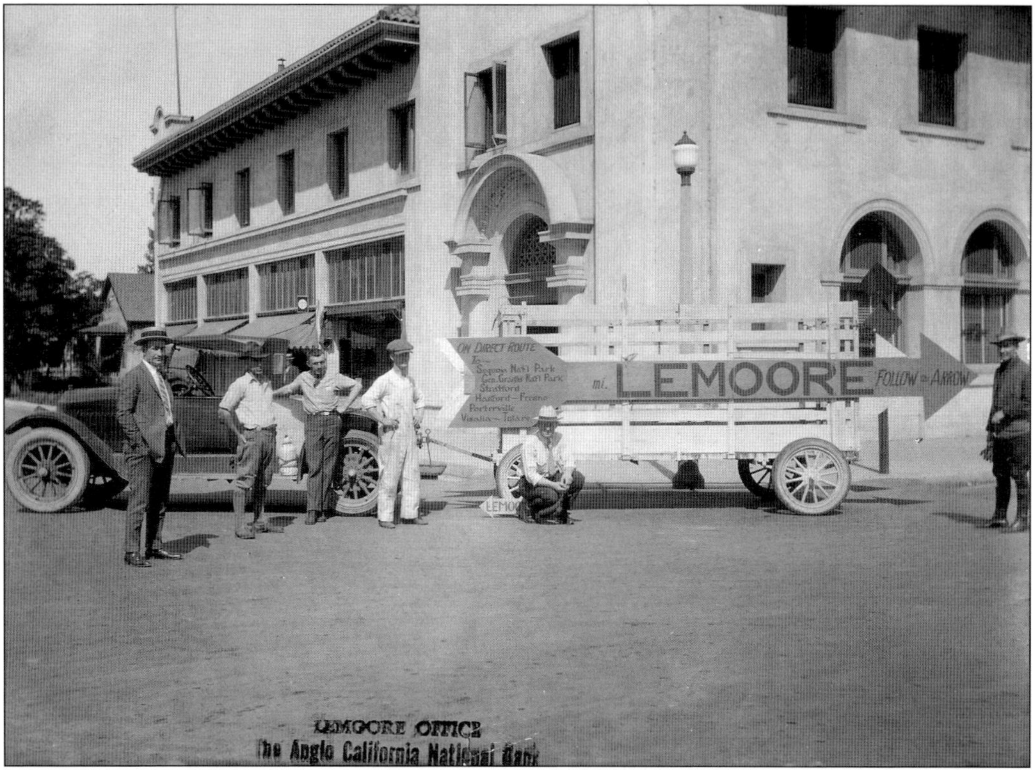

At the corner of Fox and D Streets, men pose with a large arrow that directed townspeople and visitors alike to Sequoia National Park, General Grant National Park, and points beyond. This picture was taken in front of the bank building. (Courtesy of the Sarah A. Mooney Museum.)

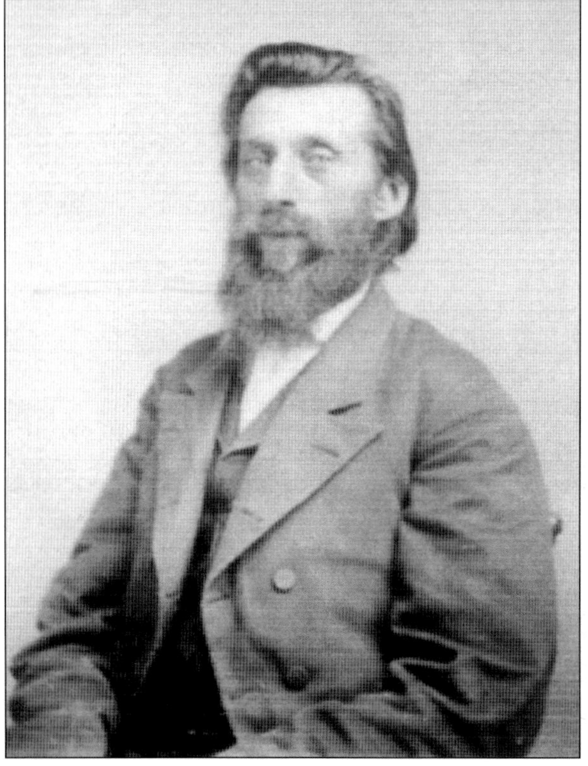

Dr. Lovern Lee Moore is considered the founding father of Lemoore. When Moore arrived in April 1871, he petitioned the U.S. Postal Service for a post office in the area. He suggested it be called La Tache, but the U.S. Postal Service changed it to Lemoore, a condensed version of Moore's name. (Courtesy of the Sarah A. Mooney Museum.)

In 1846, Daniel Rhoads moved to California from Illinois as an adult with his parents, his wife Amanda Esrey, and his siblings and their families by overland wagon train. He came to Lemoore in 1856 and built an adobe ranch house that was home to the Rhoads family for generations and still stands east of Lemoore today. It also served as one of the first schools in Lemoore. Daniel Rhoads is credited with being part of the rescue team for the ill-fated Donner party. (Courtesy of the Sarah A. Mooney Museum.)

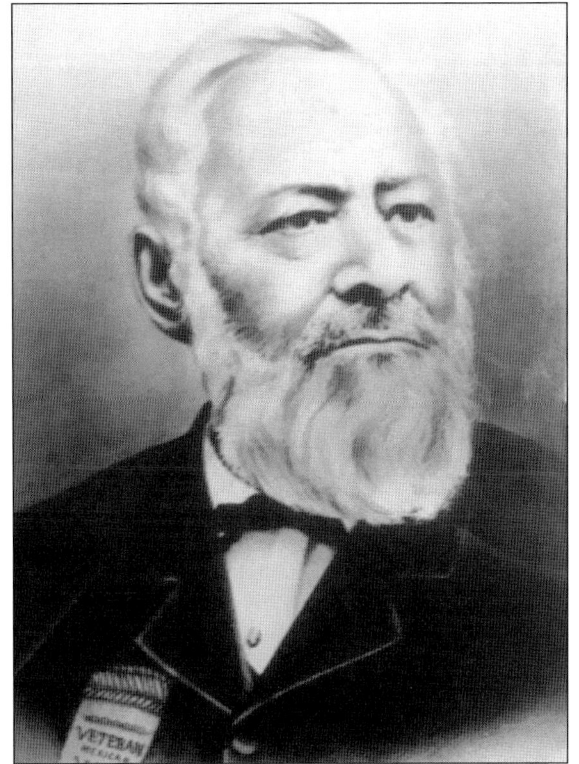

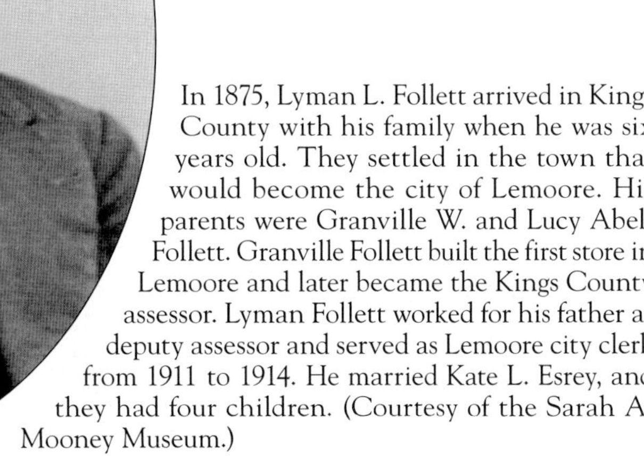

In 1875, Lyman L. Follett arrived in Kings County with his family when he was six years old. They settled in the town that would become the city of Lemoore. His parents were Granville W. and Lucy Abell Follett. Granville Follett built the first store in Lemoore and later became the Kings County assessor. Lyman Follett worked for his father as deputy assessor and served as Lemoore city clerk from 1911 to 1914. He married Kate L. Esrey, and they had four children. (Courtesy of the Sarah A. Mooney Museum.)

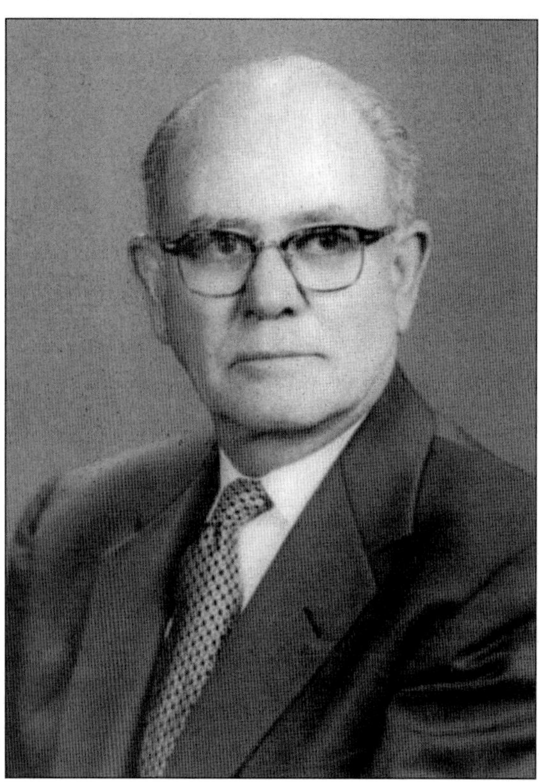

Charles Granville Follett was the eldest son of Lyman L. Follett. He was married to Peggy Inman Follett. (Courtesy of Salli Day.)

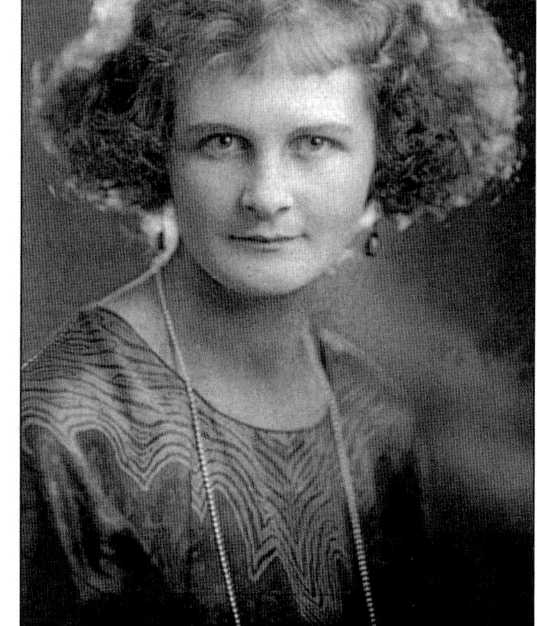

Peggy Inman Follett and Charles Granville Follett had three daughters: Janet, Sarah "Salli," and Cathryn. Salli Follett Day still lives in Lemoore and continues to be very active in the community. (Courtesy of Salli Day.)

Sarah A. Mooney came to Lemoore with her husband, Aaron, and their daughter, Harriet, in 1875. The family left a lasting legacy to Lemoore in the form of the Sarah A. Mooney Museum. The Mooney's former home contains history and many artifacts of early Lemoore. (Courtesy of the Sarah A. Mooney Museum.)

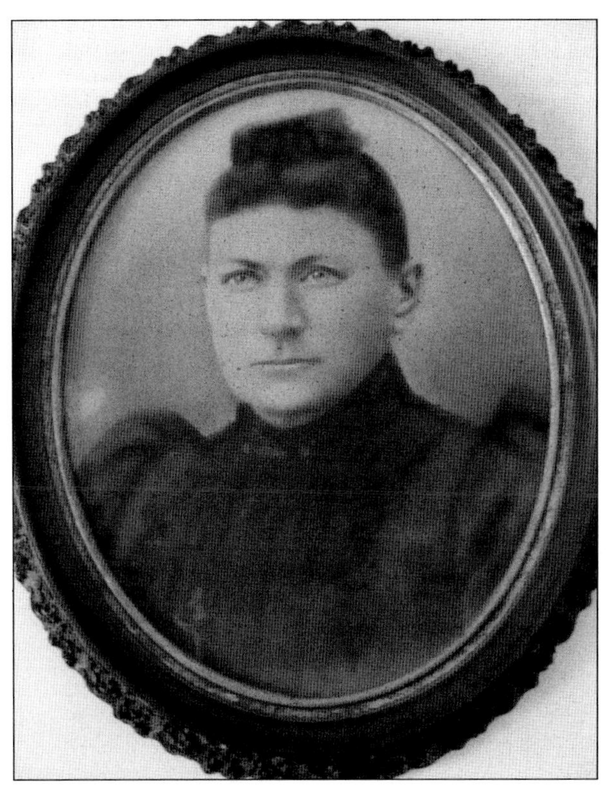

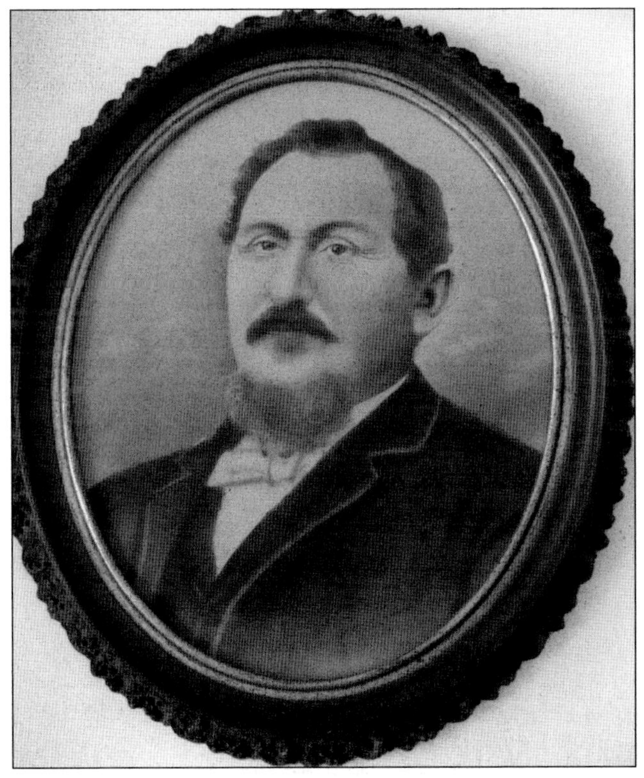

Aaron Mooney, the husband of Sarah A. Mooney, owned the home that became the Sarah A. Mooney Museum in Lemoore. (Courtesy of the Sarah A. Mooney Museum.)

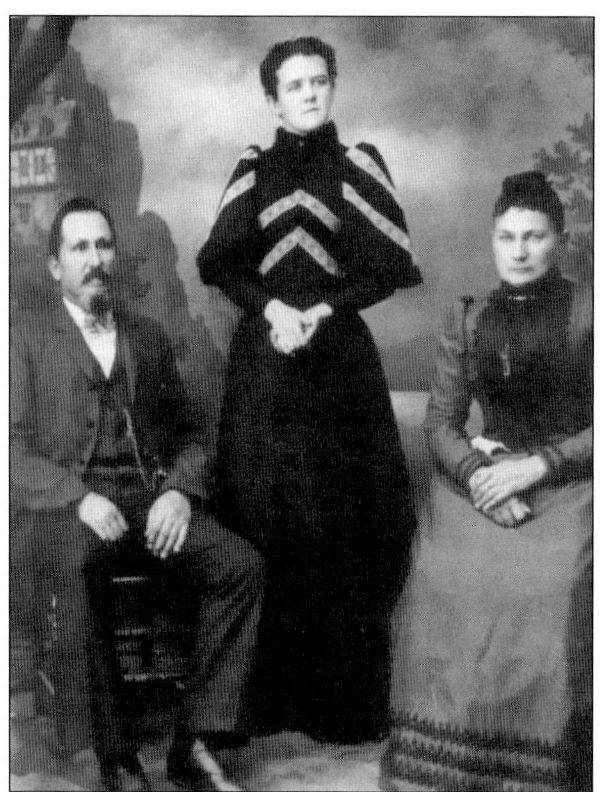

Aaron, Sarah, and Harriet (center) Mooney came to Lemoore in 1875. Aaron Mooney prospered as the proprietor of the general store and funeral director. Sarah Mooney and her daughter, Harriet, were very active in civic affairs. In 1893, Aaron and Sarah built their Victorian home at 542 West D Street. (Courtesy of the Sarah A. Mooney Museum.)

This home was left by Sarah Mooney to her granddaughter Marie Blakeley in 1925. Marie and her husband, L. M. "Buzz" Blakeley, along with Marie's family, wanted this property to stand in memory of their grandmother. In 1973, after the Lemoore Centennial, they donated it to the Lemoore District Chamber of Commerce to be used as a memorial museum. (Photograph by Cynthia J. Wright.)

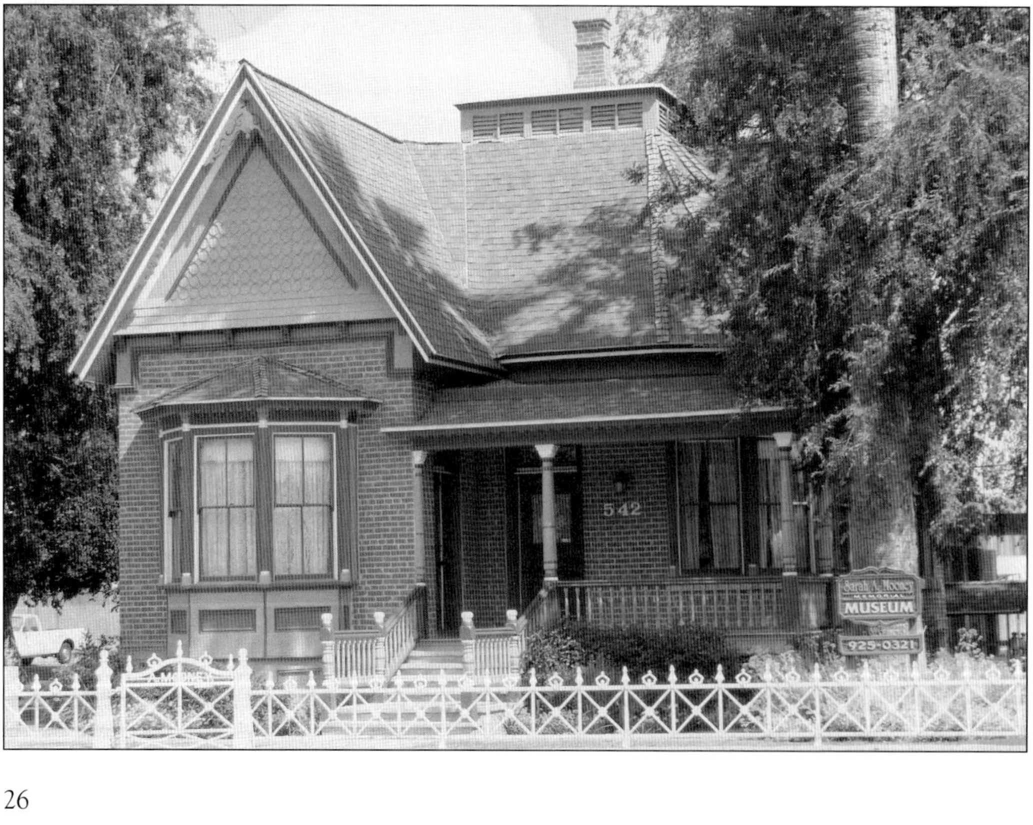

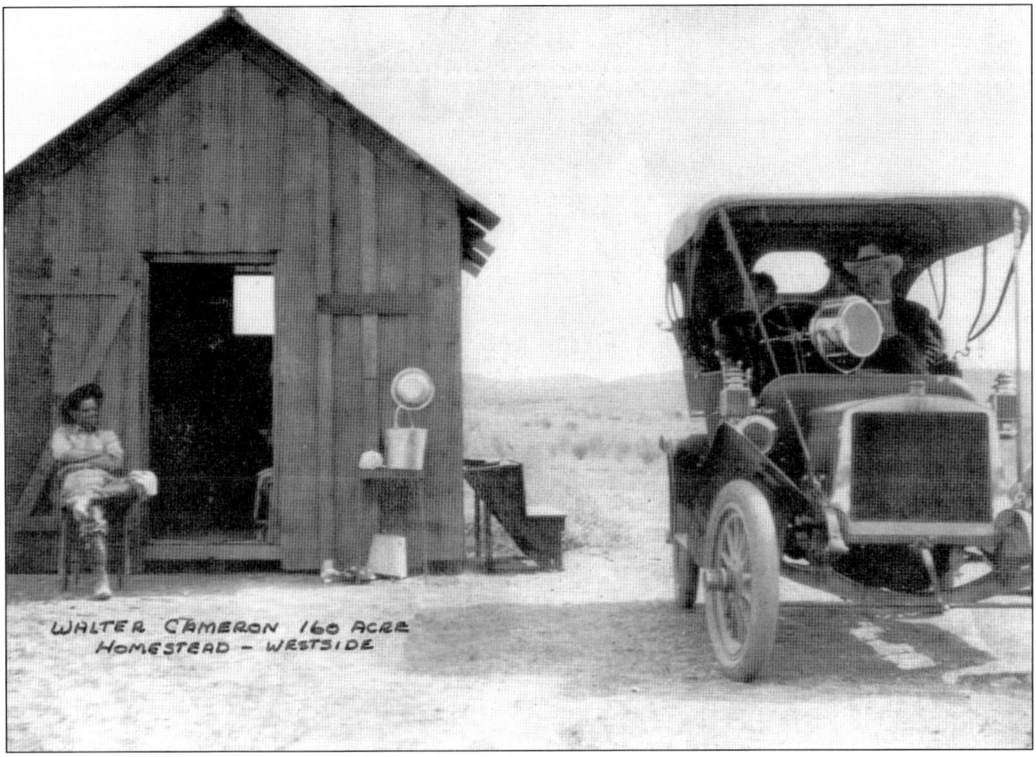

Walter Cameron sits in front of his 160-acre homestead on the far west side of Lemoore. Homesteaders in the late 1800s and early 1900s often worked in conditions of alternating floods and droughts. It was not until the mid-1900s that a secure form of irrigation was built for the west-side farmers. (Courtesy of Jack Stone.)

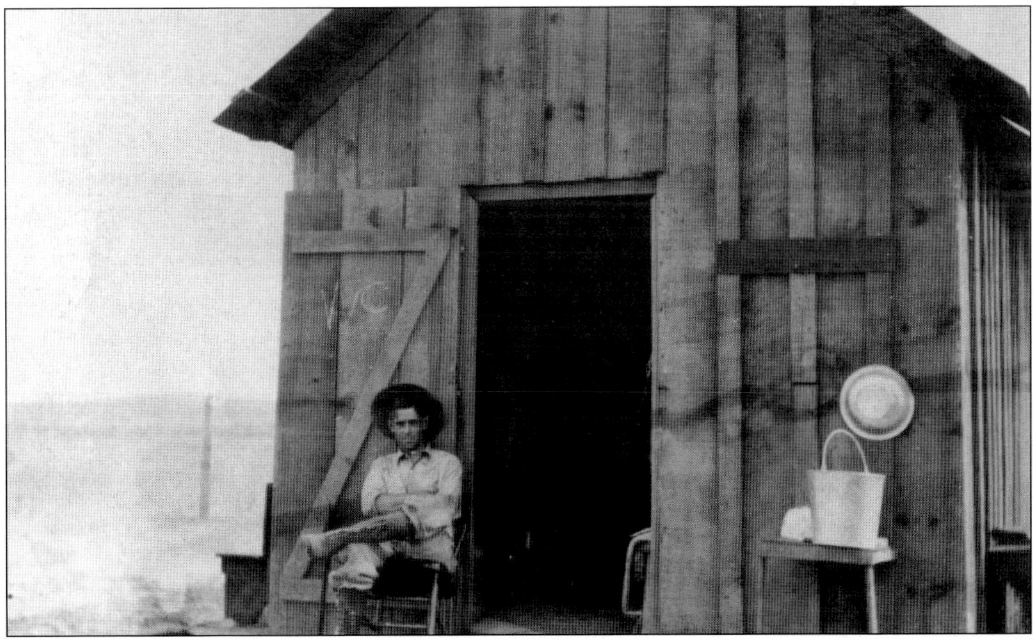

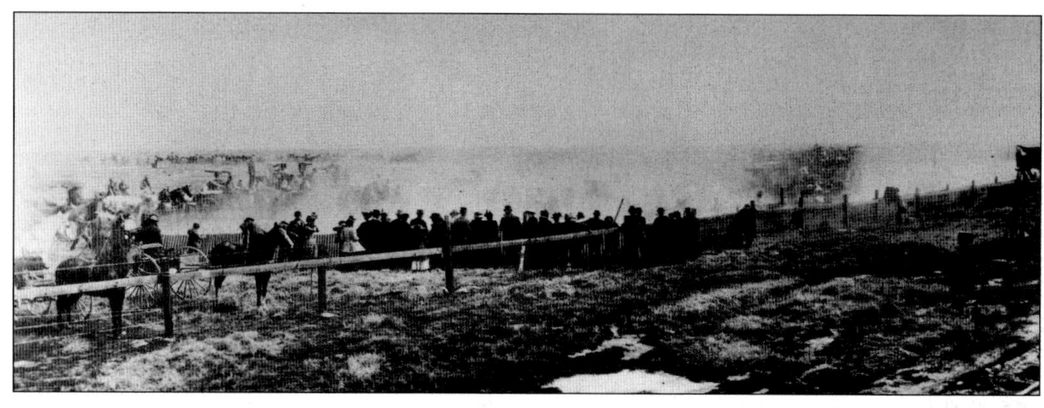

Early farmers around Lemoore held "rabbit roundups" to reduce the rabbit population. The roundups helped guard against the overpopulation of rabbits and provided a food source. (Courtesy of St. Peter's Catholic Church.)

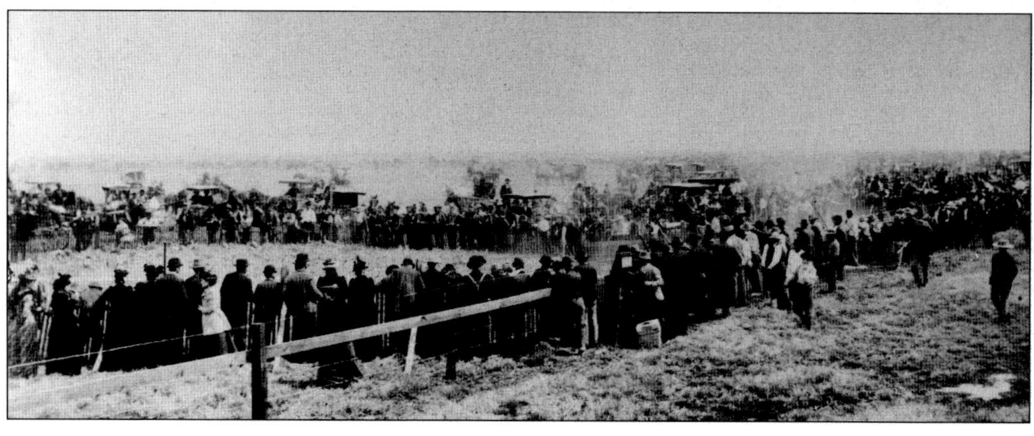

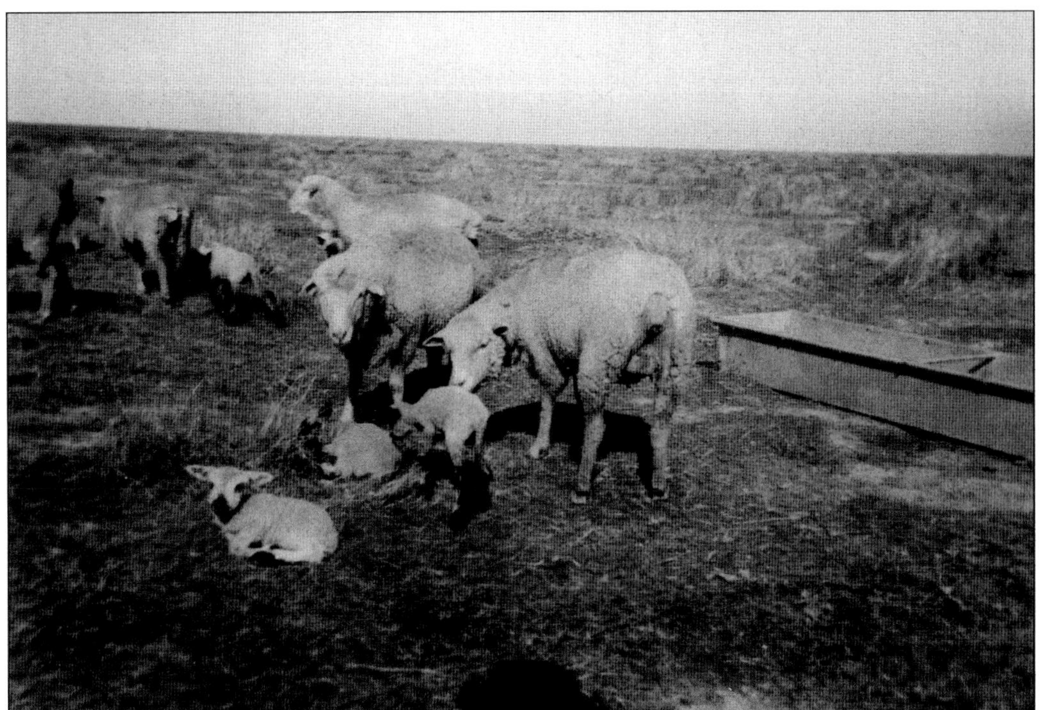

Early Basques, many from Spain, worked as migrant shepherds. They often grazed their sheep in the Lemoore area during the winter months, when grazing and lambing conditions were too harsh in the surrounding hills. (Courtesy of St. Peter's Catholic Church.)

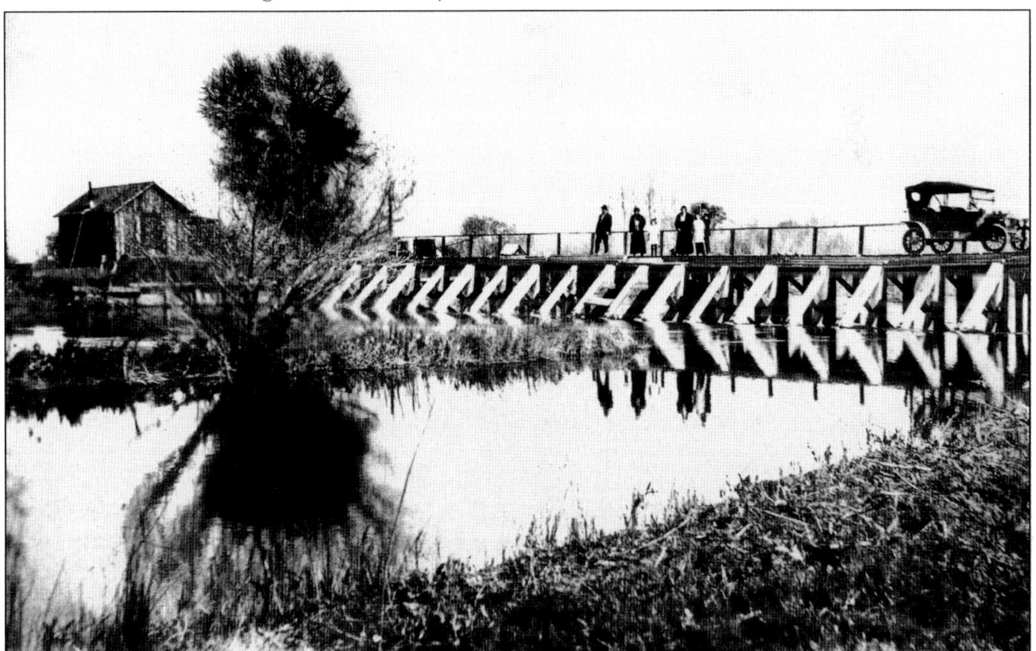

The weir at Stratford had the first telephone in town. The tender of the weir, Lee Chism, and his wife lived in the little house pictured. Stratford is just south of Lemoore and has long depended on Lemoore as a source of supplies and services. (Courtesy of Jack Stone.)

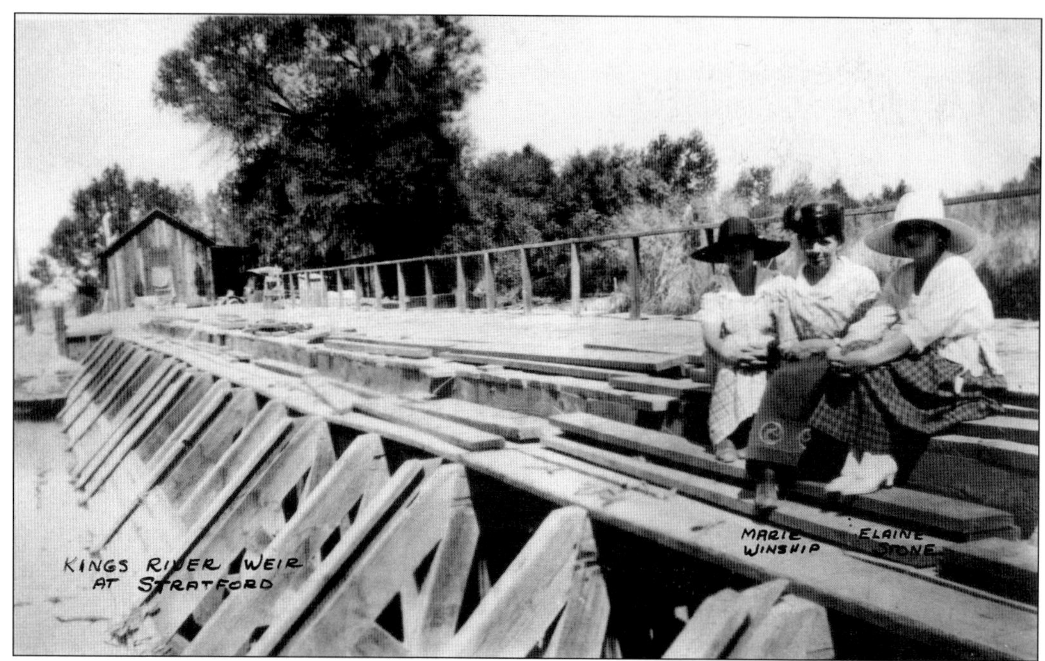

Elaine Stone (right), Marie Winsnip (center), and an unidentified girl sit overlooking the Kings River Weir at Stratford. (Courtesy of Jack Stone.)

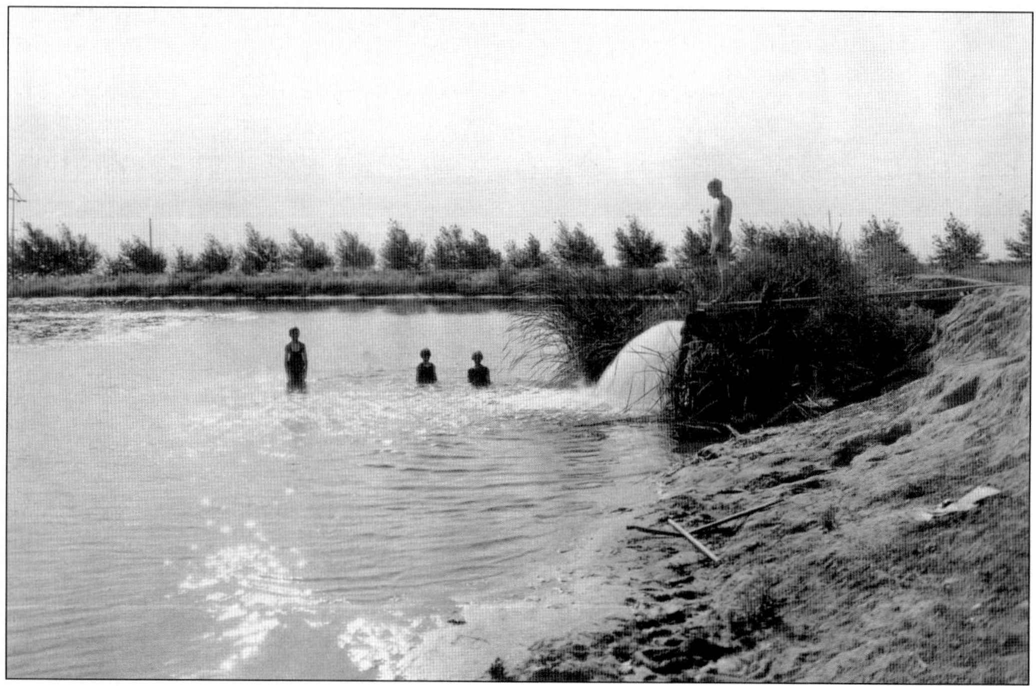

A family cools off and enjoys some down time in one of the weirs around Lemoore. (Courtesy of Jack Stone.)

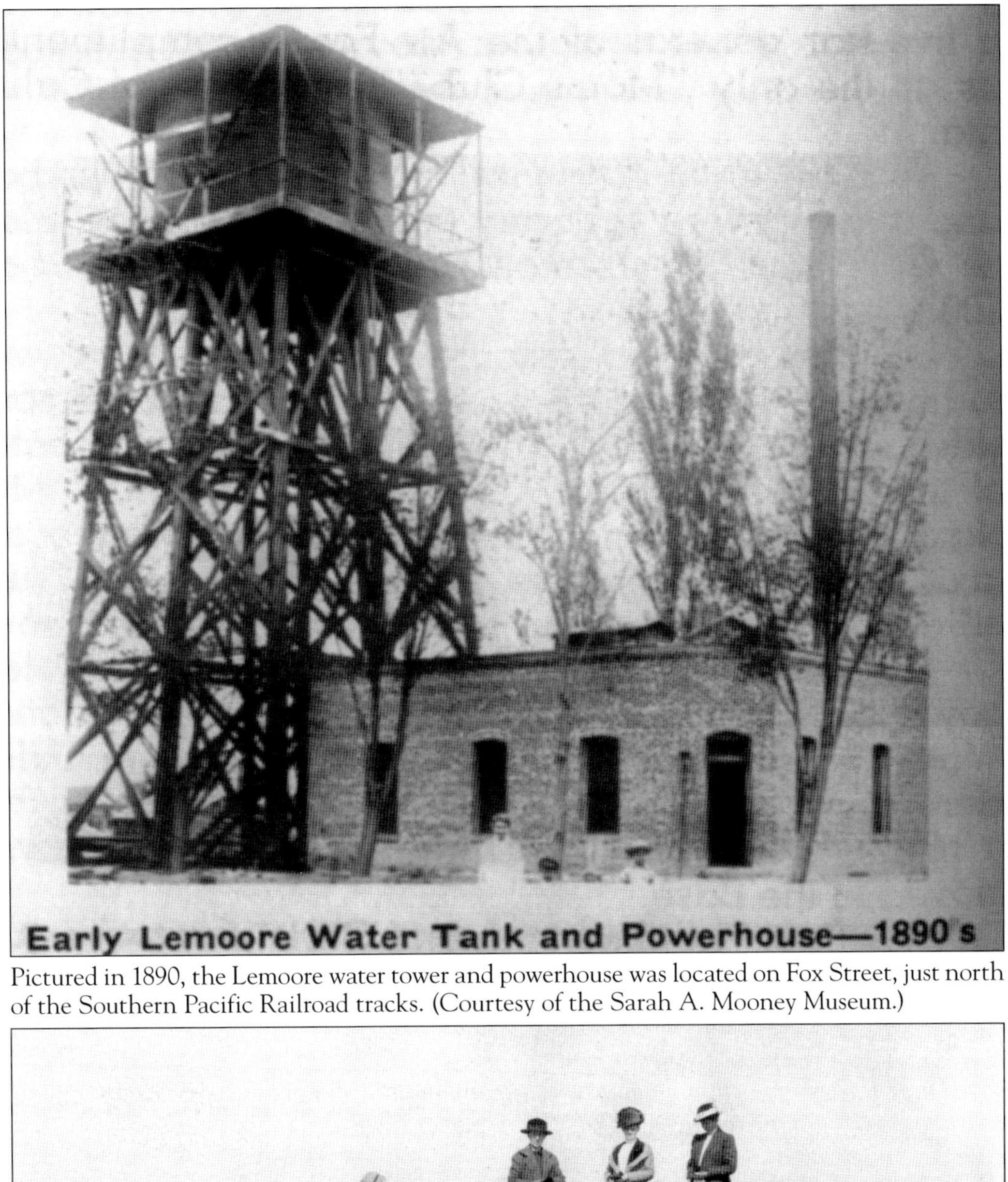

Early Lemoore Water Tank and Powerhouse—1890's

Pictured in 1890, the Lemoore water tower and powerhouse was located on Fox Street, just north of the Southern Pacific Railroad tracks. (Courtesy of the Sarah A. Mooney Museum.)

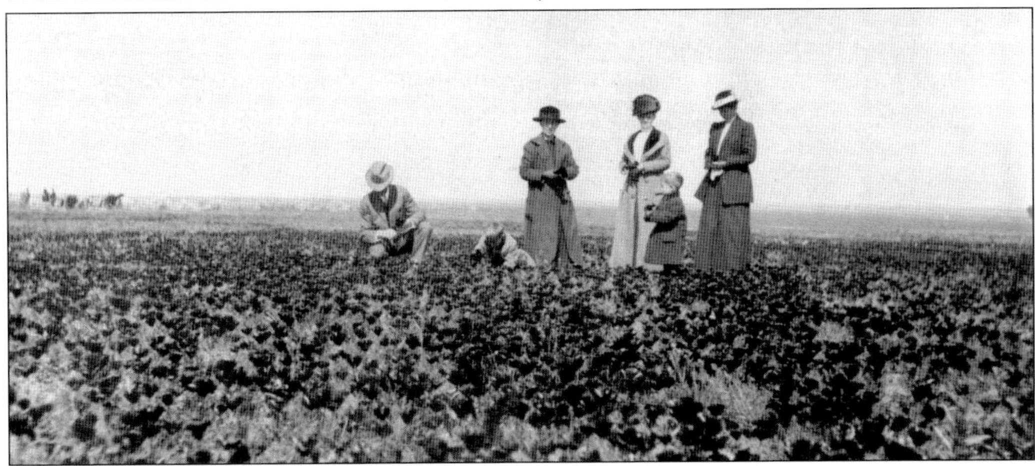

A group surveys a crop of flowers growing in a field. (Courtesy of Jack Stone.)

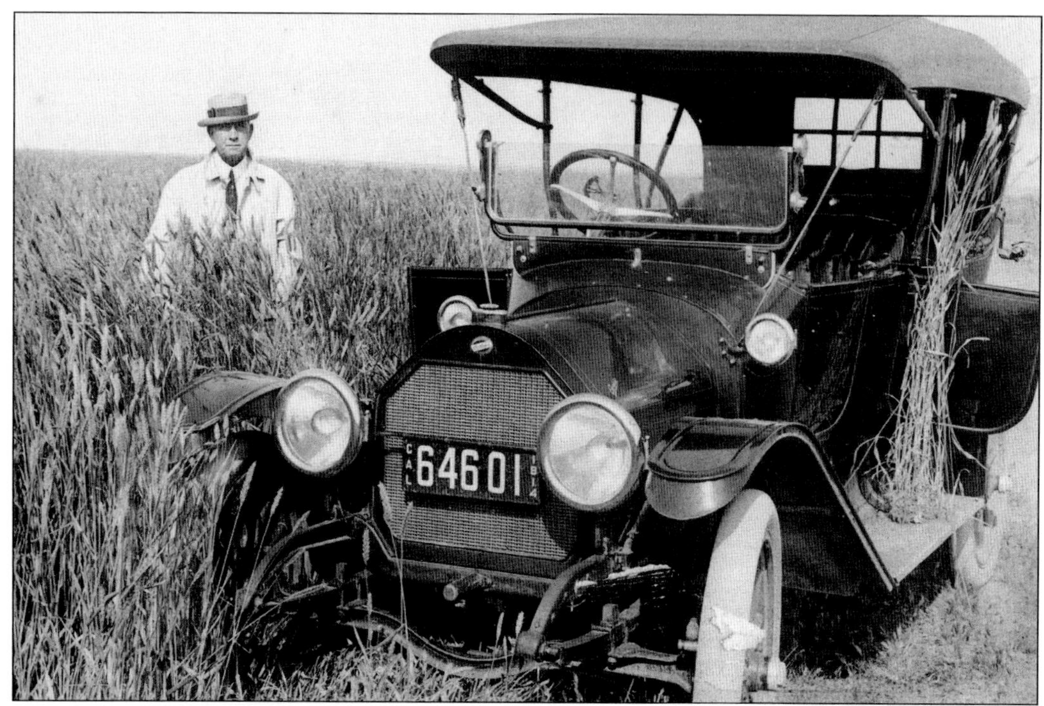

Mr. Mills stands by his car in a field of grain in the late 1910s or early 1920s. (Courtesy of Jack Stone.)

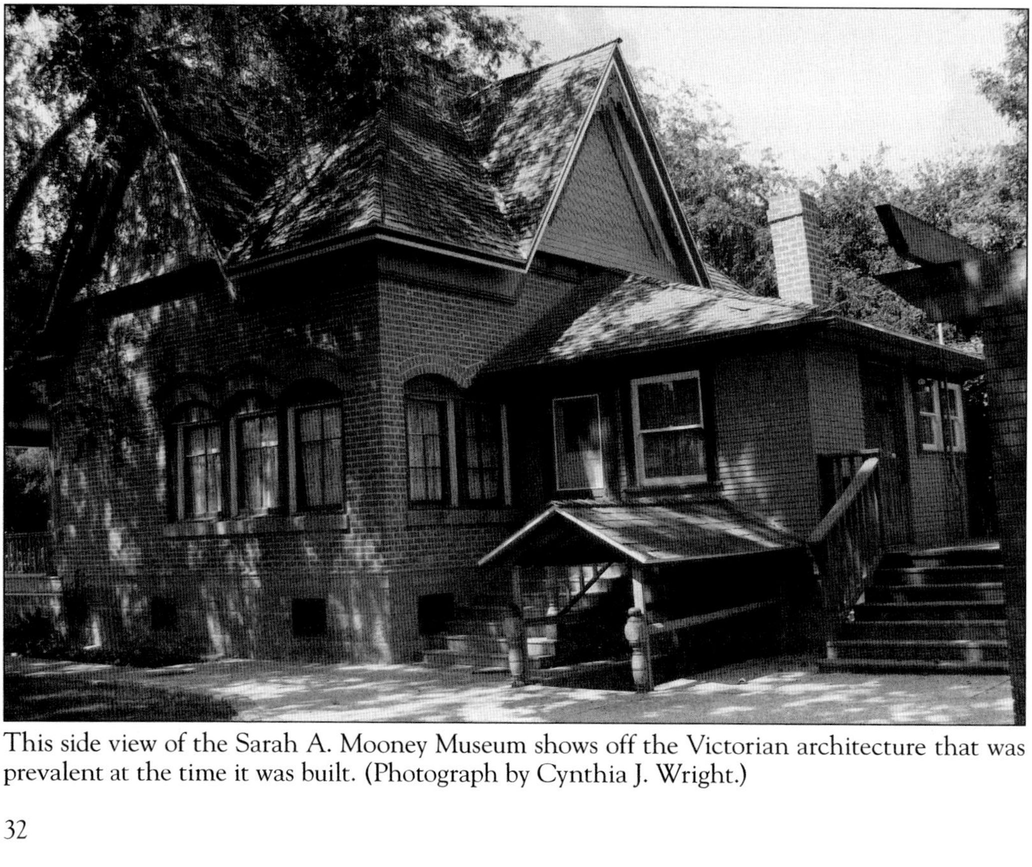

This side view of the Sarah A. Mooney Museum shows off the Victorian architecture that was prevalent at the time it was built. (Photograph by Cynthia J. Wright.)

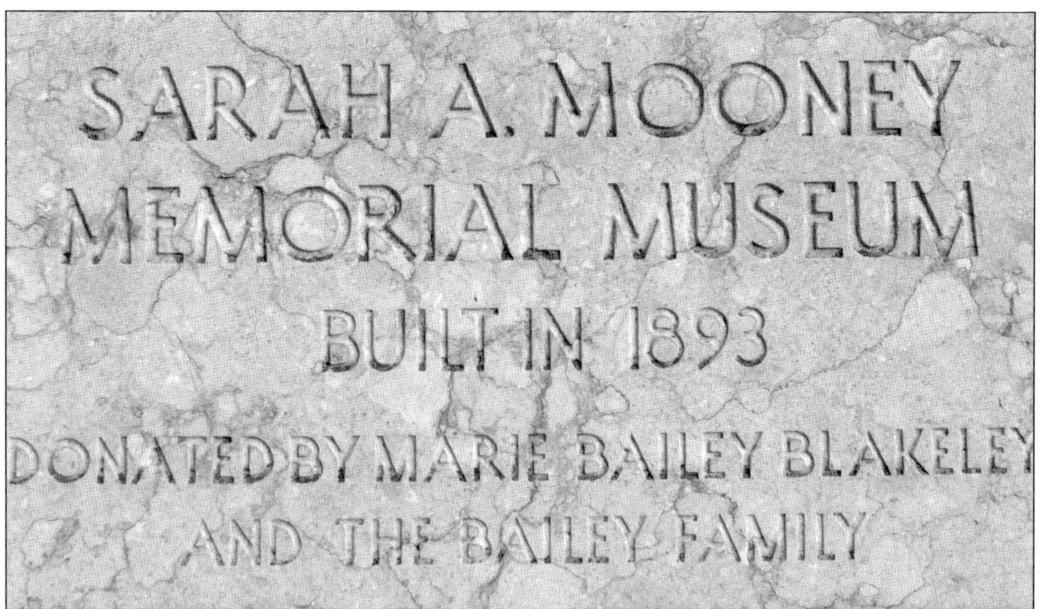

A plaque in front of the museum shows the dedication by the Blakeley family. (Photograph by Cynthia J. Wright.)

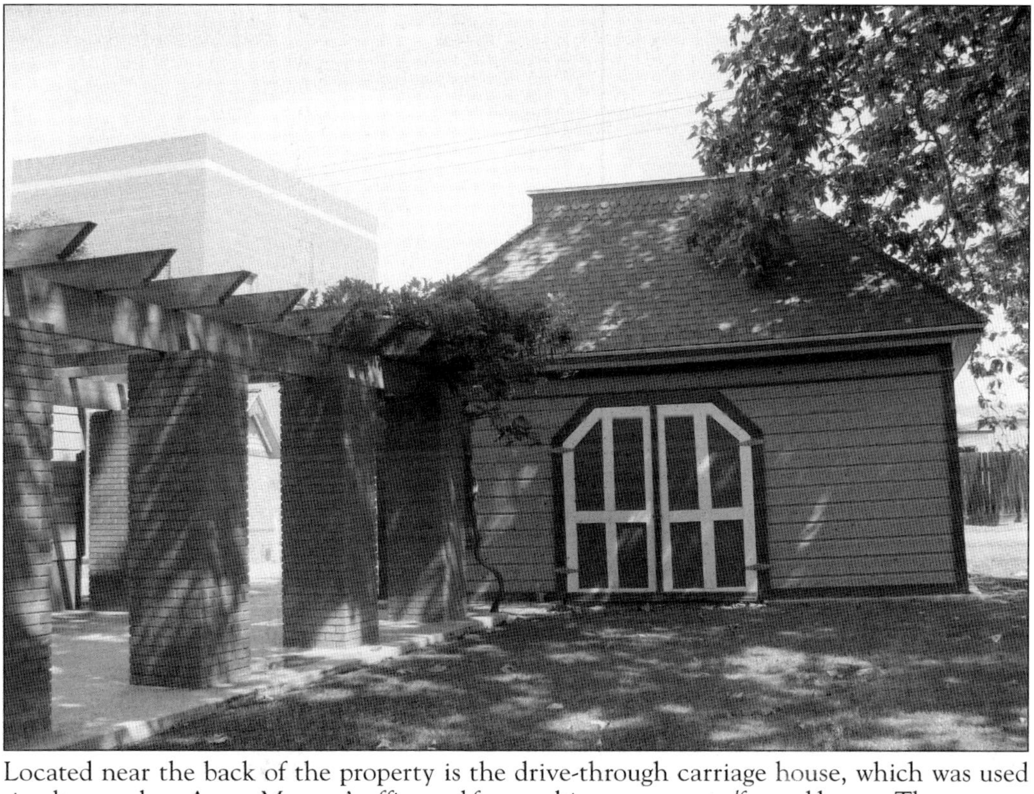

Located near the back of the property is the drive-through carriage house, which was used simultaneously as Aaron Mooney's office and for a multipurpose wagon/funeral hearse. The museum has acquired an 1890s mountain wagon that belonged to the Shore family, and the carriage house was recently restored to its original use. (Photograph by Cynthia J. Wright.)

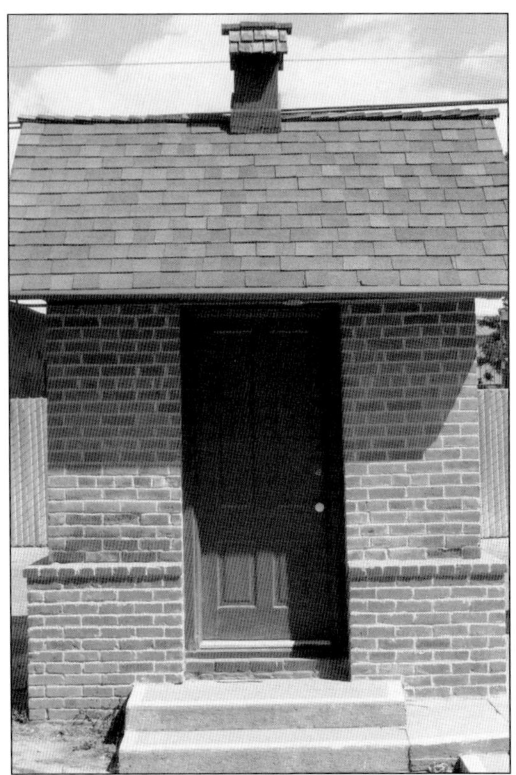

Outside the backdoor of the house is the old brick outhouse that has been plumbed and still serves as the restroom. It is reputed to be the only brick structure of this nature still in use. (Photograph by Cynthia J. Wright.)

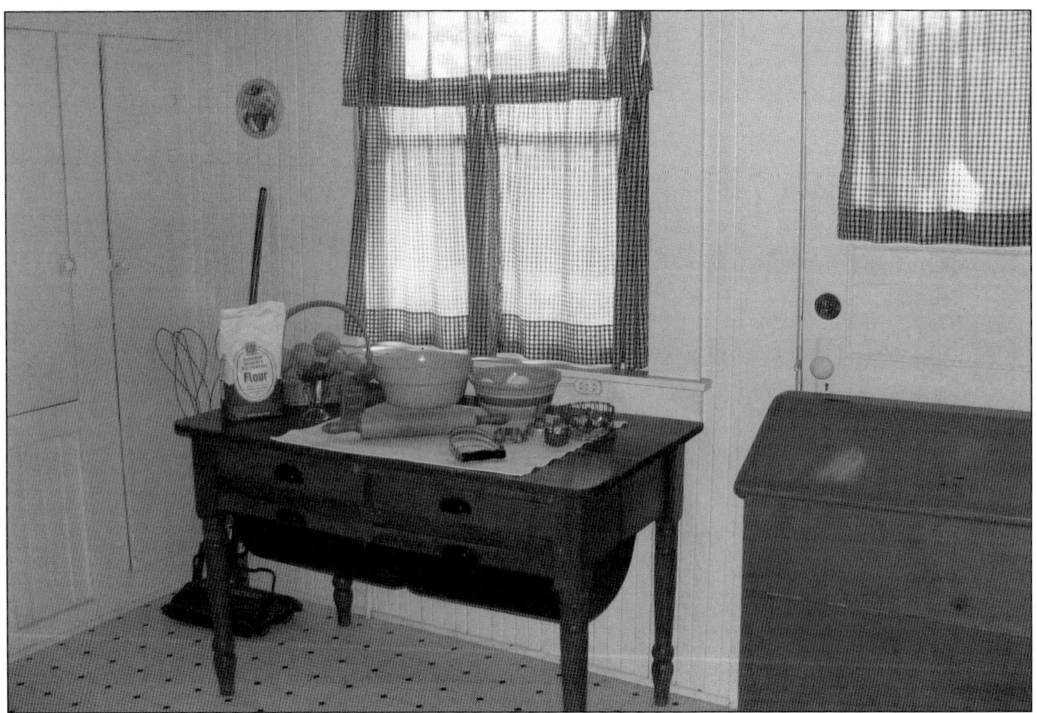

The kitchen of the Sarah A. Mooney Museum is furnished as it would have been in the late 1800s and early 1900s. (Photograph by Cynthia J. Wright.)

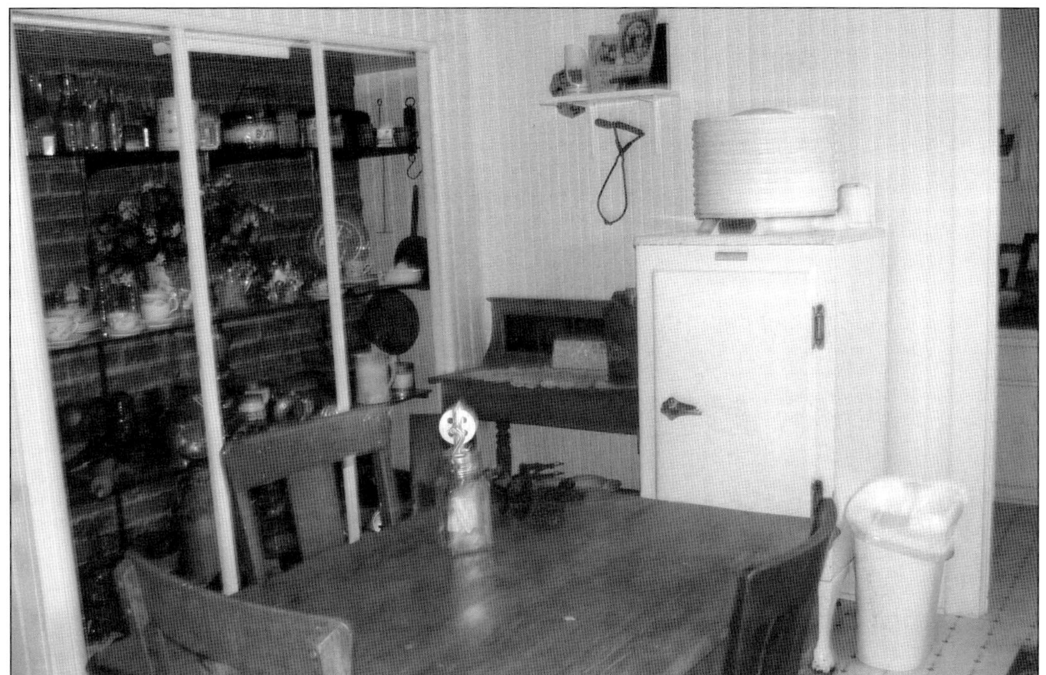

The shelves in the kitchen are full of artifacts and the implements used during the time the home was built. An early electric refrigerator made the Mooney home more convenient and modern. Prior to the electric appliance, food was often kept in an icebox. (Photograph by Cynthia J. Wright.)

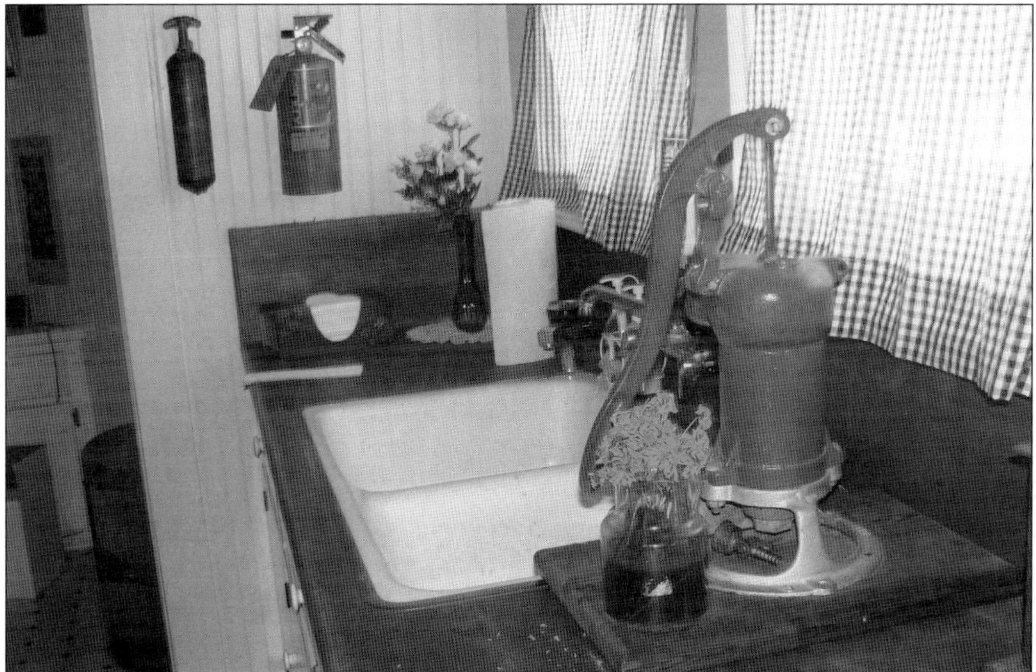

A hand pump inside the kitchen was a welcomed convenience when going outside on hot or cold days was unpleasant. The Mooney family had a pump next to their kitchen sink, as seen in the Mooney Museum. (Photograph by Cynthia J. Wright.)

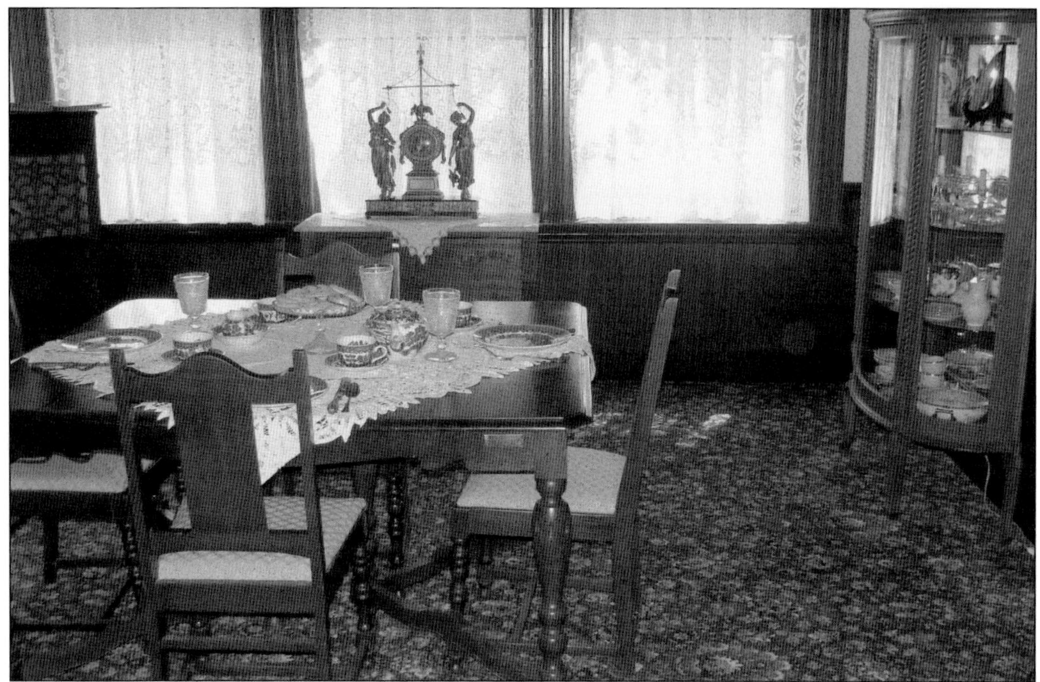

The Mooney's Victorian home is suitably furnished for the period. The dining table is set for a traditional family dinner. (Photograph by Cynthia J. Wright.)

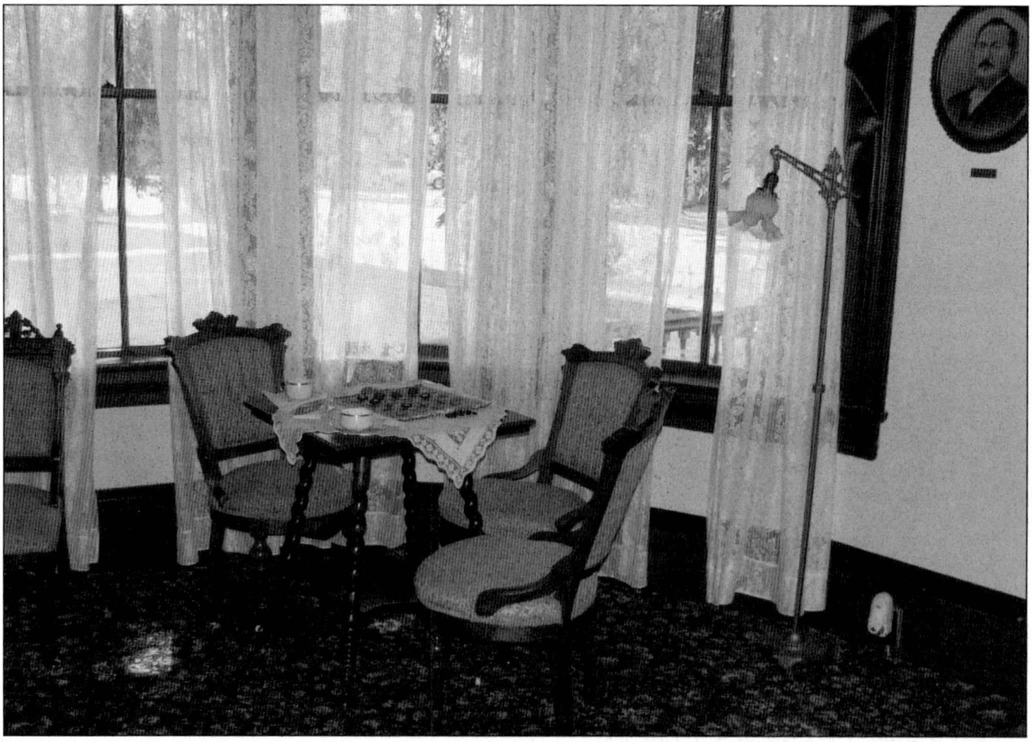

Most of the furnishings have been donated by various Lemoore families, but a few are actual artifacts given by the Mooney descendants. (Photograph by Cynthia J. Wright.)

The dresser in the Mooney bedroom displays photographs, trinkets, and hairbrushes from the era when the home was built. (Photograph by Cynthia J. Wright.)

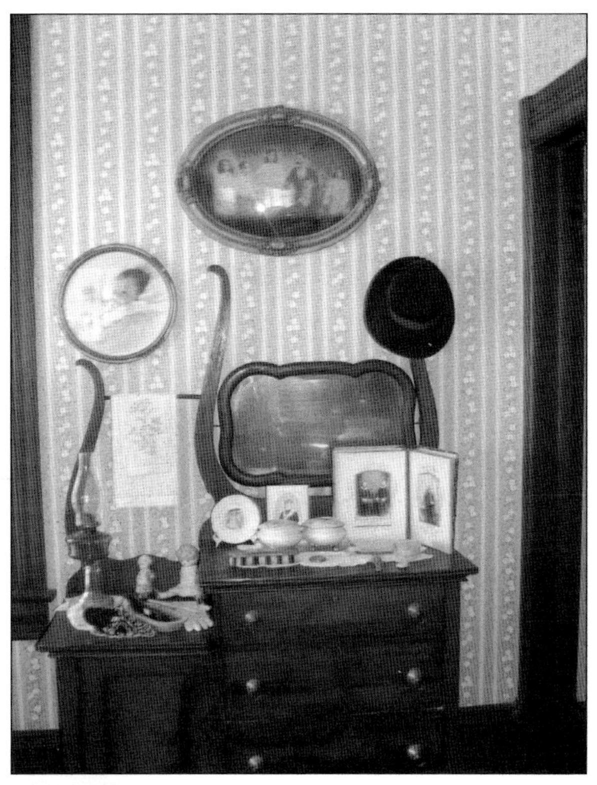

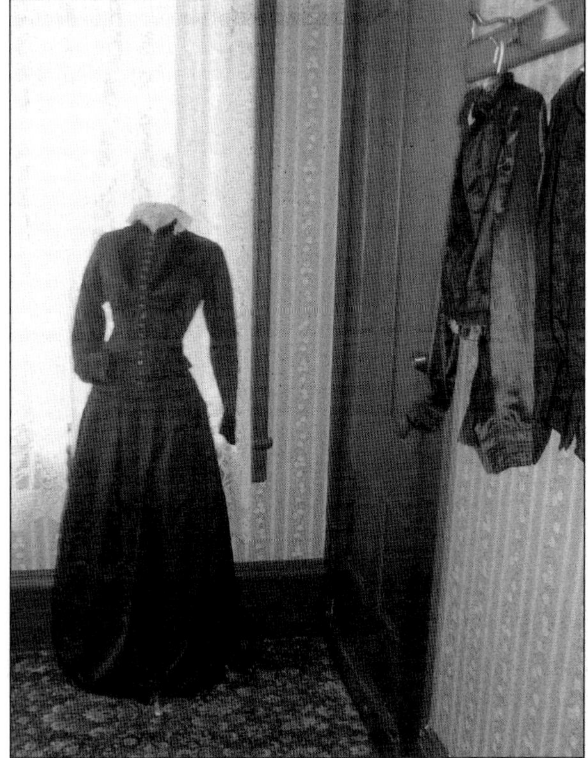

There are displays of clothing and handwork throughout the museum. A high-necked black dress is exhibited in the museum's sewing room. Shirts hang on a rack on the wall. The clothes on display are in the style of women's clothing worn during the late 19th century in Lemoore. (Photograph by Cynthia J. Wright.)

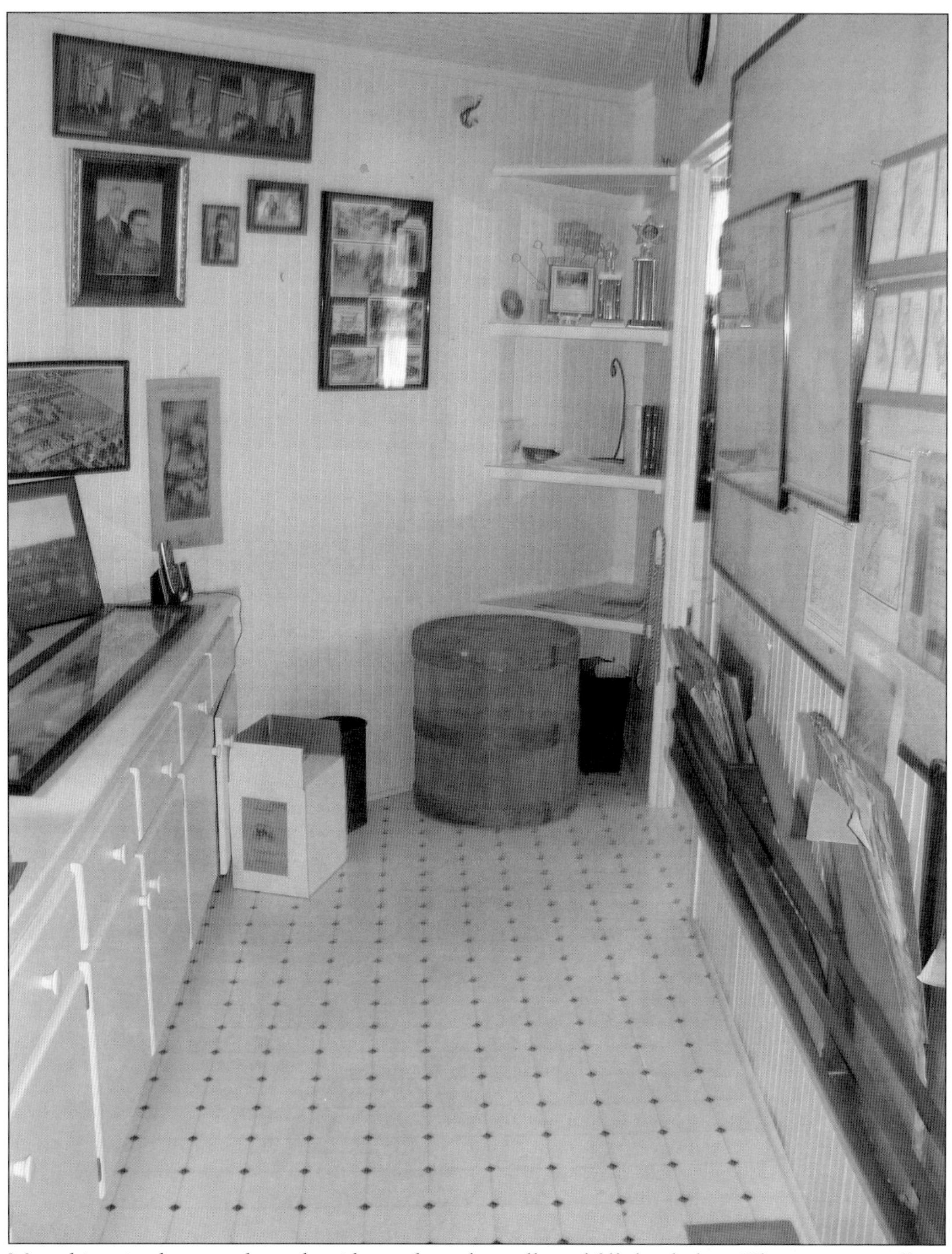

Many historic photographs and artifacts adorn the walls and fill the shelves. There is an excellent library of early Lemoore history. (Photograph by Cynthia J. Wright.)

Three

AGRICULTURE

The San Joaquin Valley's vast economy is based on agriculture. It was what brought the first pioneers to the Lemoore area, and even today, it is still the most significant industry in Kings County. The first ranchers had to deal with a yearly cycle of drought and flood, but water was not usually hard to find. Many early homesteads were built next to one of the artesian wells that bubbled water to the surface. These wells provided enough water for the household and usually enough for a garden as well. In winter, the area was ordinarily a mass of rivers and sloughs, so in the spring, the stockmen found lots of green grass for cattle, and the oak trees dropped acorns for their hogs. Spring was also the time when Tulare Lake would begin to dry up, since there was no incoming water from the rivers that fed it during the rainy season. As the lake level receded, men planted wheat in the still-wet soil. Grain farming continued on the lake in this manner for several decades.

The first real irrigation in the area was probably via the Rhoads Ditch, which tapped into the Kings River in 1861. Years later, state water engineer William Hall wrote that the Rhoads Canal seemed to be a system of natural waterways and short canals. Water flowed out of the Green Slough and went through the farms of Henry Rhoads, John Esrey, and Lancelot Gilroy on its way south. A "Claim for Water" filed in 1870 brought a canal through the Caruthers Slough from the Kings River, across the plains, to Tulare Lake and was completed in 1872. The canal watered about 6,000 acres at that time. Water has always been a sought-after commodity in the area. New waterworks in the so-called Island District of Lemoore, combined with a new dam in the Sierra, made for a water supply in the 1940s that would encourage a huge cotton-growing industry to be built. In 1963, growers to the west would benefit from the Central Valley Water Project, which brought water in from Northern California.

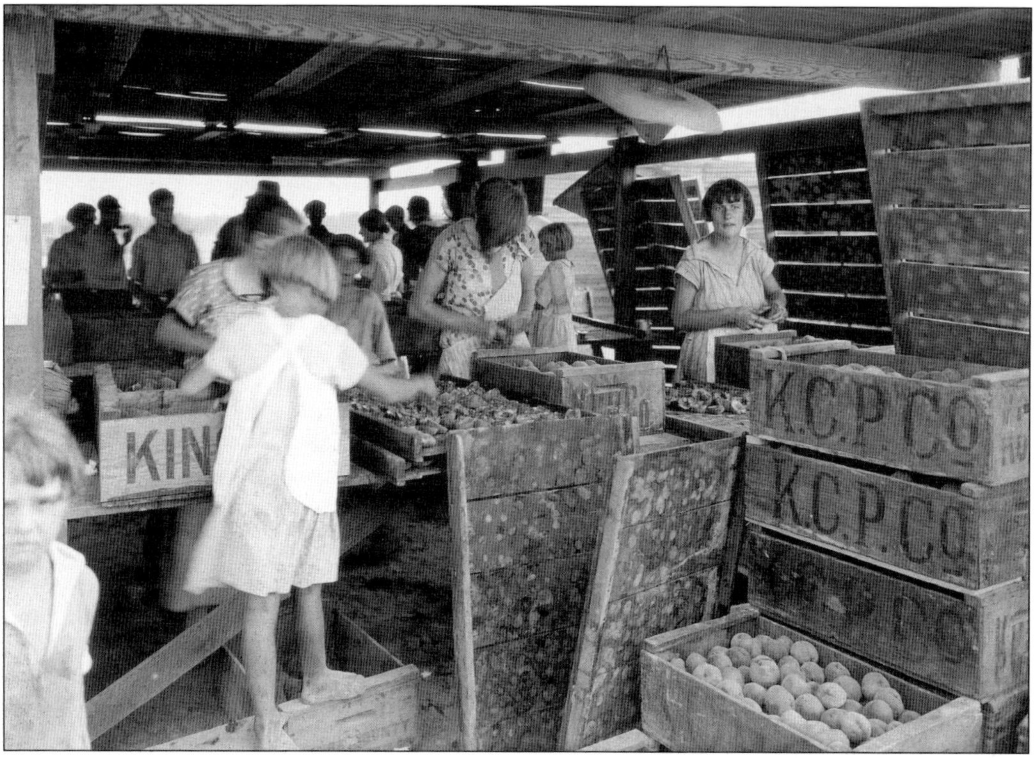

Children help as workers pack peach crates for the Kings County Packing Company in 1920. (Courtesy of Jack Stone.)

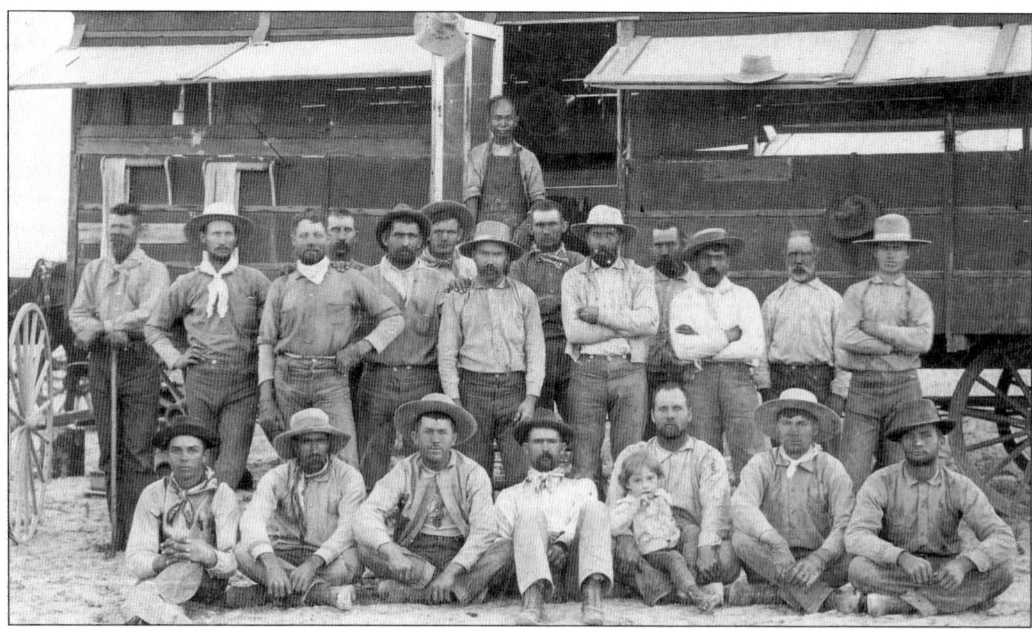

The scene on the Jacobs Ranch south of Lemoore around 1895 shows a rolling cook shack and mess hall with a Chinese cook in the doorway. L. W. Sweaney was the foreman of the ranch. The boy in front is Sweaney's four-year-old son, Ross. (Courtesy of the Sarah A. Mooney Museum.)

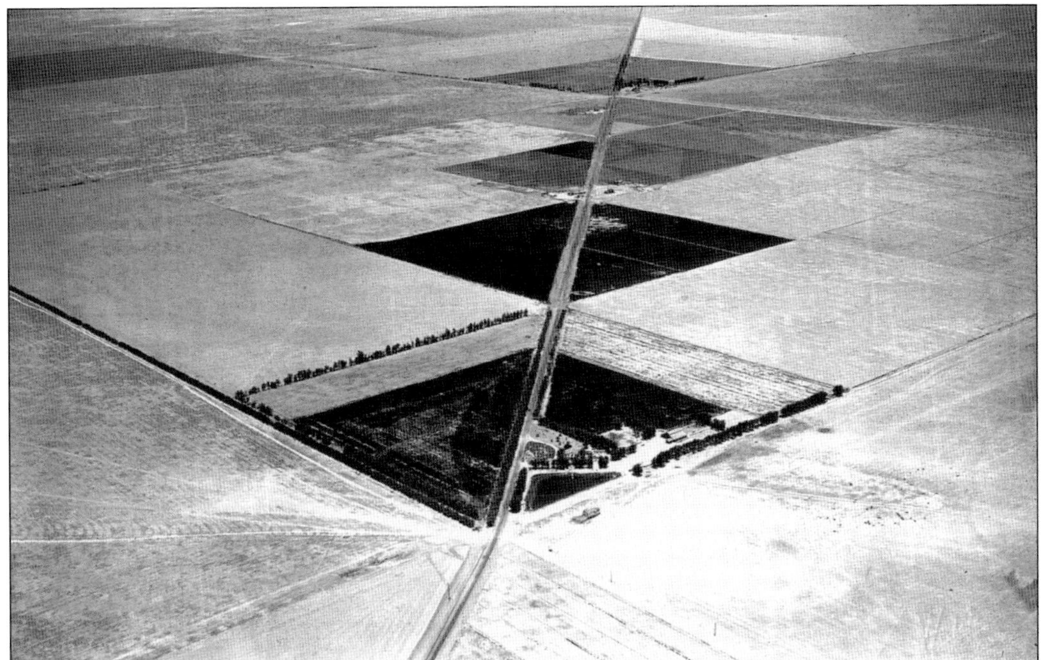

An aerial view of the original demonstration farms and sample homes built by the Kings County Development Company provided insight into what would be constructed on the west side of Lemoore. (Courtesy of Jack Stone.)

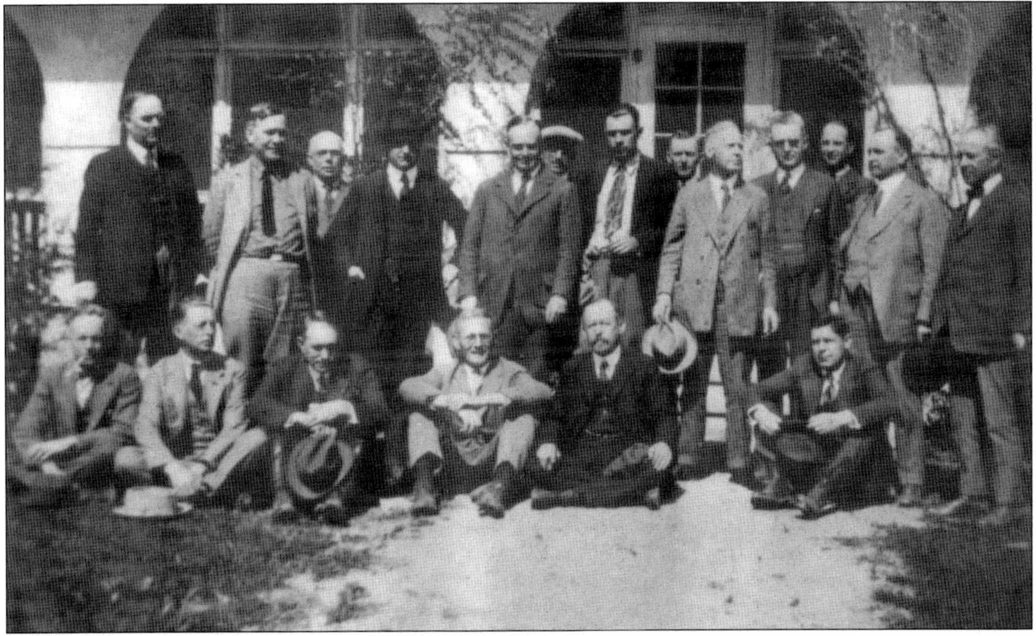

The Southern Pacific Railroad men who founded the Kings County Development (KCD) Company pose for a photograph. Pictured from left to right are (first row) Mr. Block, Mr. Burton, Mr. Wright, Mr. Nares, Mr. Wooster, and Mr. Klingensmith; (second row) Mr. Faulkner, Dr. Janes, Mr. Keisner, Mr. Cornwall, Mr. Stone, Mr. Robbins, Mr. Mendenhall, Mr. Springer, and Mr. Poundstone; (third row) Mr. Pine, unidentified, Mr. Schindler, and Mr. Massey. (Courtesy of Jack Stone.)

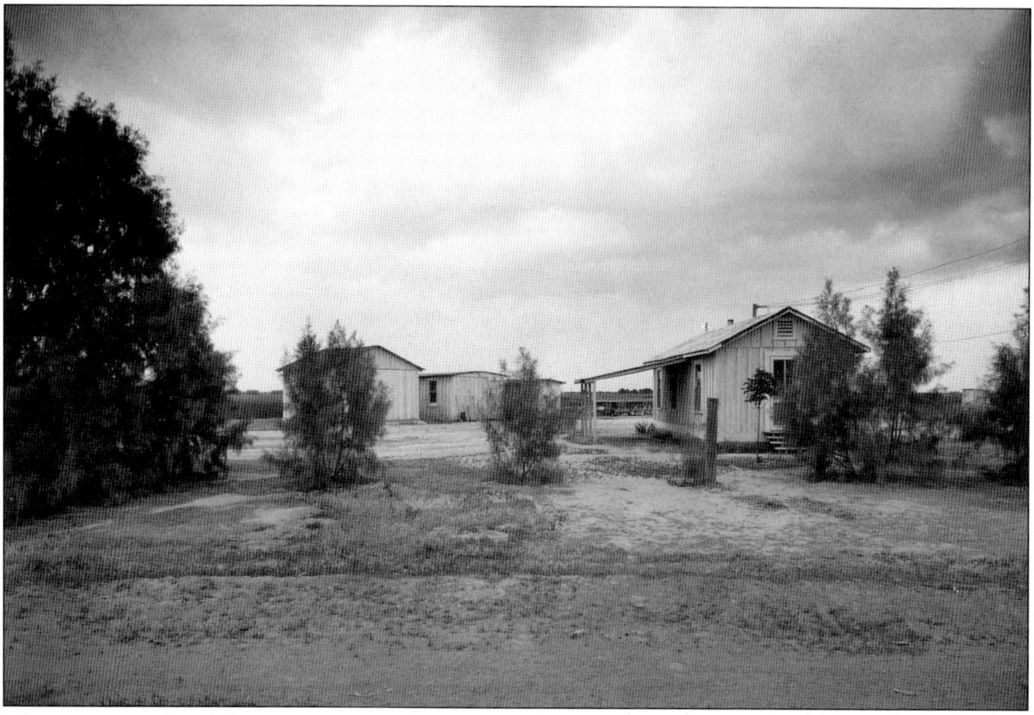

This is a sample of the Kings County Development Company ranch housing that was built northwest of Lemoore. (Courtesy of Jack Stone.)

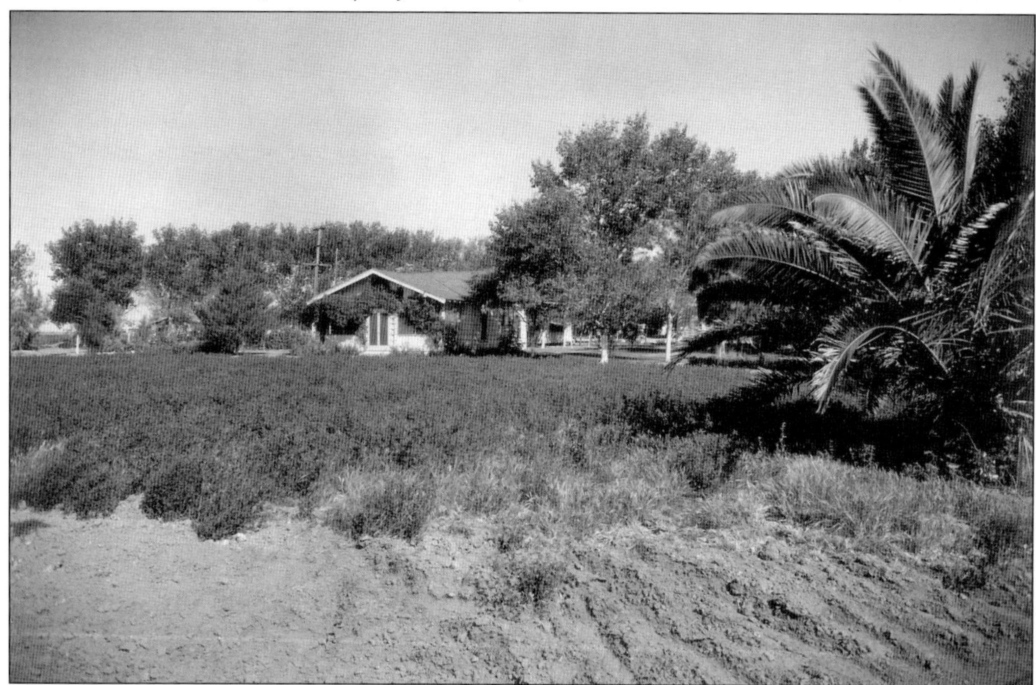

This is another view of a ranch house located on one of the demonstration farms, which were built by the Kings County Development Company to experiment with agricultural and residential expansion on the west side of Lemoore. (Courtesy of Jack Stone.)

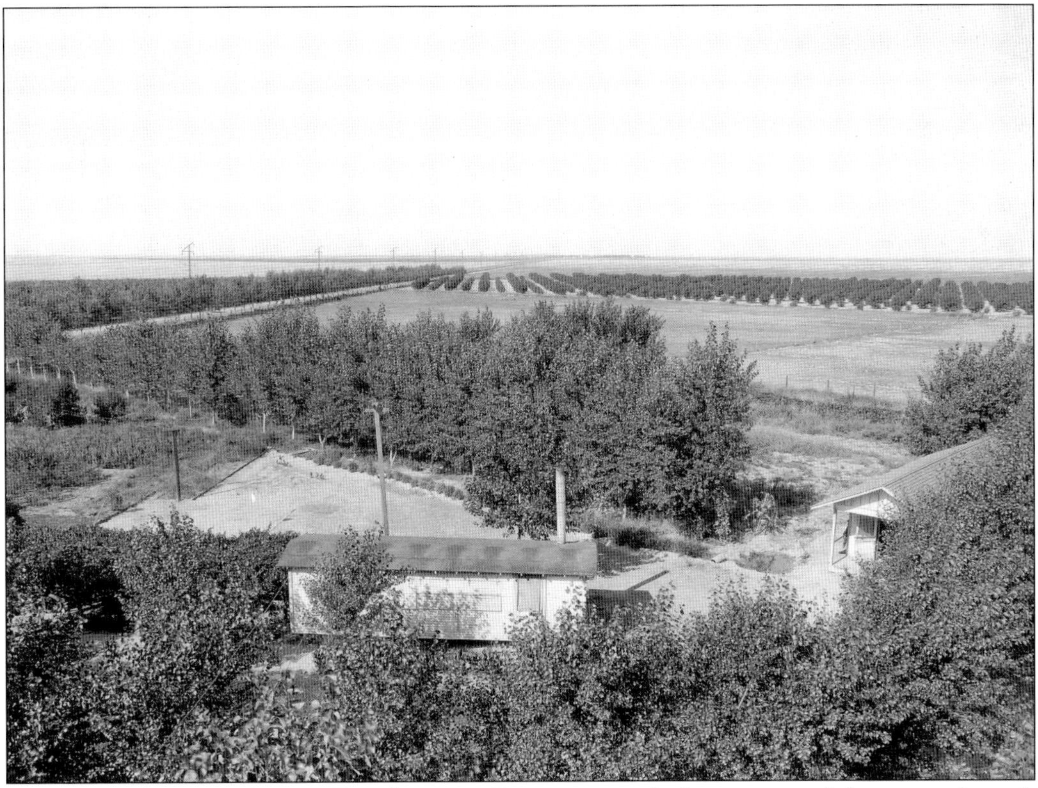

This view of a Kings County Development Company ranch shows some of the crops planted, with homes in the foreground. (Courtesy of Jack Stone.)

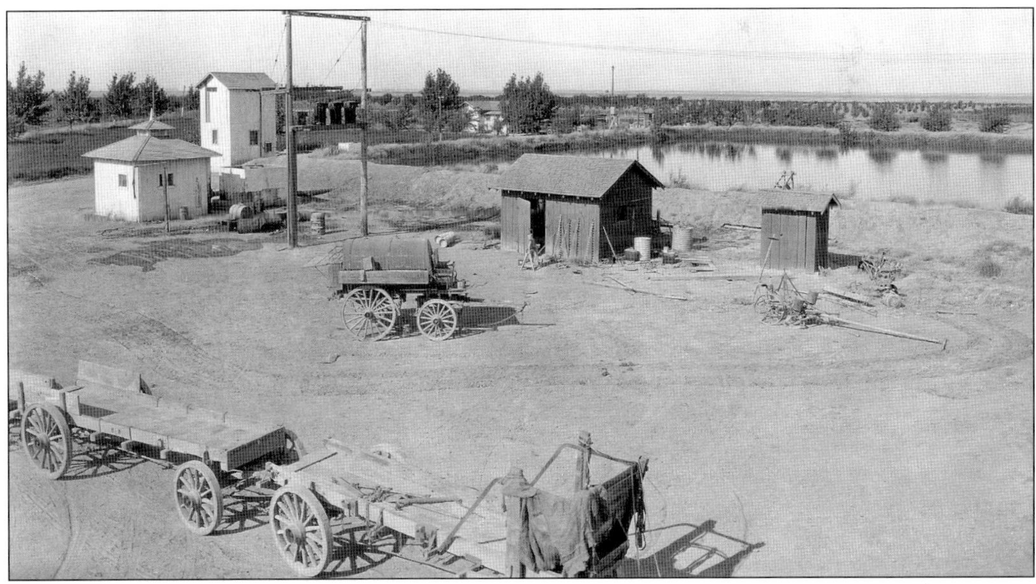

Ranch equipment sits unused at one of the Kings County Development Company ranches. Grain sacks and other commodities were carried on wagons like the one seen at the bottom of this photograph. (Courtesy of Jack Stone.)

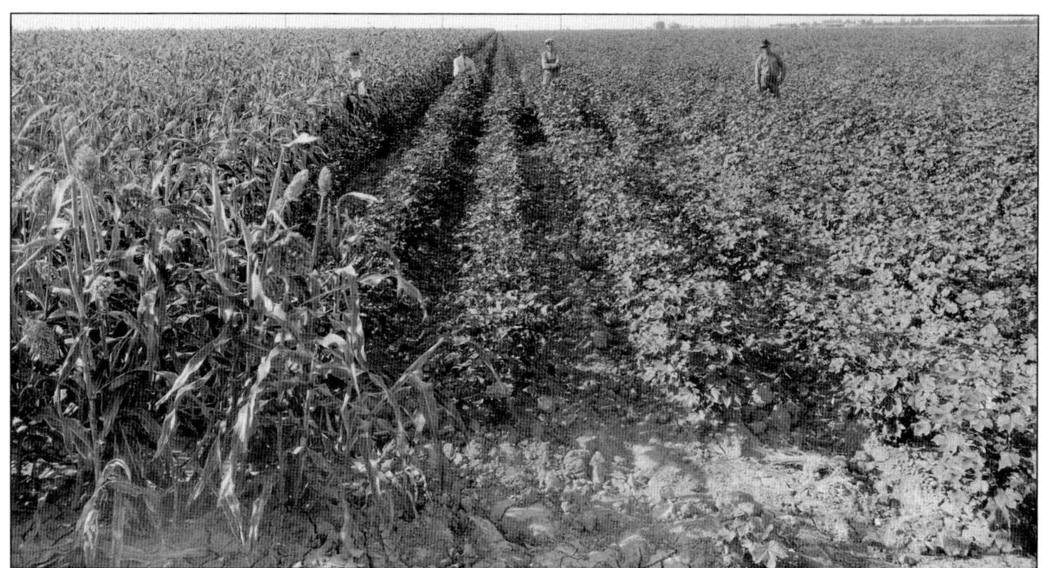

The Kings County Development Company grew a variety of crops. According to longtime area farmer Jack Stone, the company was started by a group of Southern Pacific Railroad men who retired and bought a couple thousand acres of land to prove that a crop could be raised on it. They built three successful demonstration farms in the 1910s and 1920s. They later sold the farms. (Courtesy of Jack Stone.)

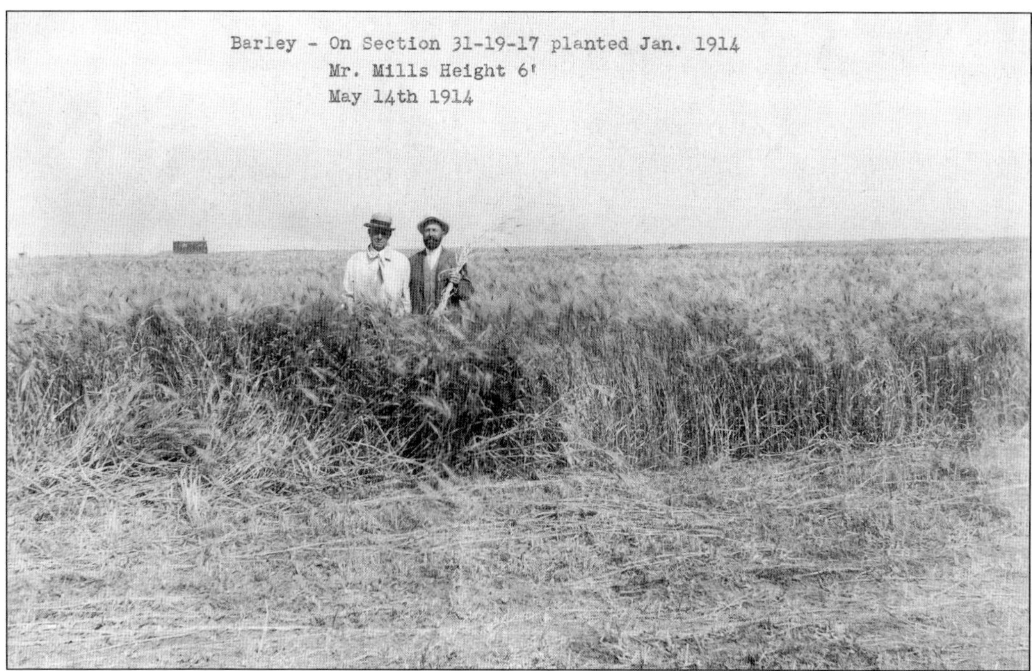

Barley was one of the crops grown by the Kings County Development Company. The men in the field, one of whom is identified as Mr. Mills, are demonstrating the height of the barley by comparing it to their own heights—6 feet. (Courtesy of Jack Stone.)

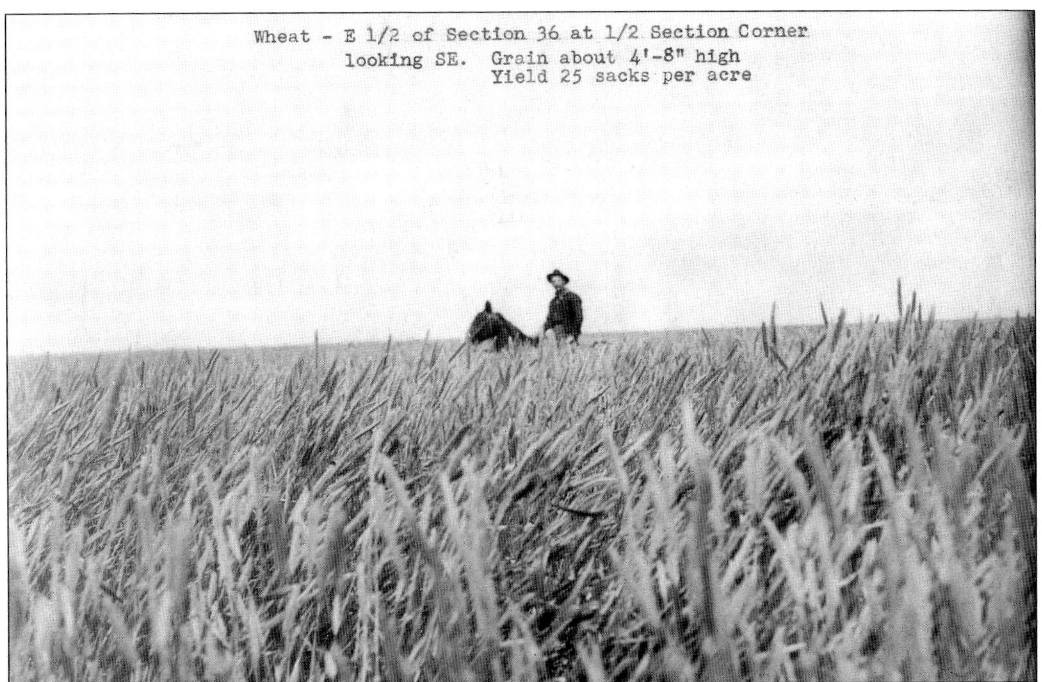

Wheat was a crop grown by the Kings County Development Company that did well in the San Joaquin Valley. (Courtesy of Jack Stone.)

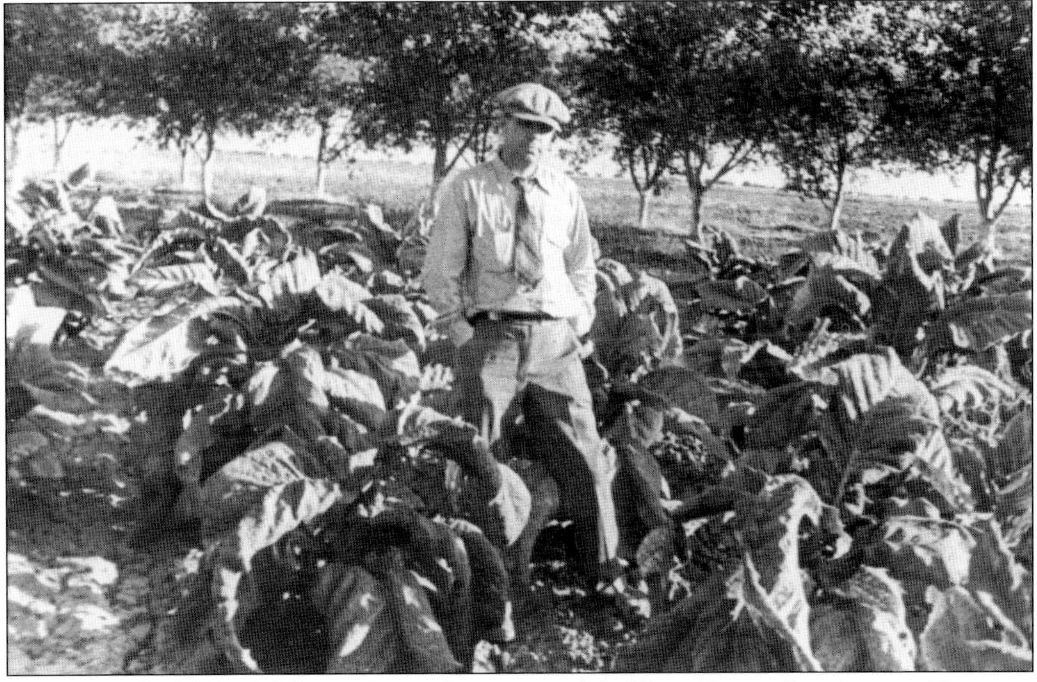

L. M. Stone, Jack Stone's father and an early manager of the Kings County Development Company, stands in a field of tobacco. This was just one of the many crops the company attempted to grow. Among the crops they tried were wheat, cotton, onions, turnips, barley, corn, grapes, cantaloupes, olives, flowers, and lettuce. Tobacco did not grow well. (Courtesy of Jack Stone.)

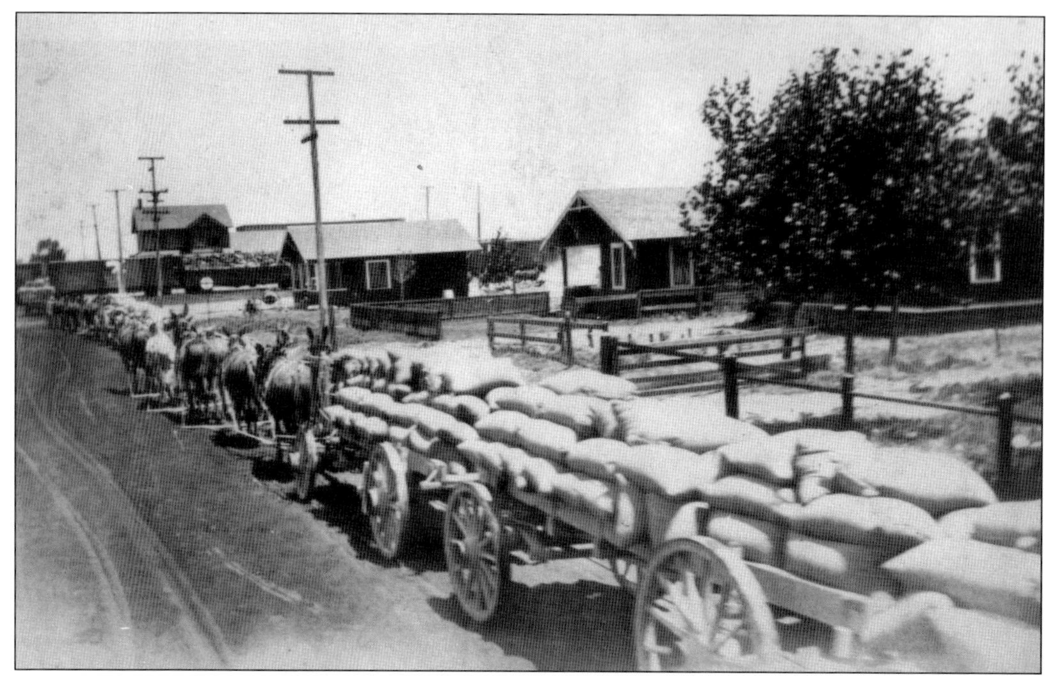

Horse-drawn wagons hauling grain from the Tulare Lake Basin wait for a train going into Stratford. (Courtesy of Jack Stone.)

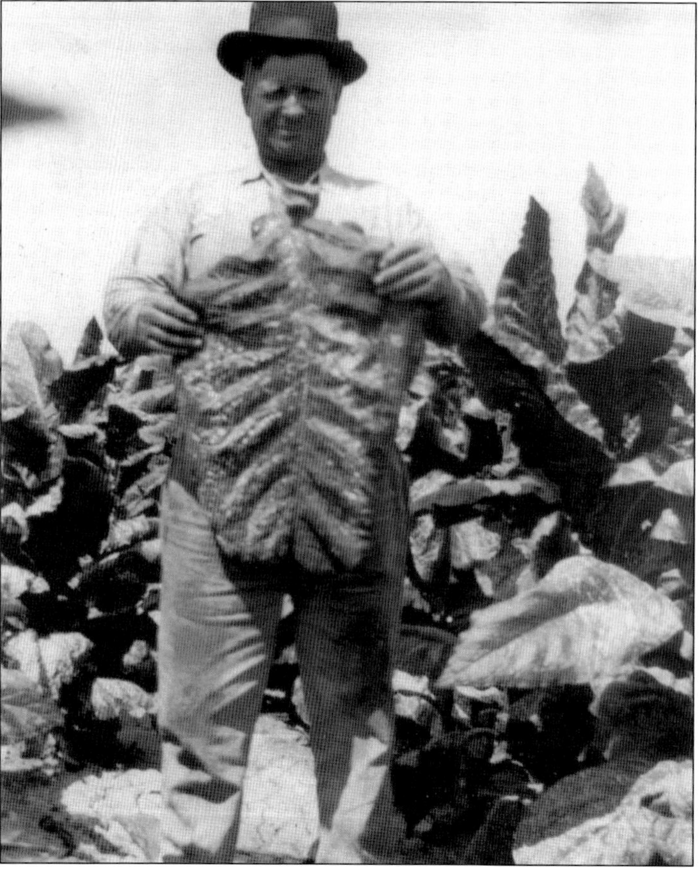

Gus Sutter shows the size of a tobacco leaf. Sutter grew tobacco in the early farming days near Lemoore. (Courtesy of Jack Stone.)

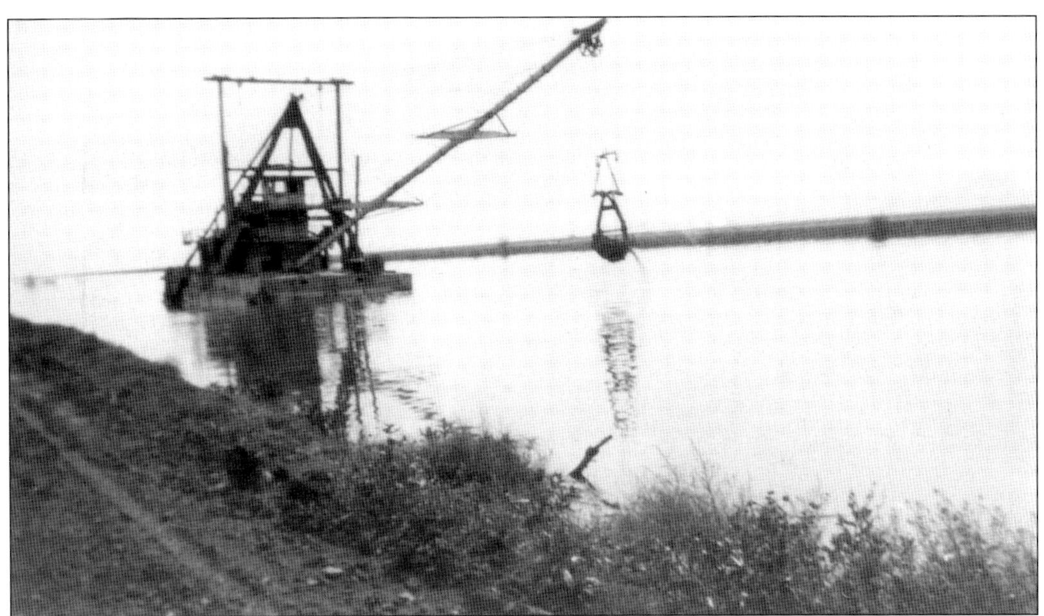

A dredge removes dirt from a canal to provide better farming opportunities near Tulare Lake after a flood broke a levee. (Courtesy of Jack Stone.)

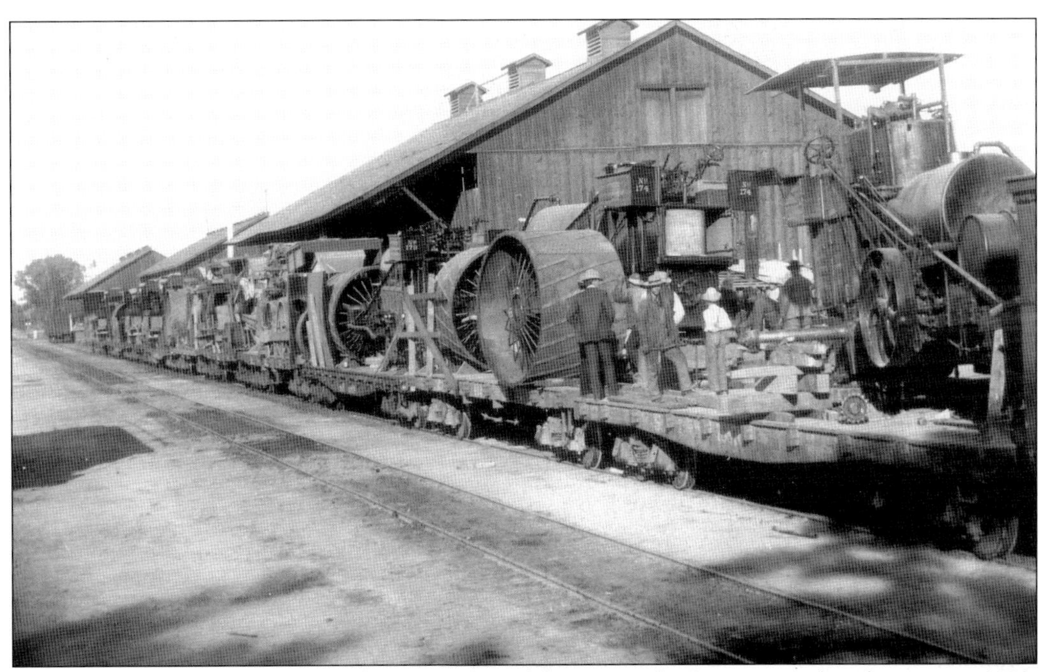

Five steam-driven tractors arrived in parts aboard flatcars at the Lemoore railroad station in 1901. Brought to the lake country by Hiram Clawson, they were reassembled at the site, E and Fox Streets, and driven out of town under their own power. (Courtesy of Jack Stone.)

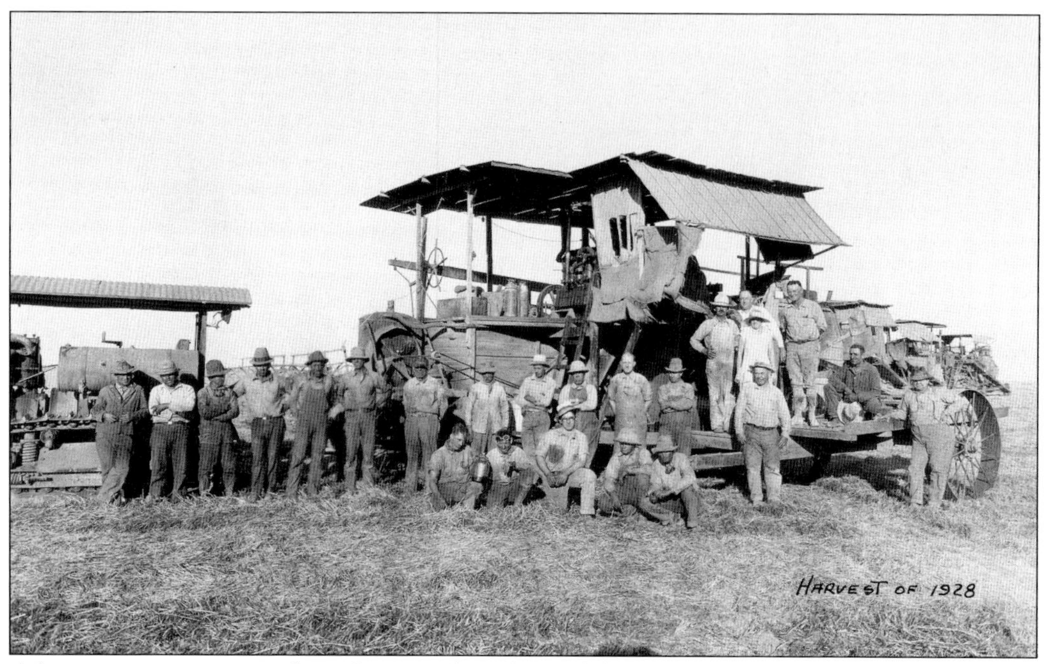

A harvesting crew pauses for a photograph in front of their farming equipment during the 1928 harvest. (Courtesy of Jack Stone.)

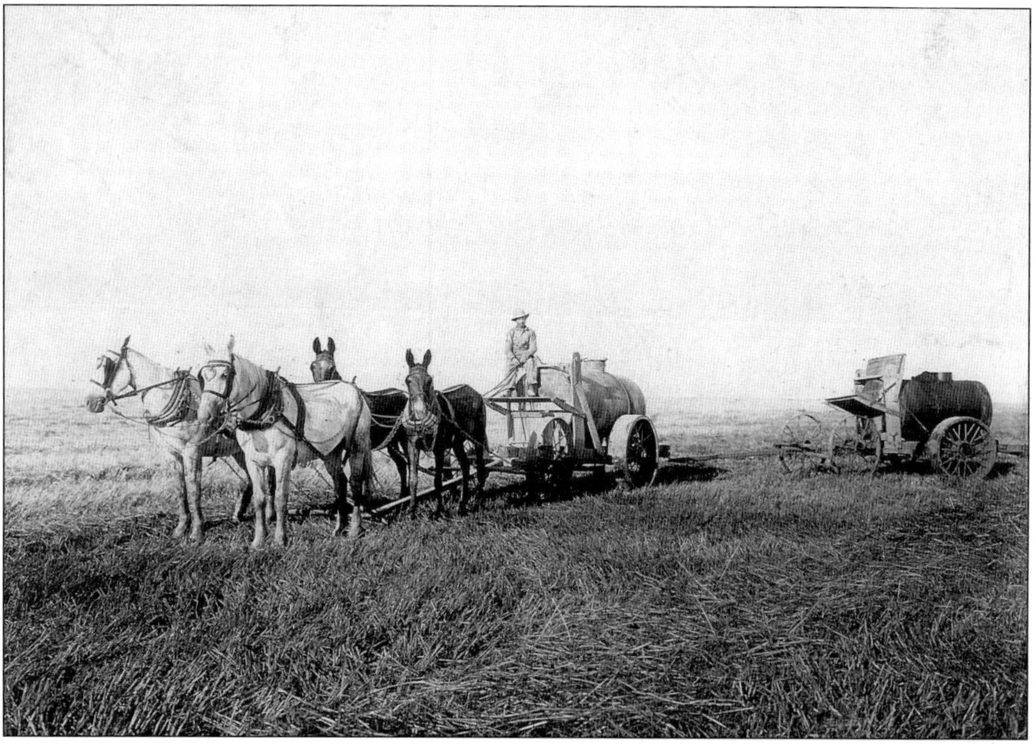

This was the Blakeley Ranch in 1912. Water and oil backup tanks were used to supply these harvesters, which needed to be refueled about every two hours. (Courtesy of the Sarah A. Mooney Museum.)

Bud Blakeley and his family lean against his ditching plow. According to Jack Stone, "Blakeley didn't have anything to do that summer so he took this plow and dug a ditch over to the coast and then put a pipe in it." (Courtesy of Jack Stone.)

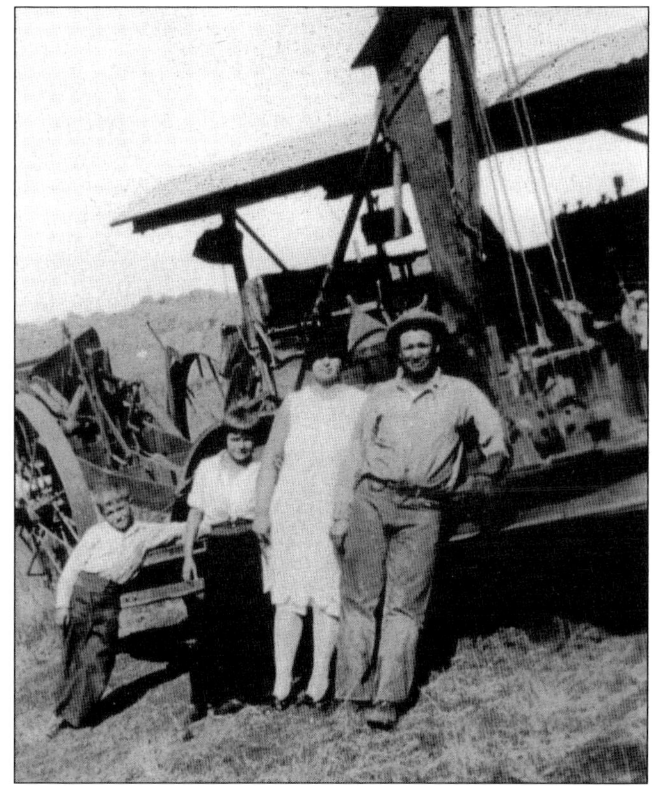

Art Wolfson (left) and L. M. Stone survey a break in the levy on Tulare Lake. The levee broke during the flood of 1938. Breaks in the levees on Tulare Lake happened every 10 years during floods. (Courtesy of Jack Stone.)

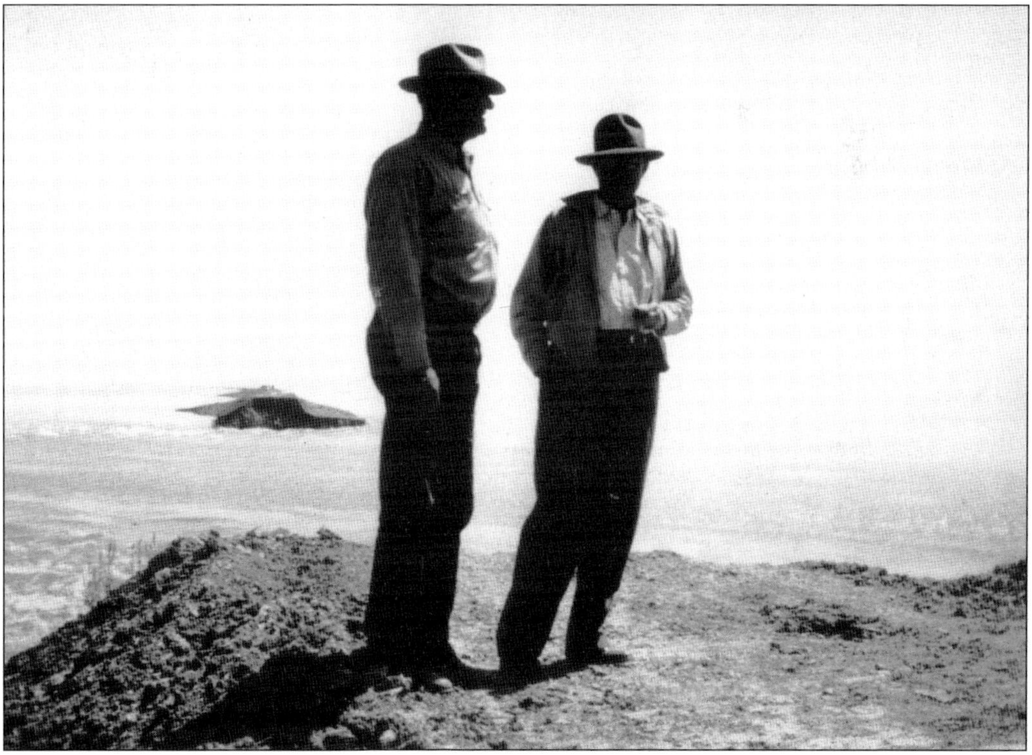

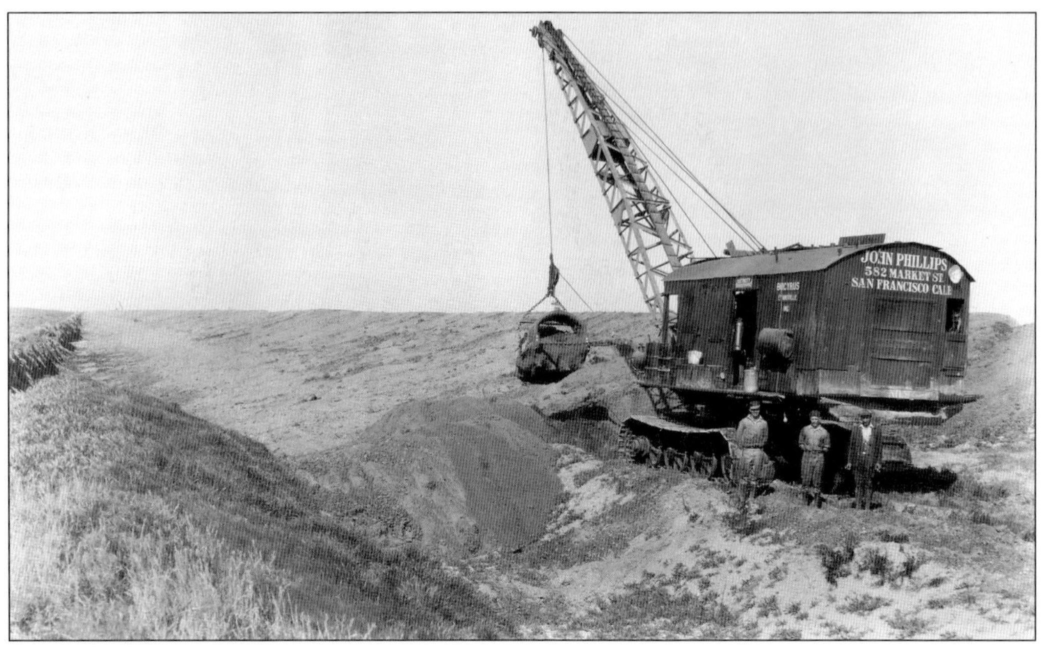

Local farmers hired John Phillips to build a levy in 1938. (Courtesy of Jack Stone.)

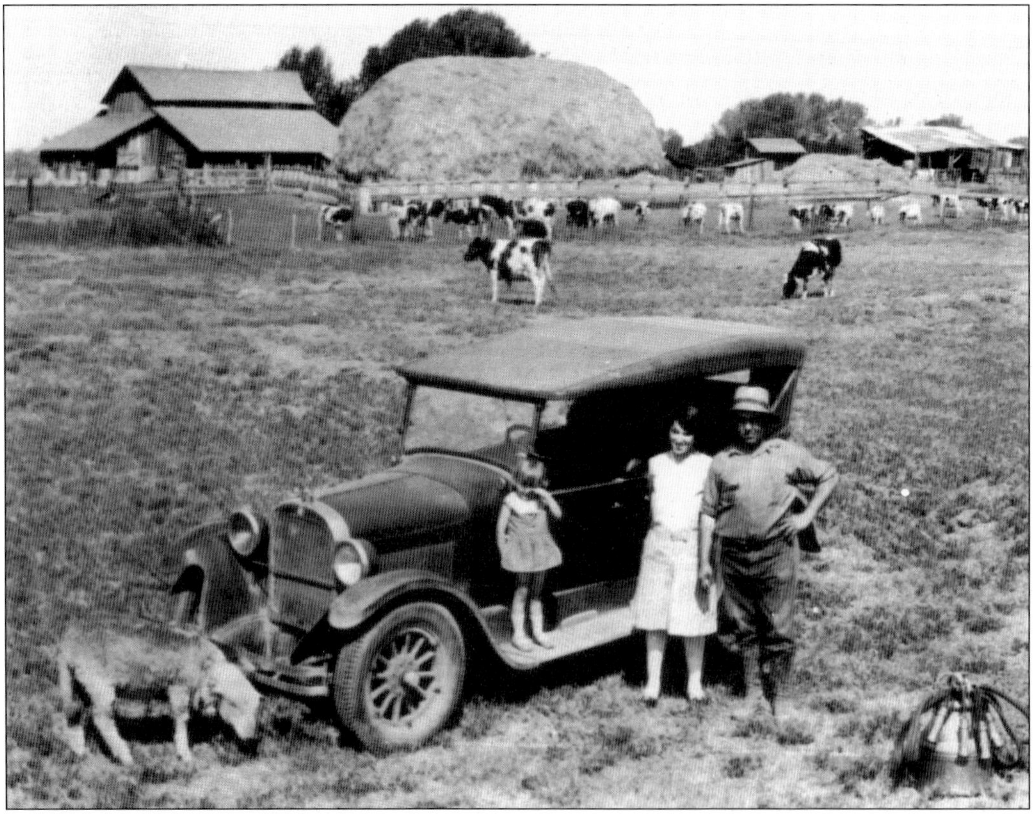

Emma McGill stands on the running board of the family car at the Rocha Dairy in 1929. (Courtesy of Jack Stone.)

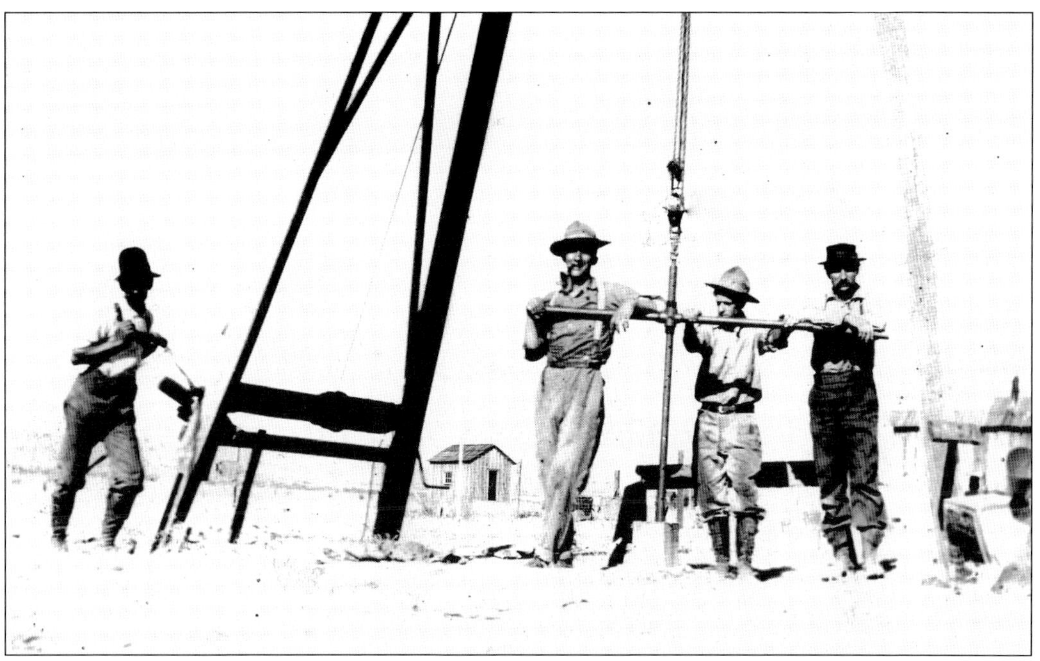

Walter Cameron and three men work tirelessly at drilling for water. Cameron, the shortest in the photograph, was one of the early homesteaders on the farms created by the Kings County Development Company. (Courtesy of Jack Stone.)

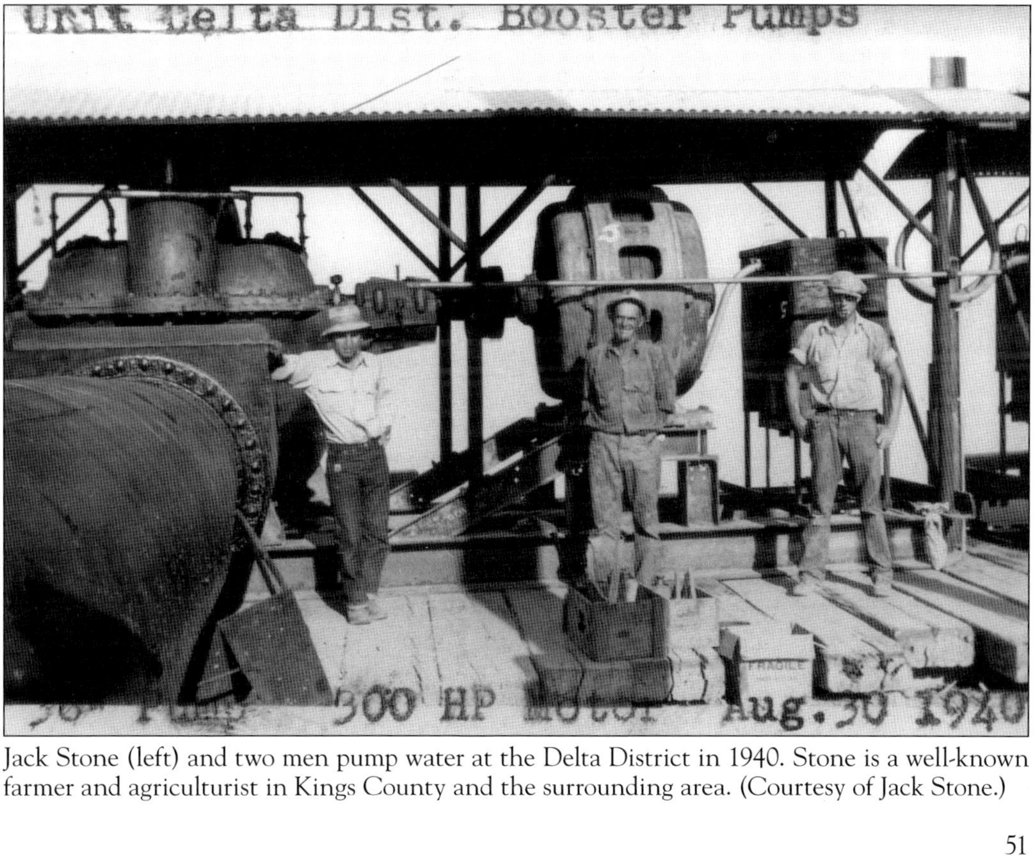

Jack Stone (left) and two men pump water at the Delta District in 1940. Stone is a well-known farmer and agriculturist in Kings County and the surrounding area. (Courtesy of Jack Stone.)

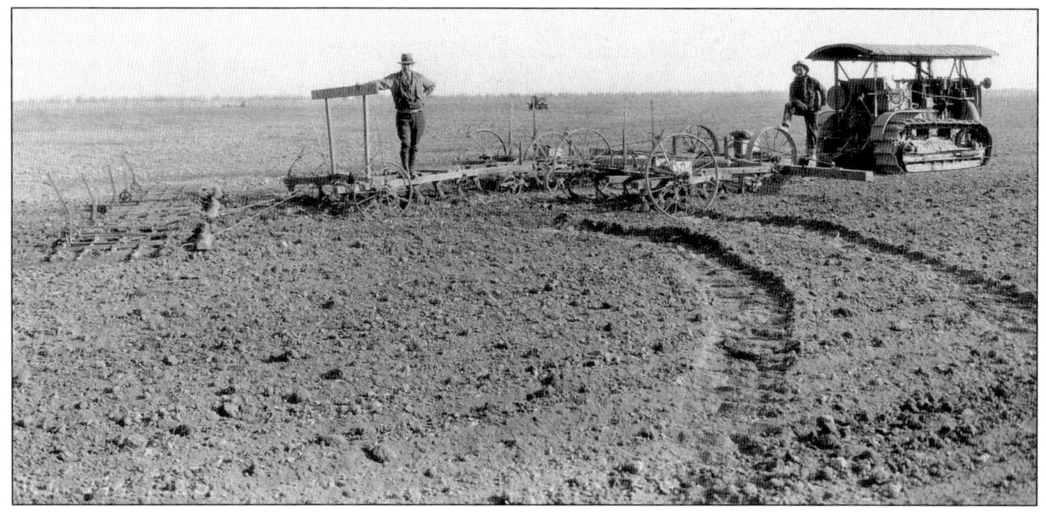

A Caterpillar tractor drags a spring tooth and disc through this field to prepare the ground for the next year's farming season. Workers take a break during the long, hard process to catch their breath and pose for a picture. (Courtesy of Jack Stone.)

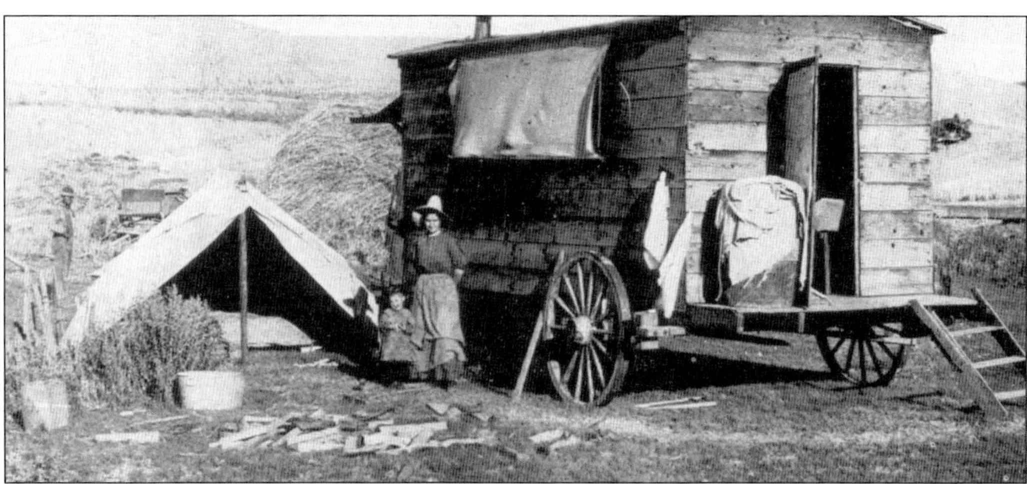

Portable cookhouses kept the farmers fed while out in the field, saving time during the harvest. (Courtesy of Jack Stone.)

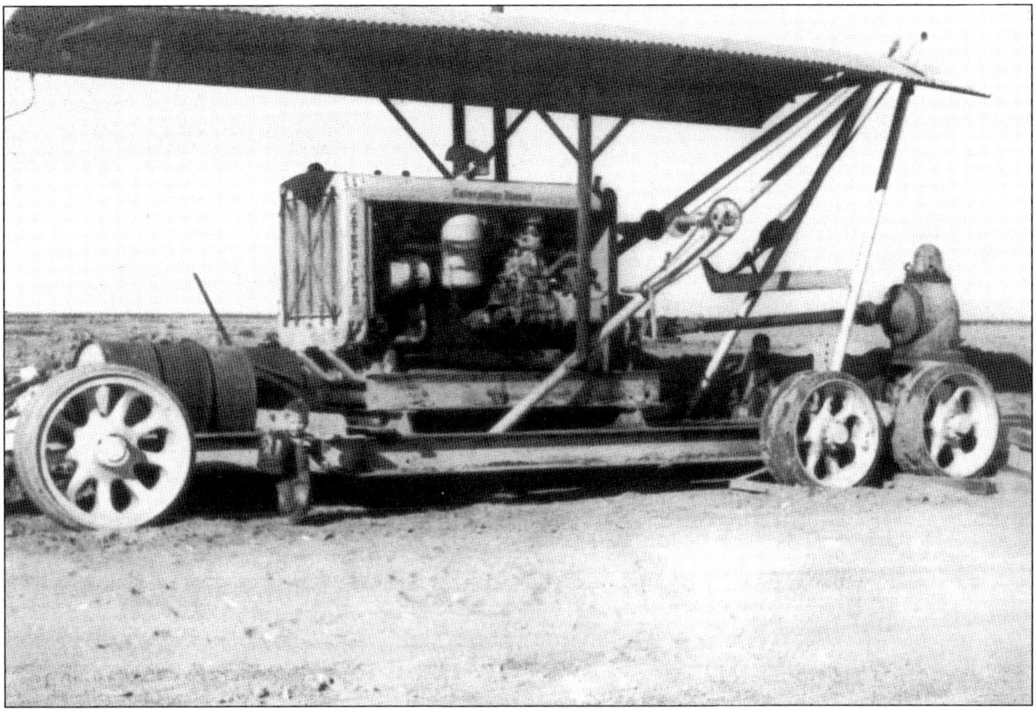

A little boy holds a bucket in front of an early diesel-powered Caterpillar in the field. (Courtesy of Jack Stone.)

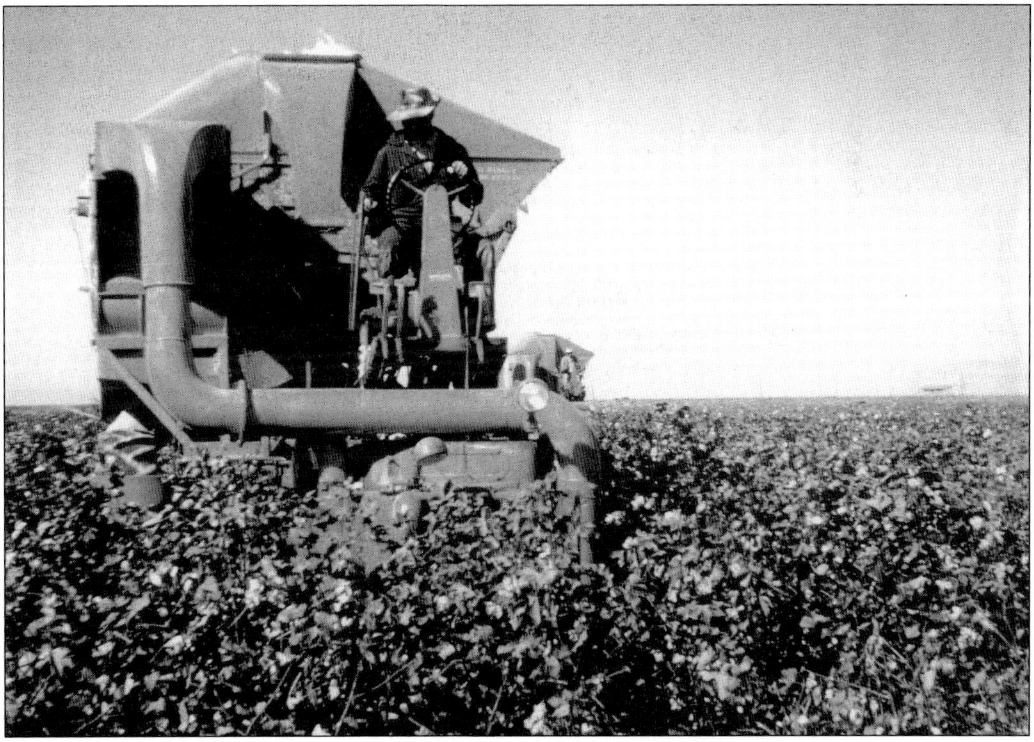

One of the earliest automated cotton-pickers harvests the cotton crop. (Courtesy of Jack Stone.)

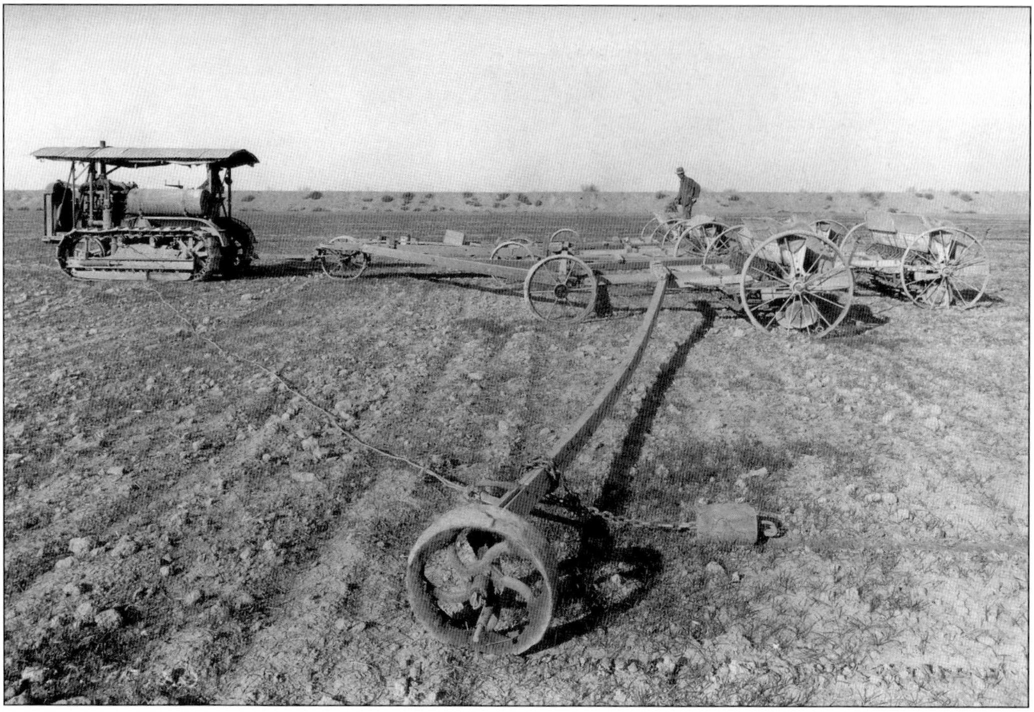

These two photographs depict the great advancement in farming capabilities from the beginning to the middle of the 20th century. The above image shows an early Caterpillar tractor towing planters in a field. Notice the difference in size of the planter in the below photograph, taken in the late 1920s. Farm sizes increased from approximately 100 acres per person to thousands of acres with the development of new equipment and enhanced farming and irrigation practices. (Courtesy of Jack Stone.)

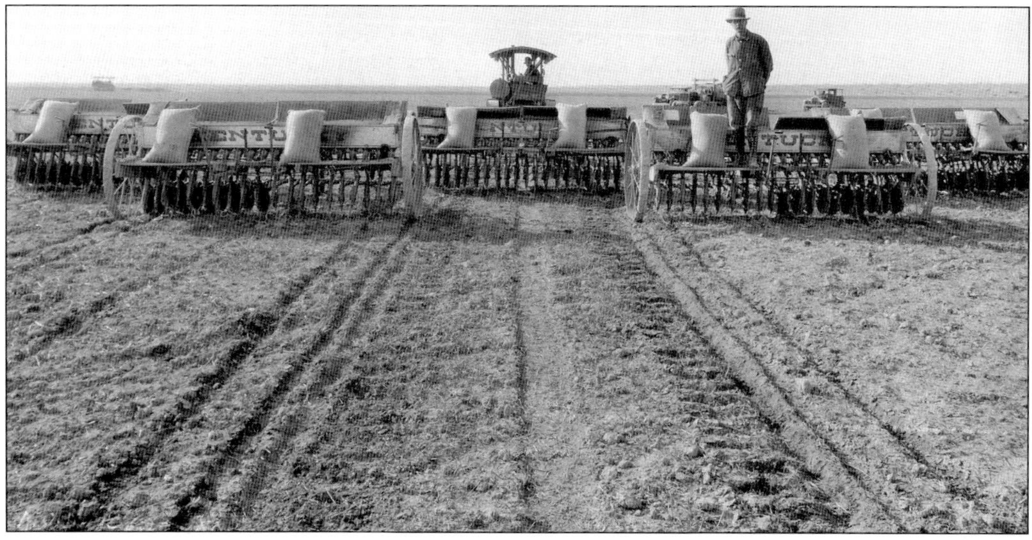

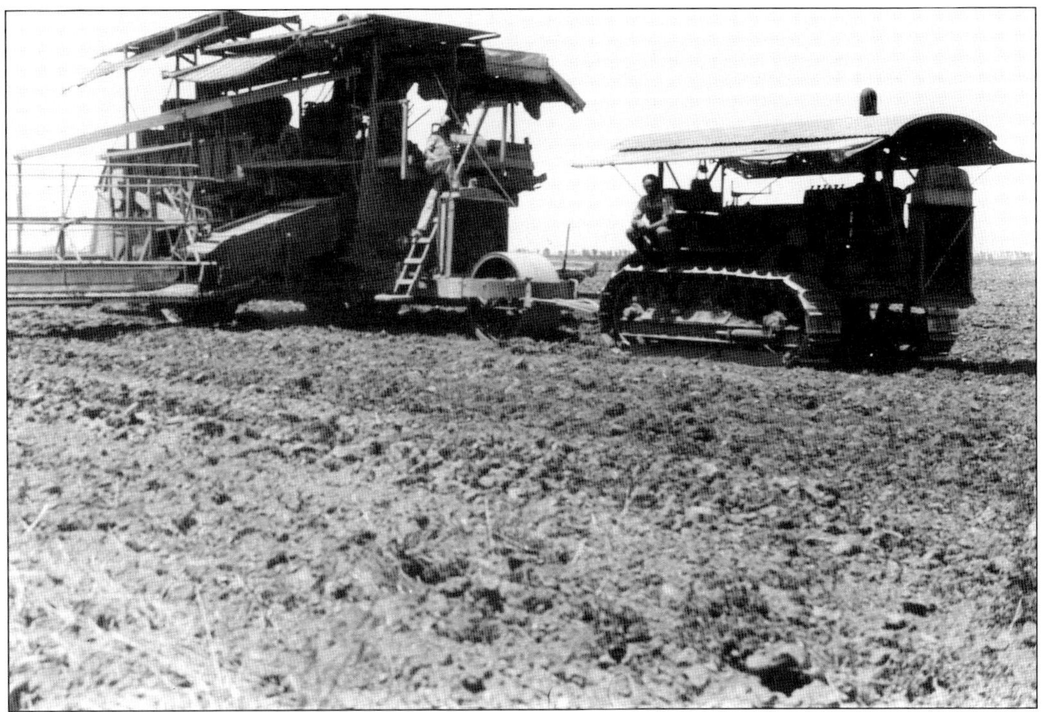

A grain harvester is pulled through the field by a tractor. (Courtesy of Jack Stone.)

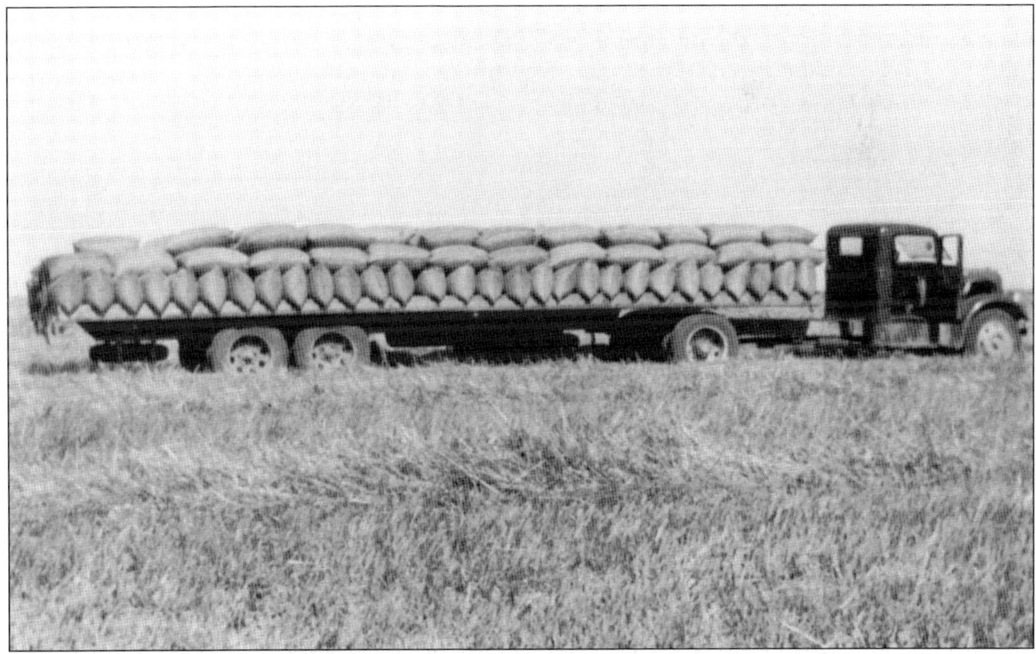

A truck with a long flatbed hauls grain out of the field. Once on the flatbed, the grain heads out to be made into wheat for hungry humans. Much grain from the Lemoore area is used to fatten animals for human consumption and dairy cattle feed. (Courtesy of Jack Stone.)

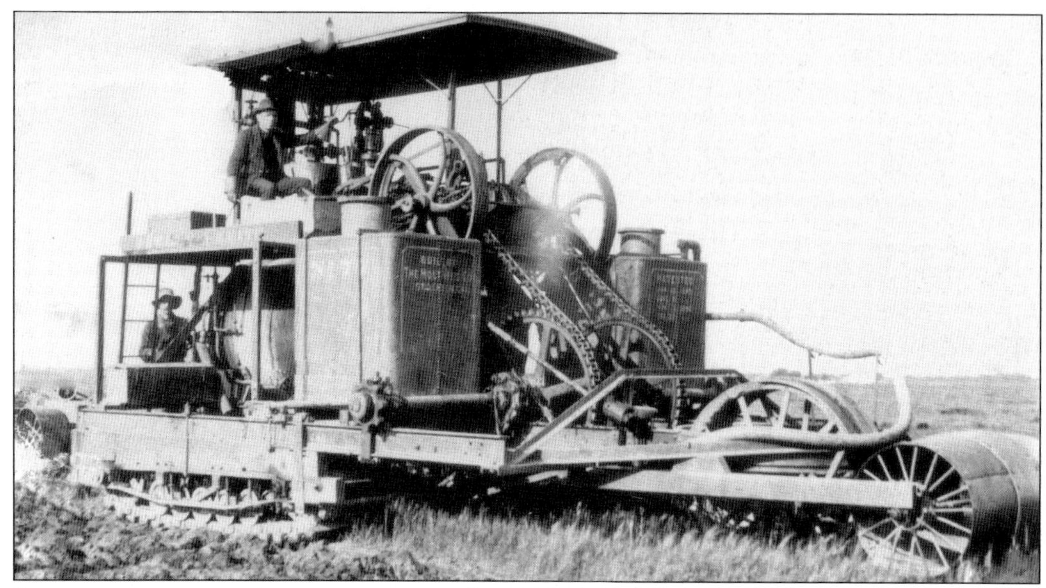

Farmers operate an early steam tractor in the 1940s. (Courtesy of Jack Stone.)

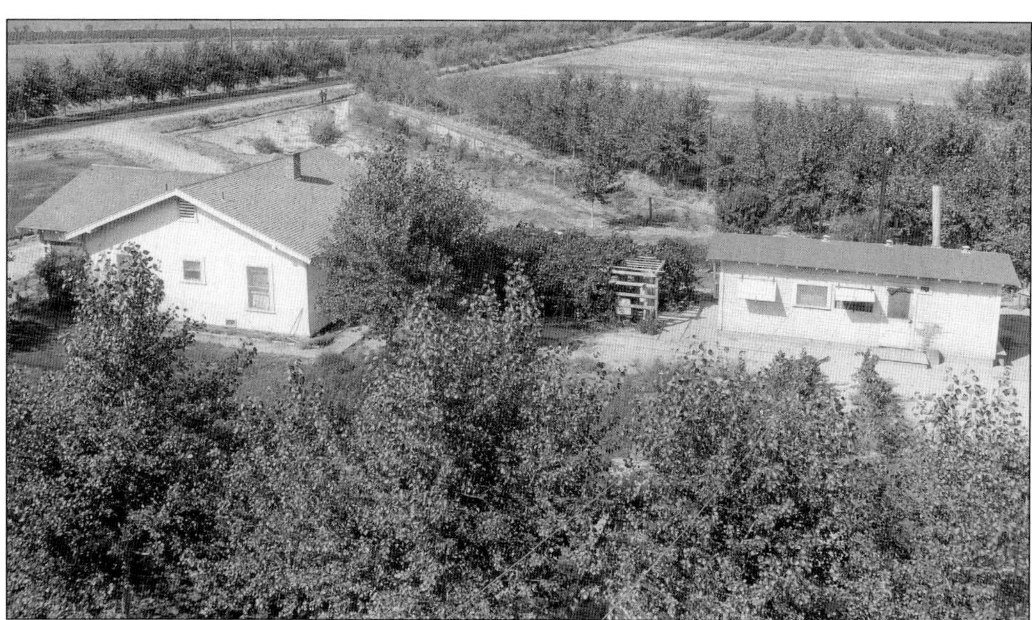

Pictured is one of the homes on the original sample farms built west of Lemoore by the Kings County Development Company. (Courtesy of Jack Stone.)

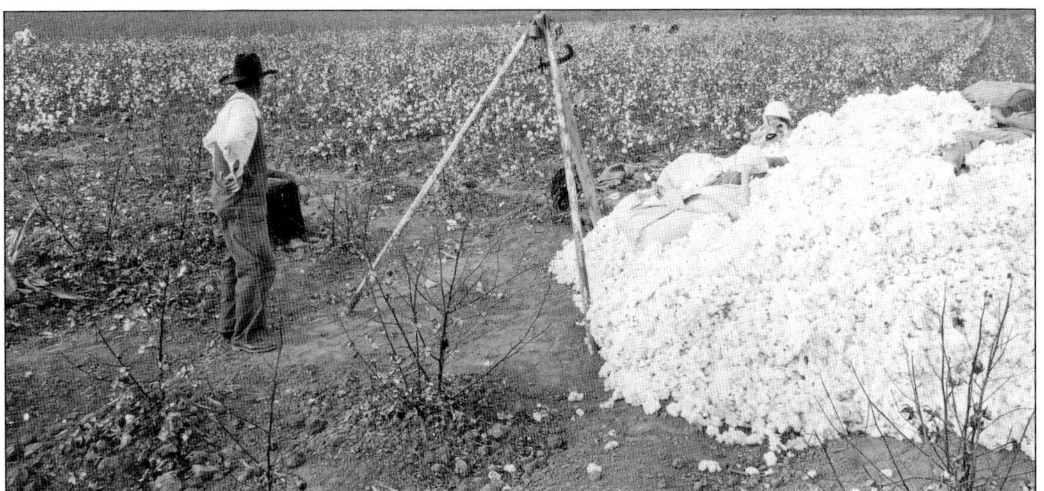

A farmer surveys his field and the fruits of a cotton harvest in 1947. (Courtesy of Jack Stone.)

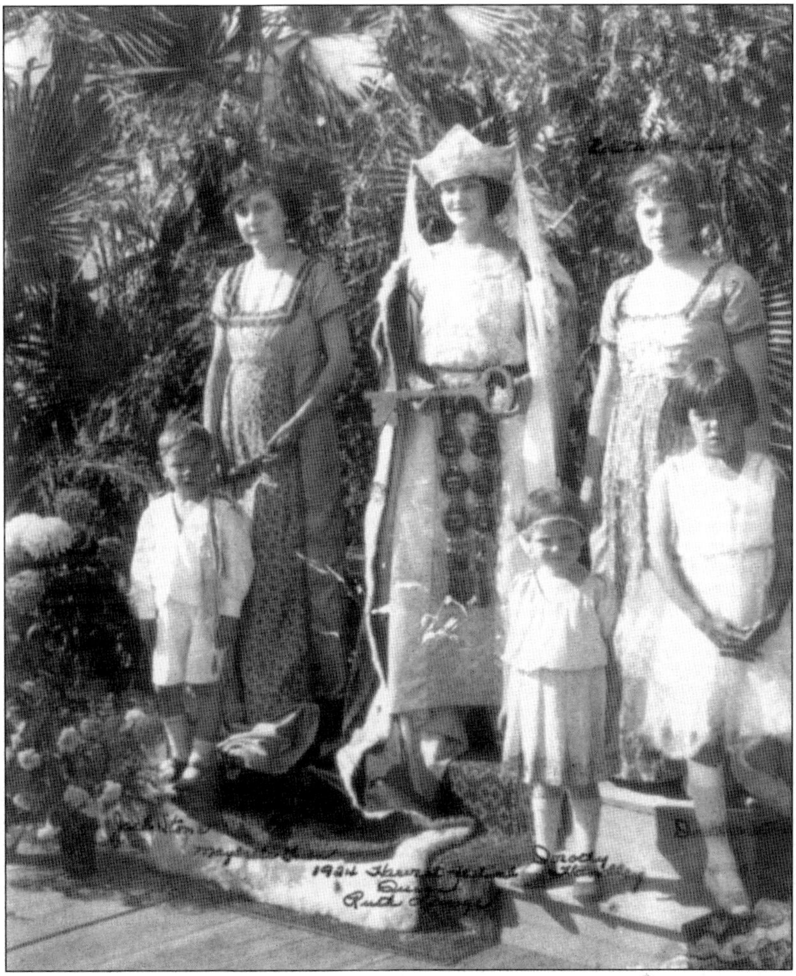

Harvest was celebrated with a festival in the 1920s. In this 1924 photograph, Harvest Festival queen Ruth Lange stands in the middle. The small boy to the left is Jack Stone, standing next to Maybelle. The small girl in front is Dorothy Handley, behind her is Edith, and to the far right is Dorothy Stone. (Courtesy of Jack Stone.)

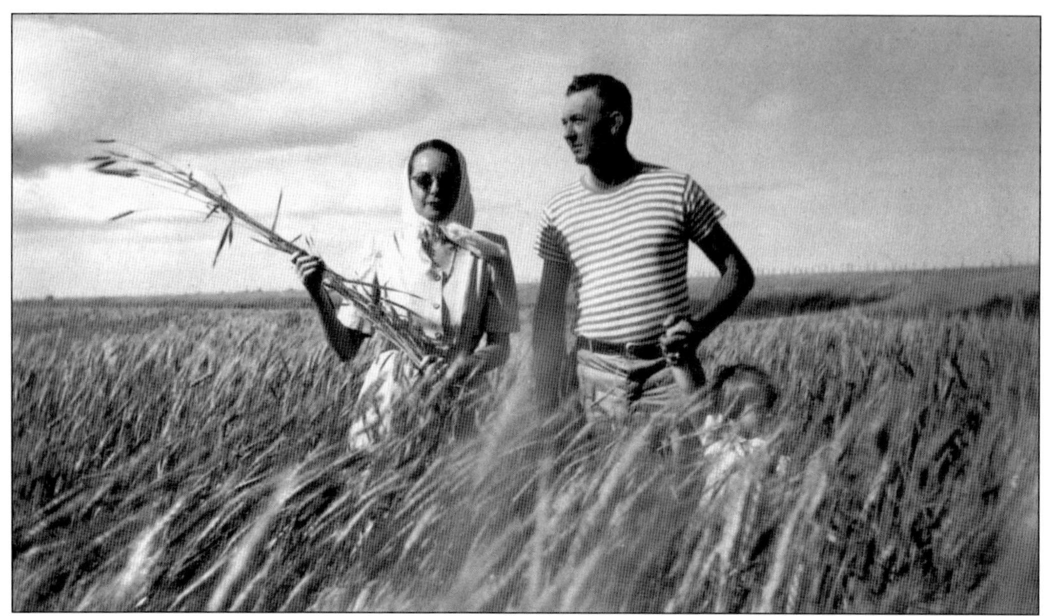

Hilda Stone, who is Jack Stone's wife, and Norman Wolfson, along with an unidentified child, show off some wheat while standing in the wheat field in 1946. (Courtesy of Jack Stone.)

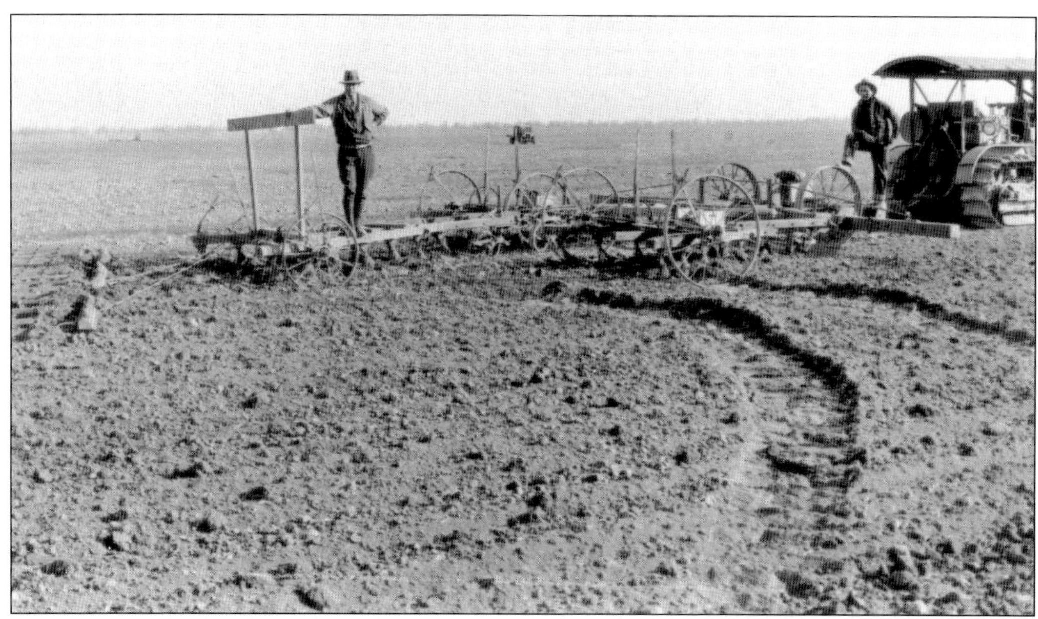

L. M. Stone, Jack Stone's father, supervises work on his farm in 1927. L. M. Stone was a civil engineer who had worked for the railroad before becoming a manager of the Kings County Development Company. (Courtesy of Jack Stone.)

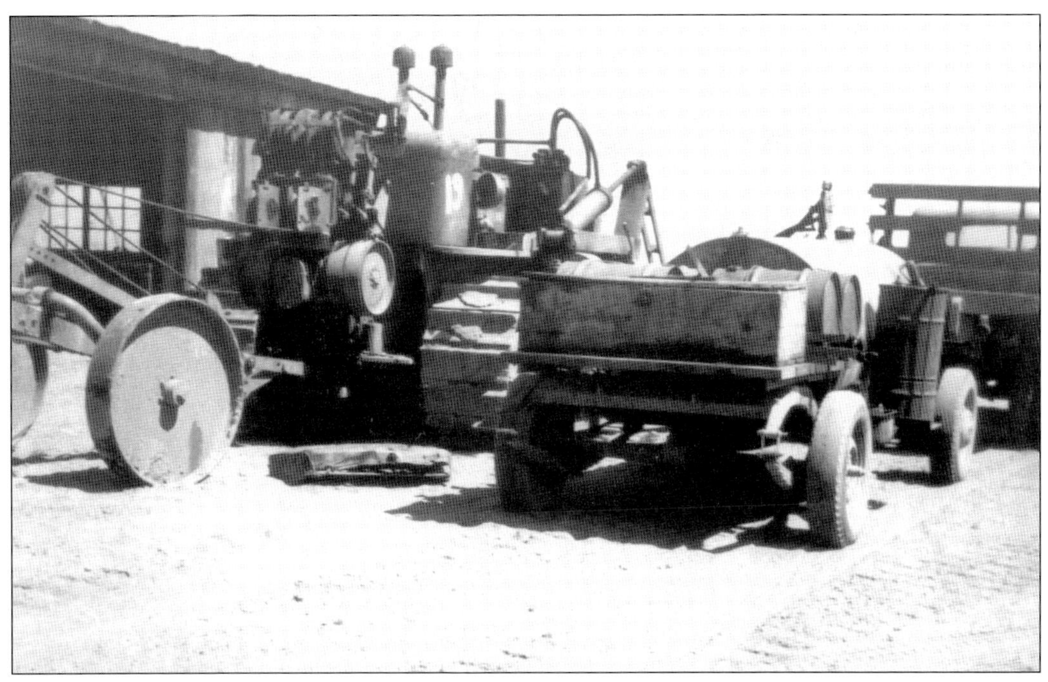

Farming equipment and tractors in various stages of maintenance remain idle at Jack Stone's shop on his west-side ranch in 1948. (Courtesy of Jack Stone.)

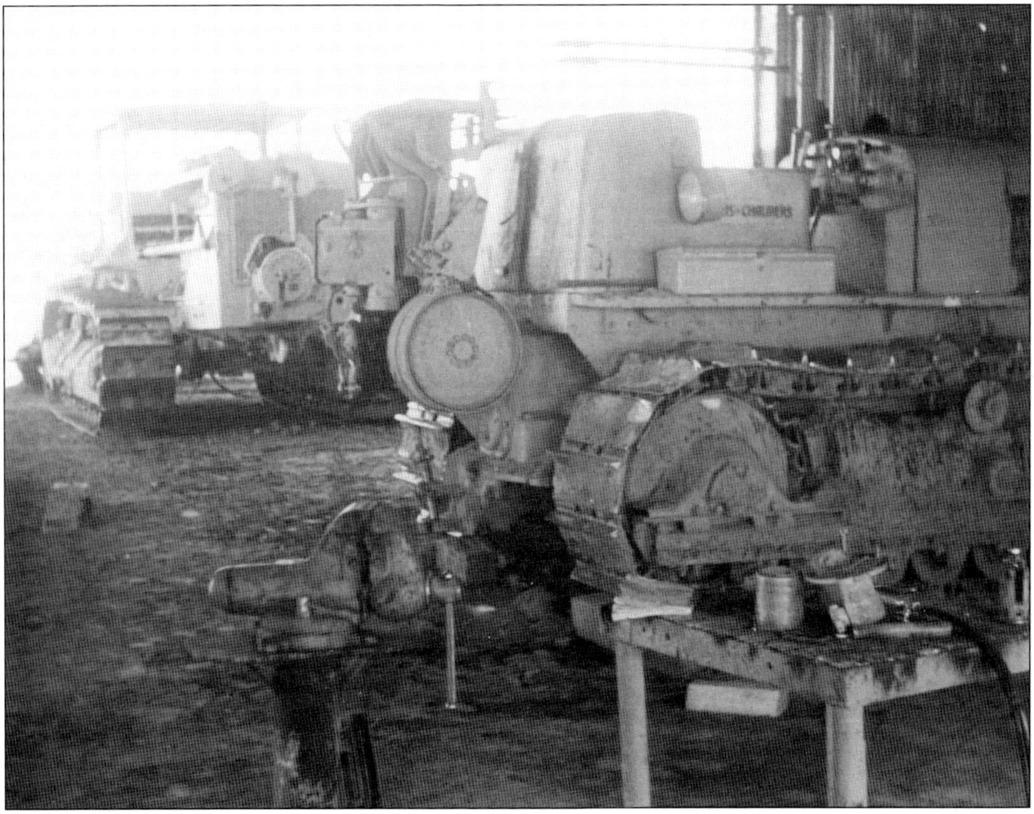

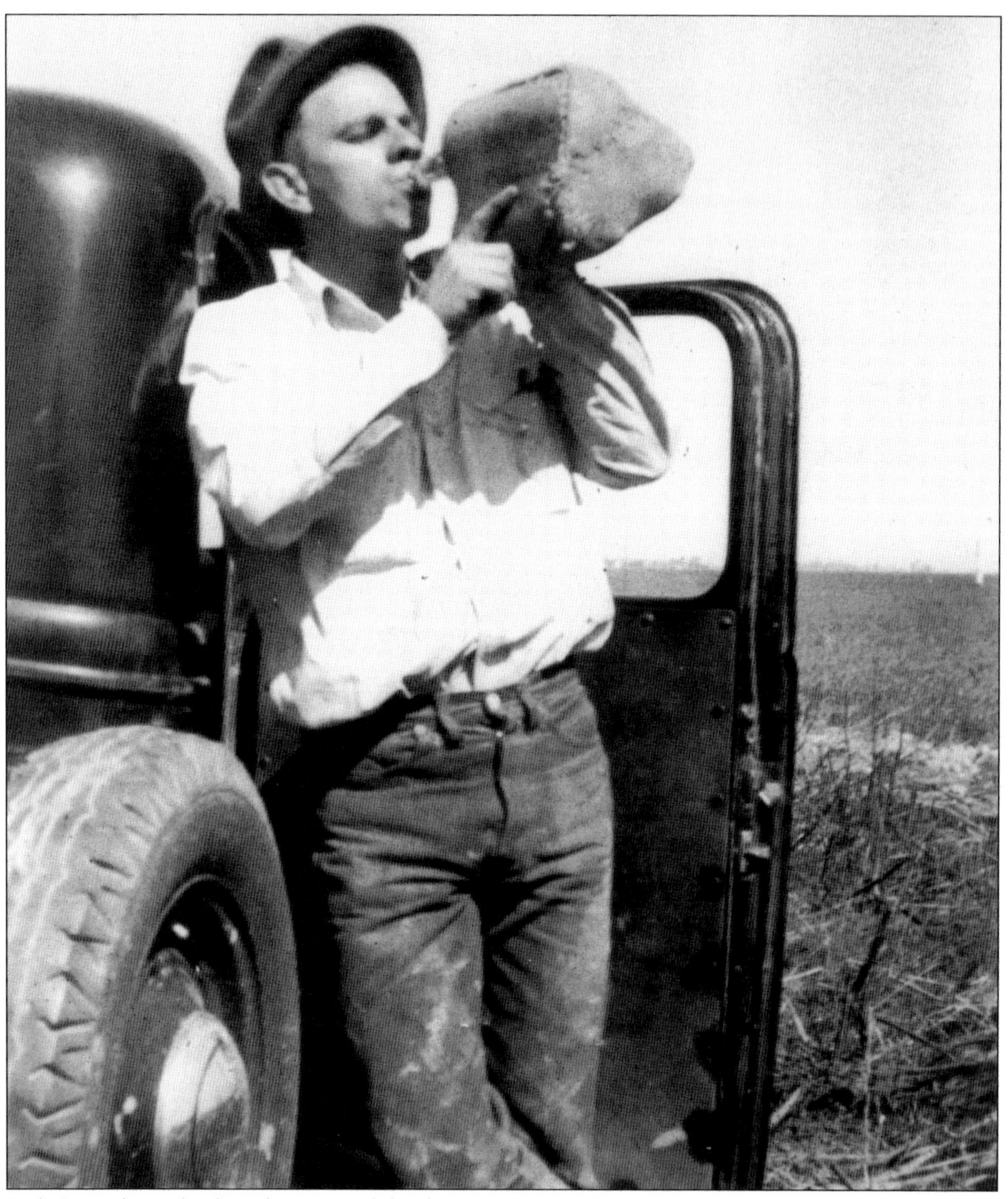

Jack Stone leans back on his car and drinks water pumped from one of the west-side pumps while out surveying the fields around 1950. (Courtesy of Jack Stone.)

Four
Business

Hot on the heels of early agricultural pioneers were those who provided them with necessary services. Early businesses in Lemoore included stables, liveries, banks, cafés, rooming houses, and saloons. By 1875, Lemoore had Granville Follett's grocery and dry goods store and Dr. Benjamin Hamlin's drugstore. When Dr. Benjamin Hamlin came from Santa Cruz in 1875, he was doctor, dentist, and druggist all rolled into one. He had been a surgeon during the Civil War. The railroad came through in 1877, but not where Dr. Lee Moore thought it would. Tracks were laid about a mile north. Every business in the fledgling town relocated up to the railroad along Front (E) Street.

Businesses included packinghouses for fruits and vegetables and a flour mill, which produced up to 200 barrels per day. The local newspaper, the *Lemoore Leader*, became a popular read among area residents in the late 1880s. A thriving Chinatown grew in the 500 block of G Street and offered stores, homes, restaurants, and entertainment catering to Asian immigrants. The Lee family went into grocery sales and built Lincoln Market, which was a thriving family business for many years. The store is still in operation, though with a new name and owner. The Lee family still owns the shopping center in which the grocery store is located.

More businesses came following an agricultural growth at the beginning of the 20th century. Two creameries and a winery were built, and clothing and hardware shops, lawyers, and other professionals added to Lemoore's character. Downtown Lemoore became D Street between Fox and Heinlen Streets. There were at least five different automobile retailers in the city during the mid-1900s, and large manufacturers located their production facilities in Lemoore. Leprino Foods currently has two plants in Lemoore—the largest of which is on the western edge of town and is the most abundant producer of mozzarella cheese in the world. Olam Vegetables has a tomato and vegetable processing plant in the south industrial complex. Drawing on the ample availability of cheese, wheat, and tomato products, Lemoore established the annual Central Valley Pizza Festival. Everything that goes into a great pizza is found right here in Lemoore.

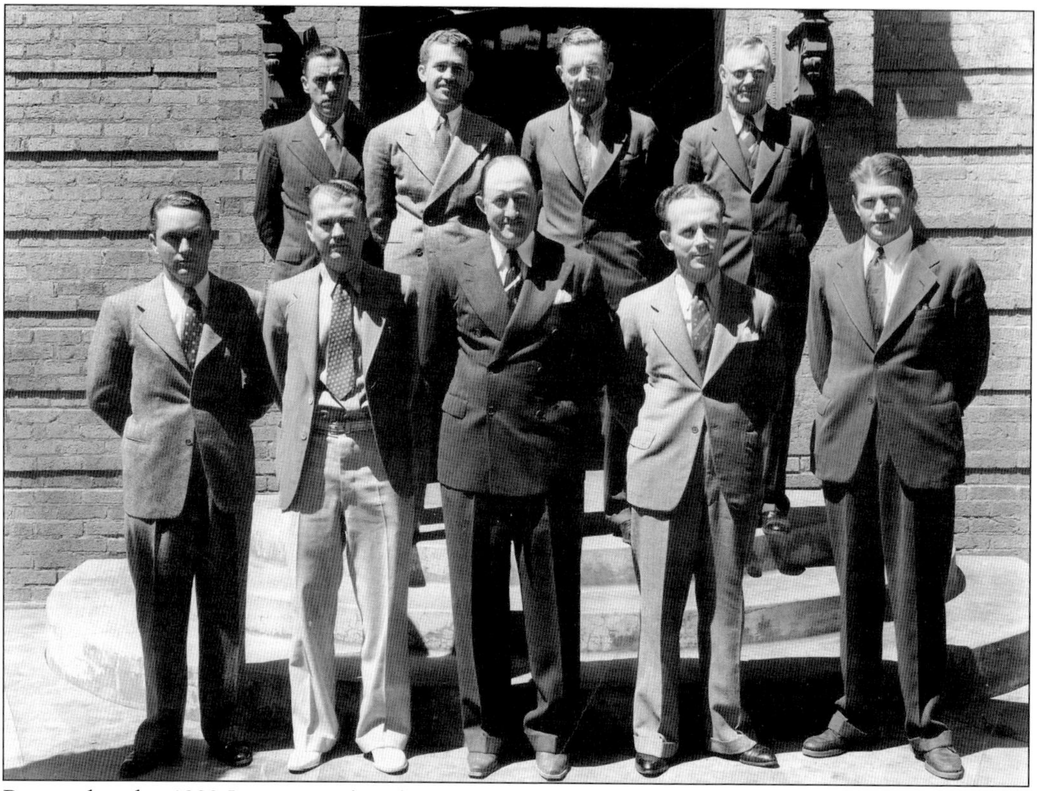

Pictured is the 1939 Lemoore Chamber of Commerce. From left to right are (first row) James Burke, Tubby Hamblin, T. W. Patton, Oliver Pereira, and C. N. Phipps; (second row) Stan Myrick, Vernon Chinn, P. W. Engvall, and Steve Ross. (Courtesy of the Sarah A. Mooney Museum.)

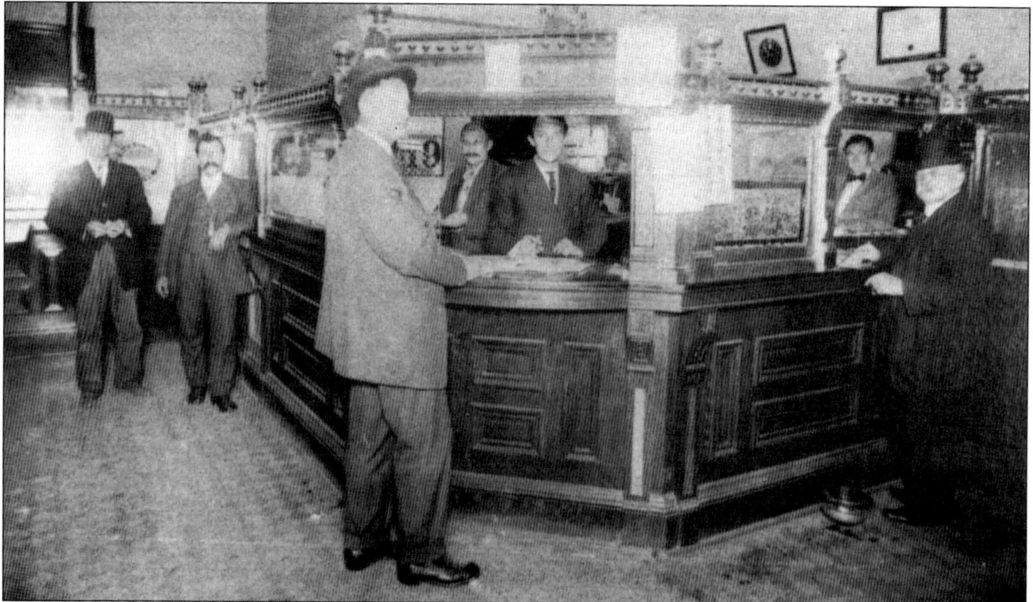

Ford Sorrick and Art Campbell (seen behind the counter at the center window) were tellers at the Bank of Lemoore. (Courtesy of the Sarah A. Mooney Museum.)

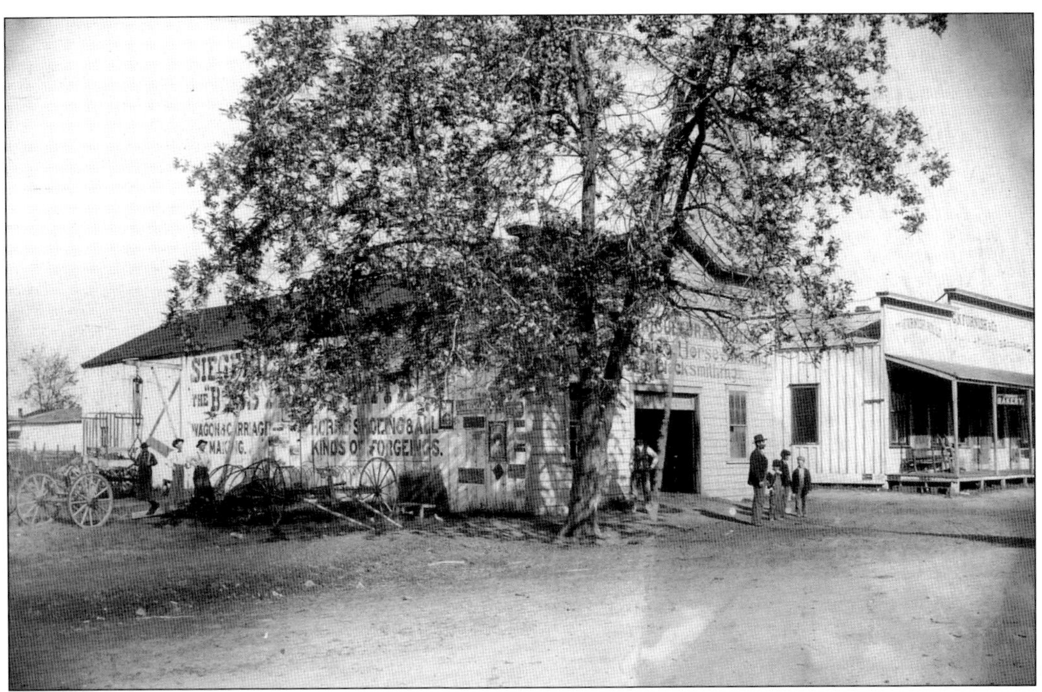

J. H. Young's blacksmith shop above was located at Front and Follett Streets. Shown at work below are Francis Yousty, Tom Thompson, and John Henry Siegfried. (Courtesy of the Sarah A. Mooney Museum.)

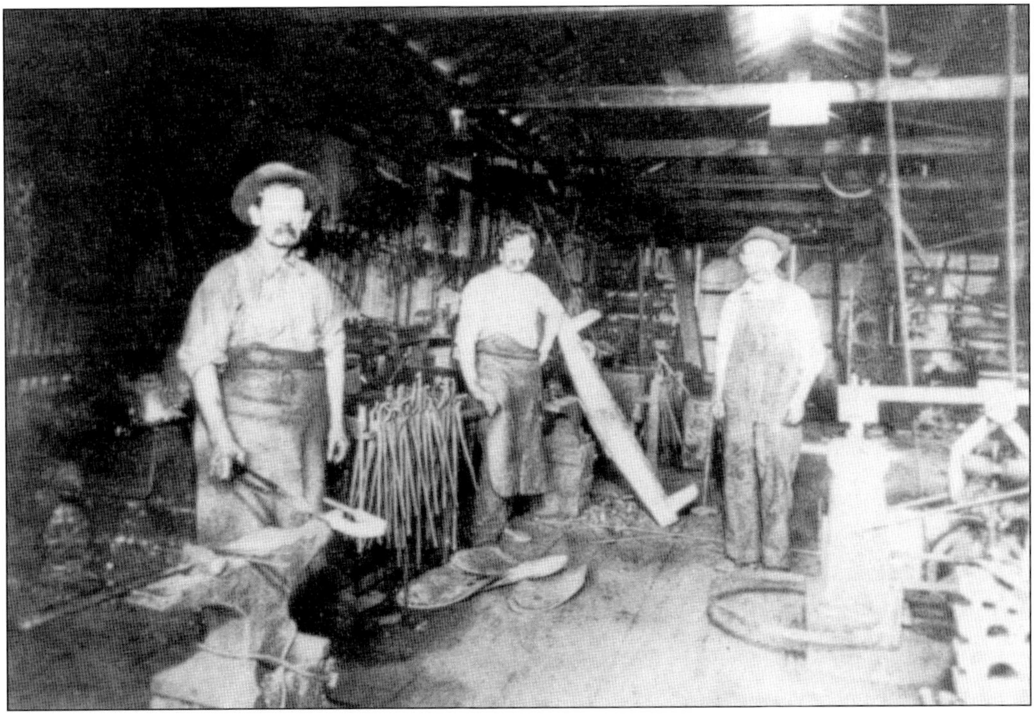

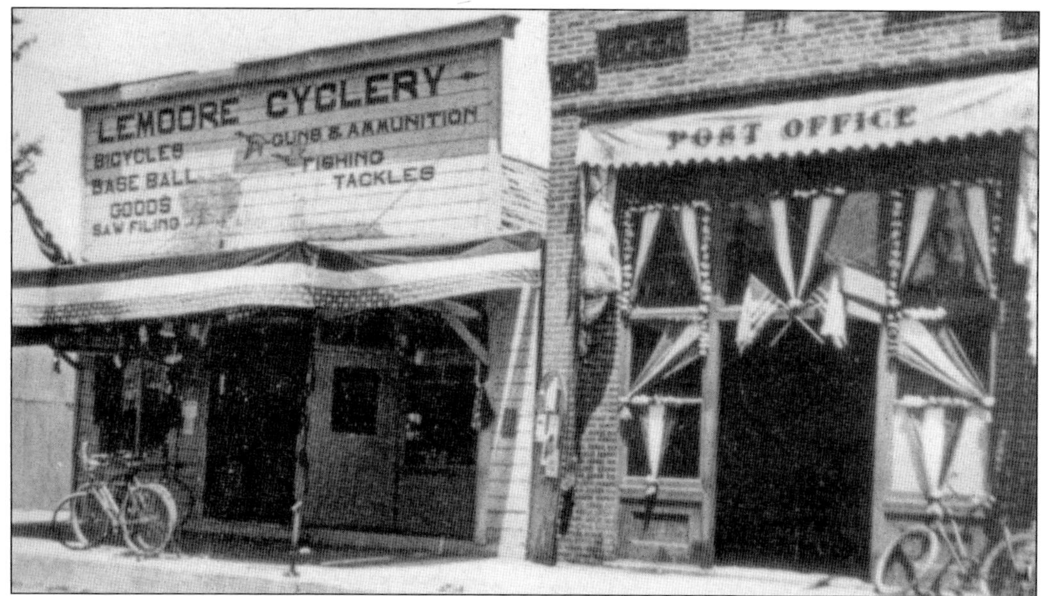

On September 1, 1875, a Lemoore post office was established in Copeland's store on Front Street. It then moved next to the Lemoore Cyclery on Heinlen Street, as seen here in 1898. Soon after, it was relocated again to the Mooney building on D Street. It has been in its current location on C Street since 1947. (Courtesy of Jack Stone.)

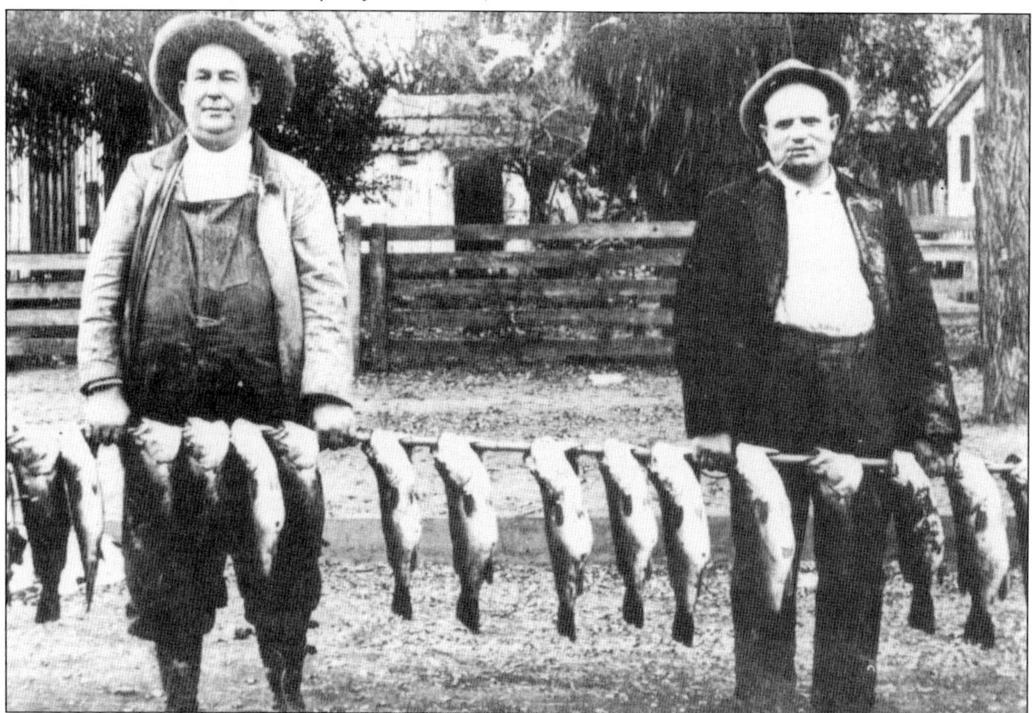

Minor L. Doss (left), the owner and editor of the *Lemoore Republican* newspaper and his employee, Tom White, took a day off for fishing. Lemoore, at times, had two newspapers publishing at once, the *Lemoore Leader* and the *Lemoore Advance*. While Doss owned the paper, from 1904 to 1914, he renamed the *Lemoore Leader* to the *Lemoore Republican*. (Courtesy of Kings County Museum.)

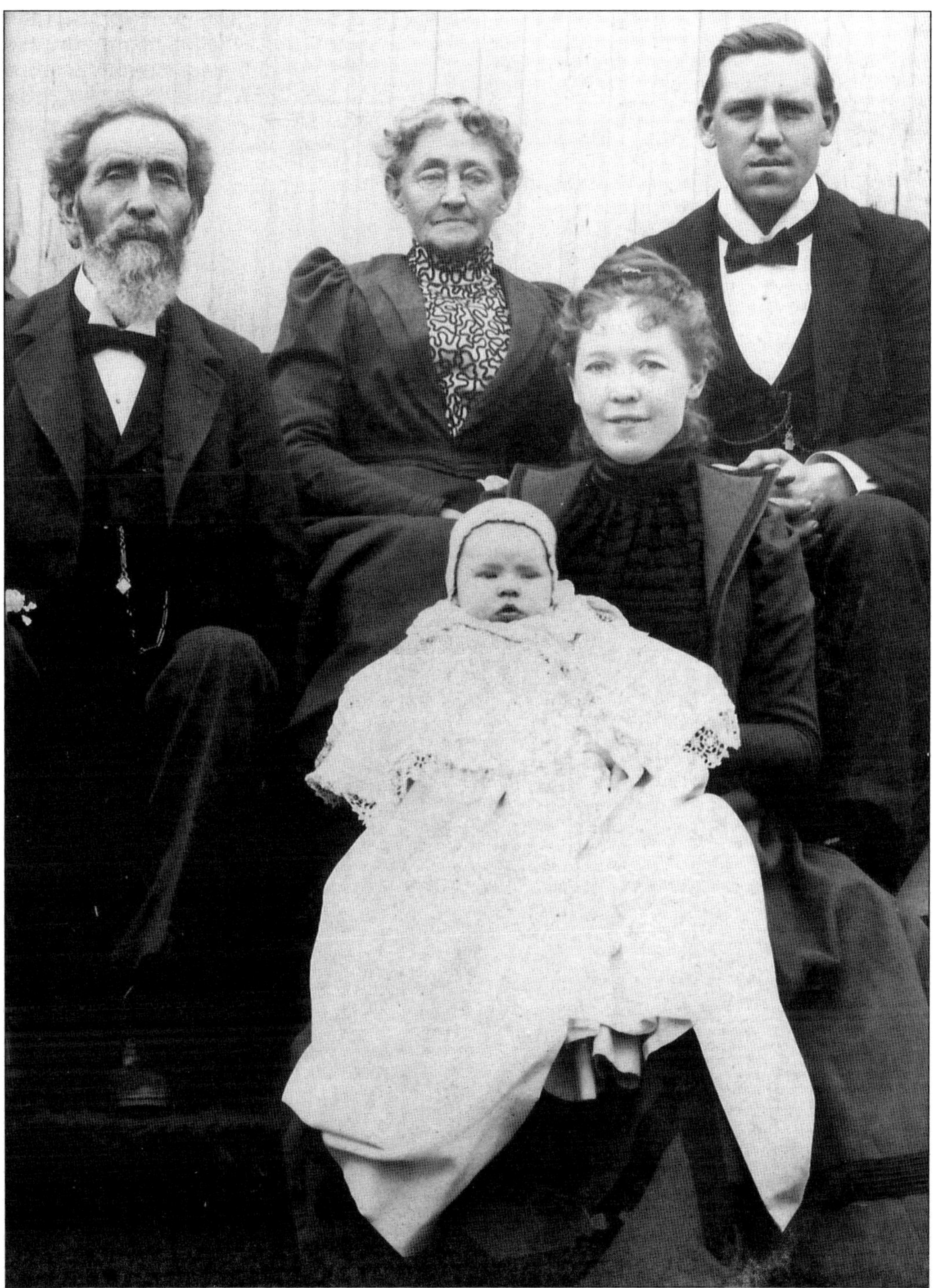

Col. B. O. Carr (left), the bank president, and his family are pictured in 1899. To his right are Sarah Pratt Carr, founder of the Alpha Club, and Dr. R. A. Moore (not Lee Moore). In front are Mary Carr Moore and her baby. The photograph was taken November 30, 1899, and was loaned to the Sarah A. Mooney Museum by the Reed sisters. (Courtesy of the Sarah A. Mooney Museum.)

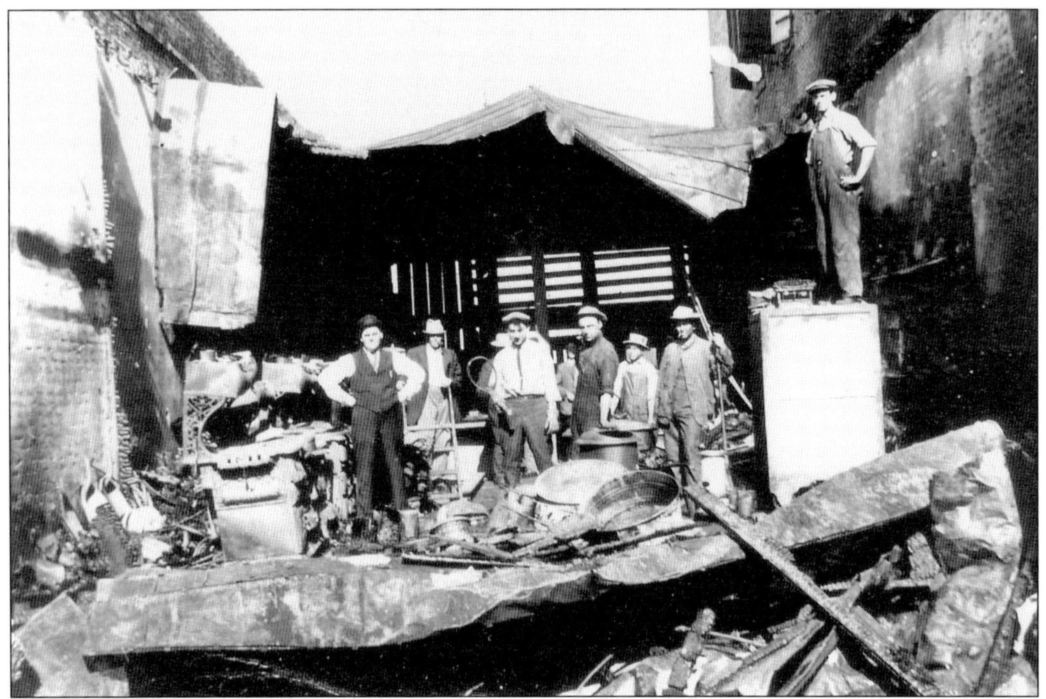

Pictured is the Lemoore General Store after being burned down in a fire about 1917. Tadeo's Mexican Restaurant is now located on the site of the old store. (Courtesy of the Sarah A. Mooney Museum.)

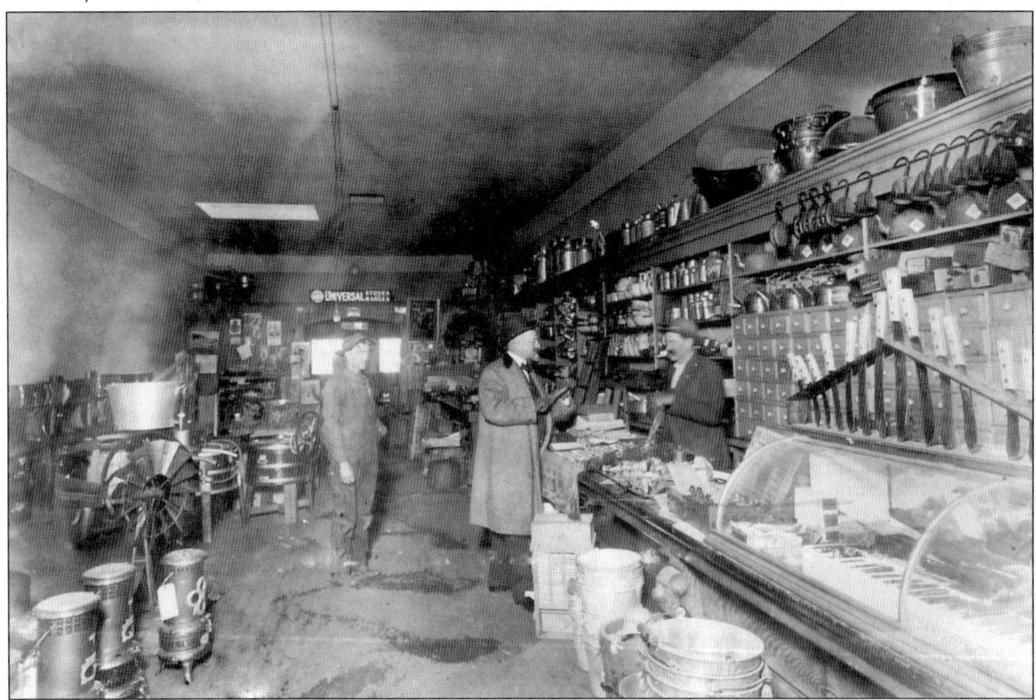

Mr. Moore, Max Leeper, and a Gideon salesman are shown in the Lemoore General Store on March 22, 1911. (Courtesy of the Sarah A. Mooney Museum.)

The Gem Saloon was on Front (E) Street in Lemoore in the early 1900s. Standing on the porch are Charlie Parker, Bill Wilson, Howard Tharp, Thomas Rhoads, and Dee Rhoads. (Courtesy of the Sarah A. Mooney Museum.)

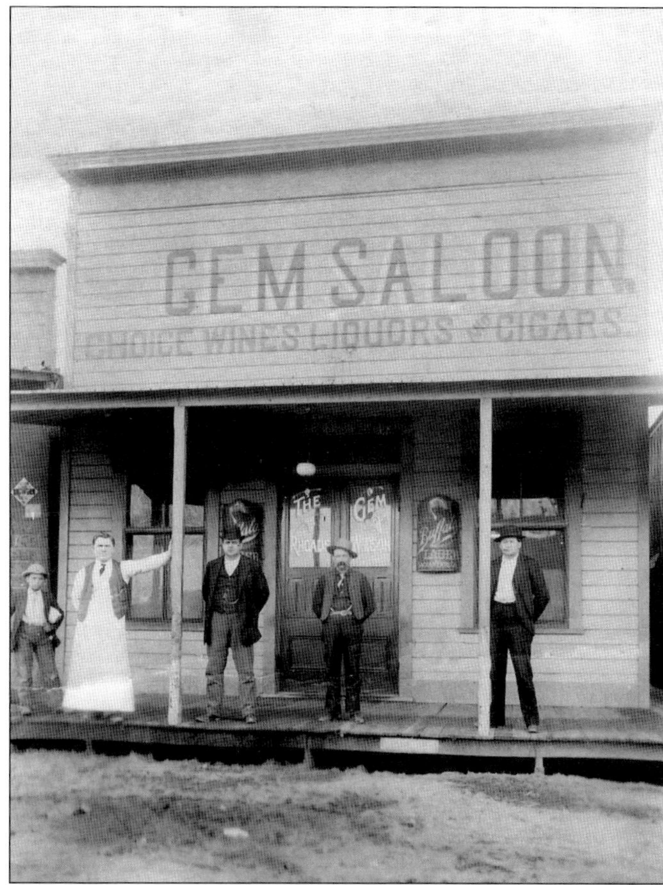

The L. S. Stepp General Merchandise store at the corner of Heinlen and E Streets was a popular place. The store moved several times over the years. Stepp is in the center wearing a vest and white shirt. (Courtesy of Jack Stone.)

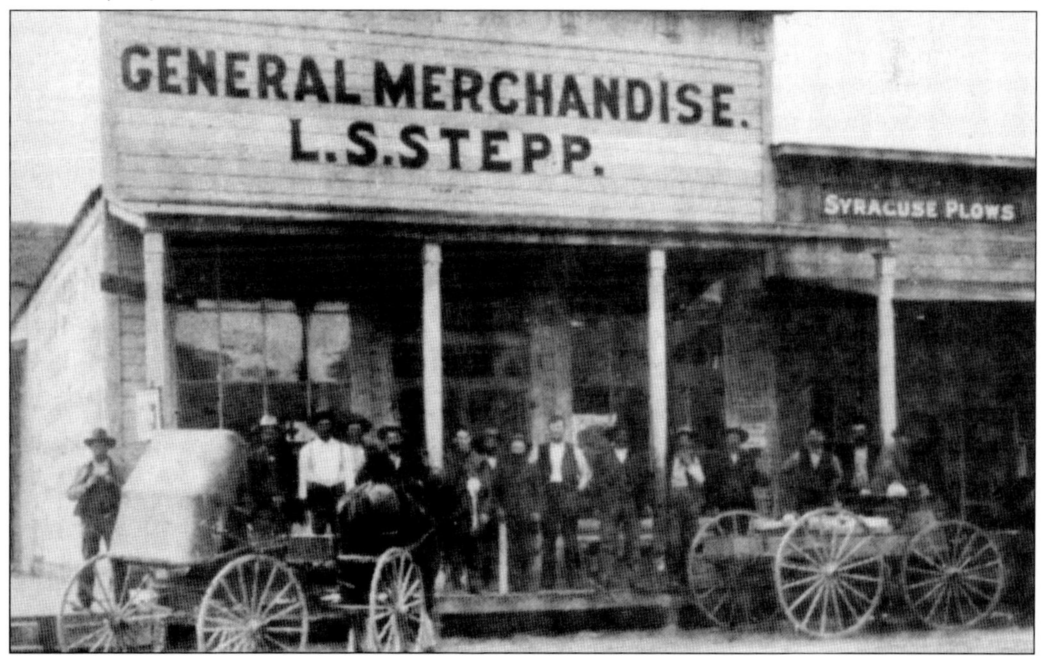

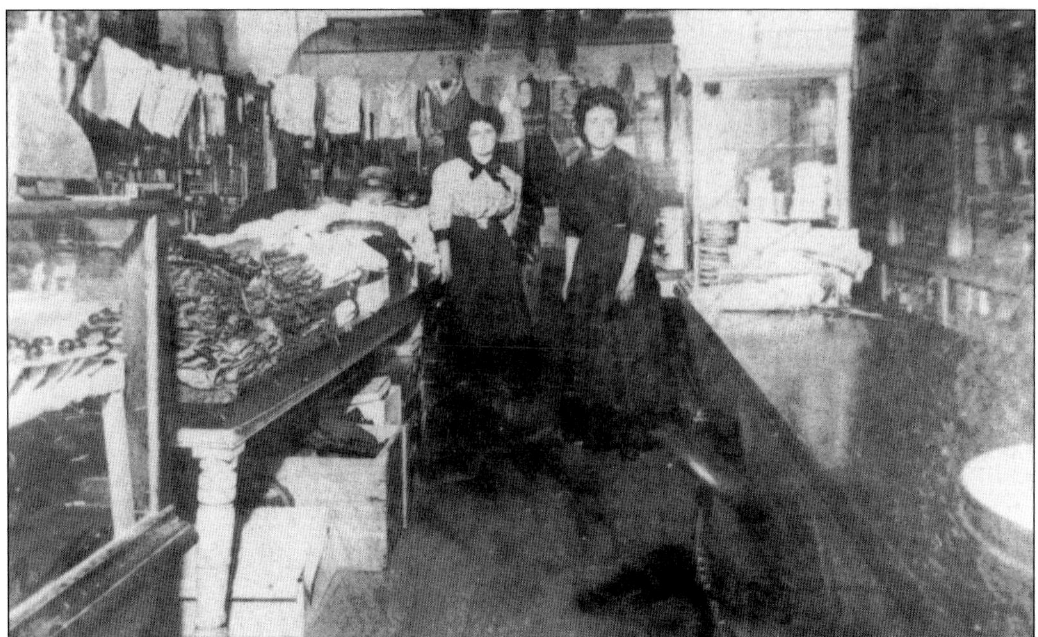

Nanette Brothers and Ila Sorrick Mahon are shown inside Brownstone's General Merchandise store. (Courtesy of the Sarah A. Mooney Museum.)

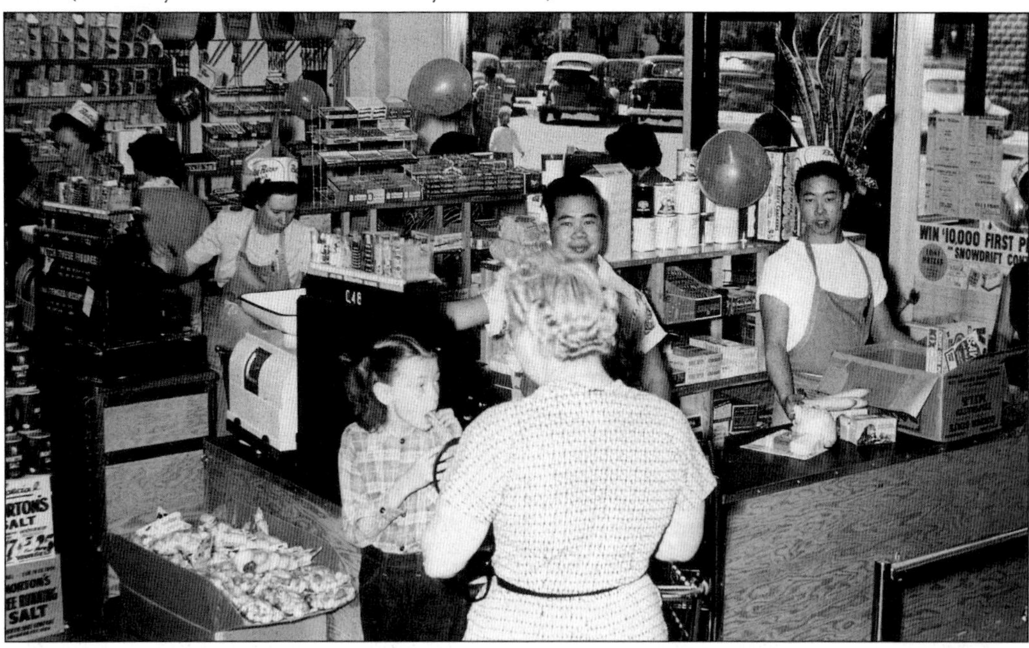

The Lee family of Lemoore opened their first grocery store, Lincoln Market, on Heinlen Street in 1929. Shown serving customers at the first checkout counter in this early April 1952 photograph are Art (left) and Jim Lee. They middle checker is Theda Green, and in the back is Pauline Kurtz. Fook Loy Lee opened the store and passed it on to his five sons: Mike, Dick, Tim, Art, and Jim Lee. The market was named for F. L. Lee's hero, Abraham Lincoln. The store moved to Bush Street and Nineteenth Avenue in 1962. The family also owned the Mid-Town Market on D Street for a time. (Courtesy of the Sarah A. Mooney Museum.)

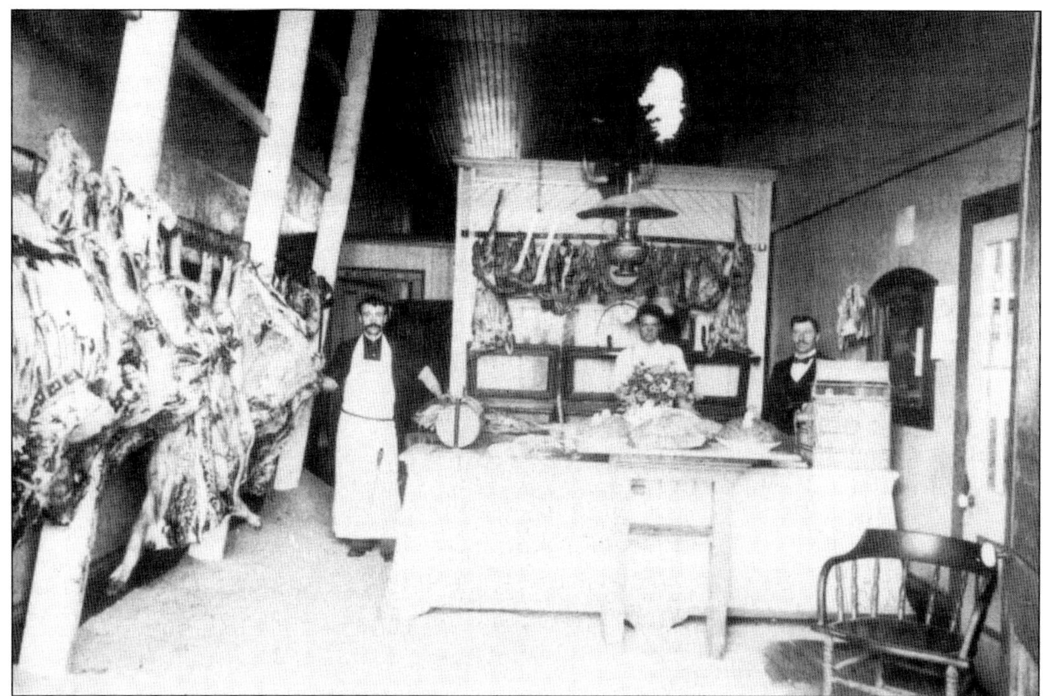

This meat market was located on Front Street. (Courtesy of the Sarah A. Mooney Museum.)

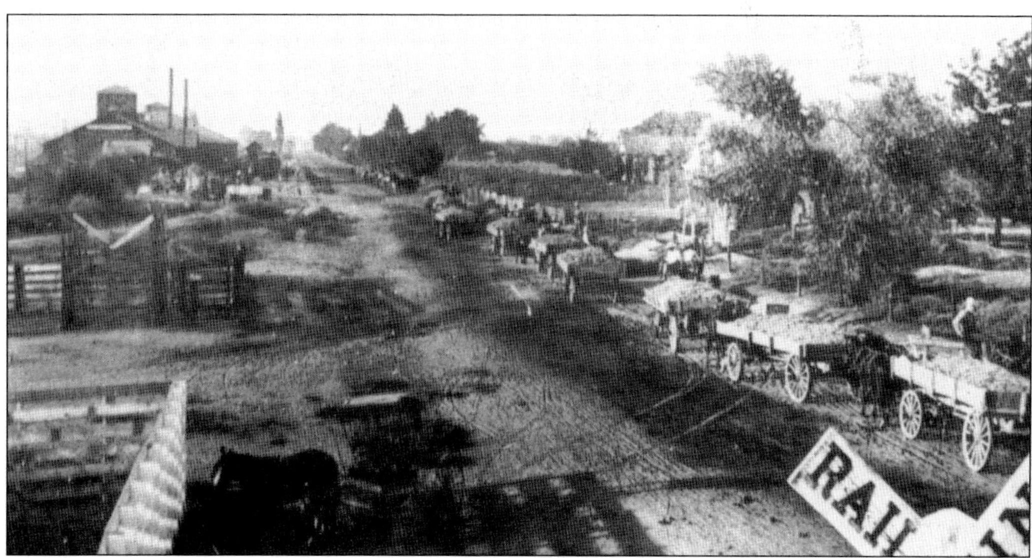

The Italian Swiss Colony Winery was built on Lemoore Avenue in 1902. This view is from the railroad tracks looking north. In 1907, the plant produced 500,000 gallons of wine and 50,000 gallons of brandy. (Courtesy of the Sarah A. Mooney Museum.)

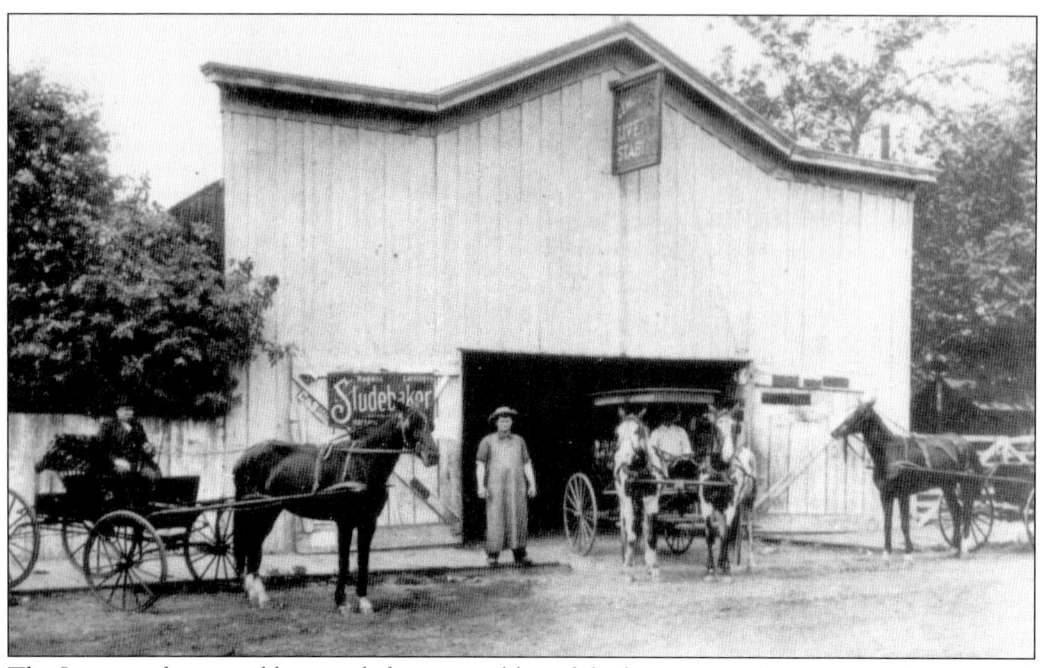

The Lemoore livery stable provided room and board for horses in early Lemoore. (Courtesy of Jack Stone.)

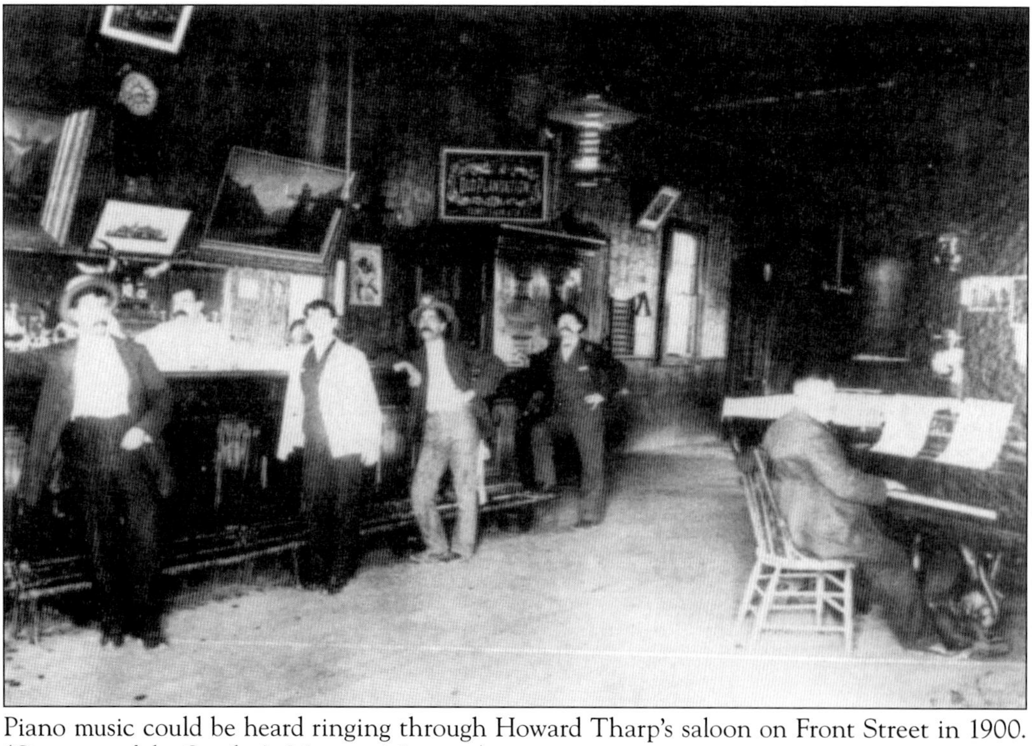

Piano music could be heard ringing through Howard Tharp's saloon on Front Street in 1900. (Courtesy of the Sarah A. Mooney Museum.)

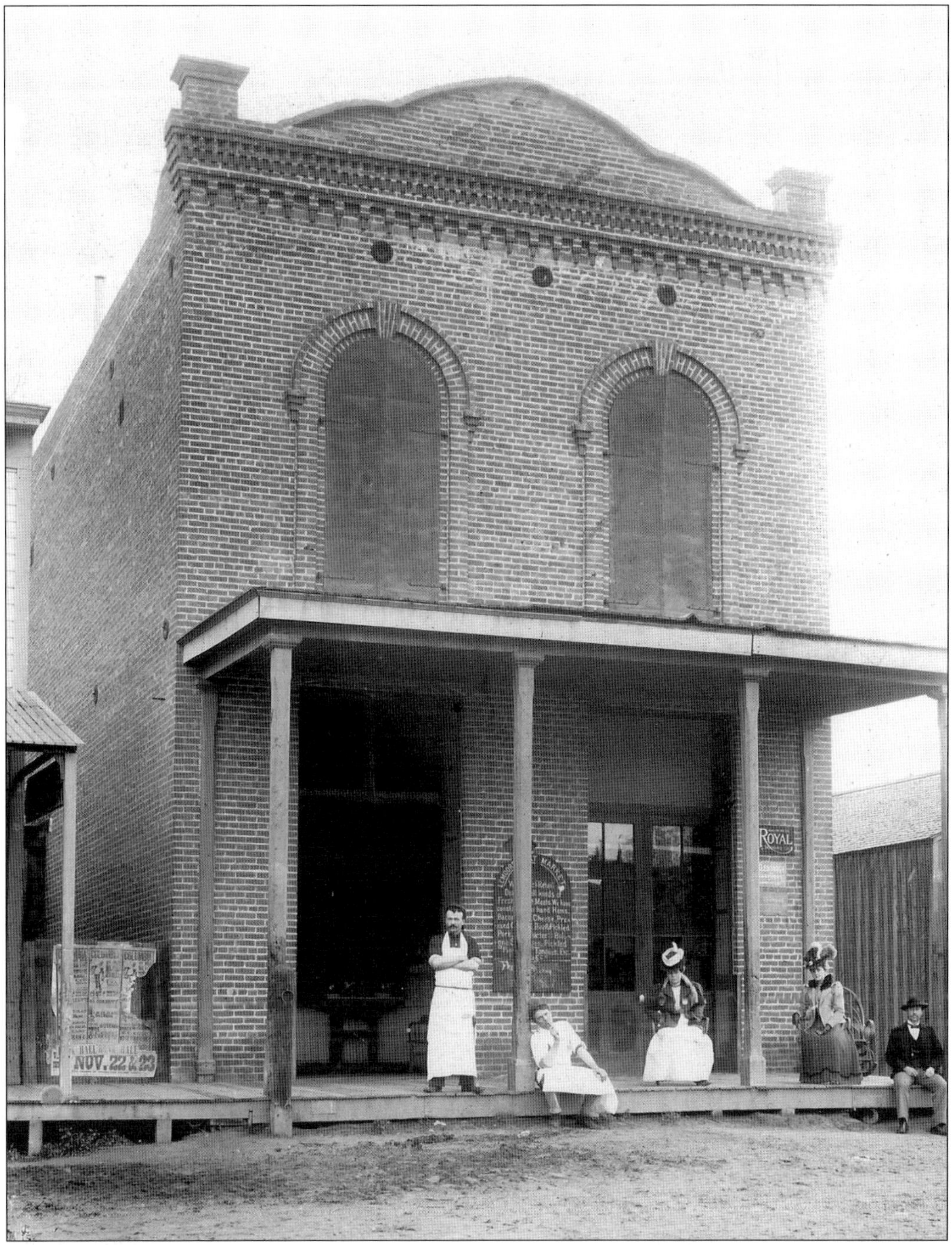

The Lemoore Meat Market and Royal Insurance Company were located in the same building on Front (E) Street. The building still stands today and houses a gift shop. (Courtesy of the Sarah A. Mooney Museum.)

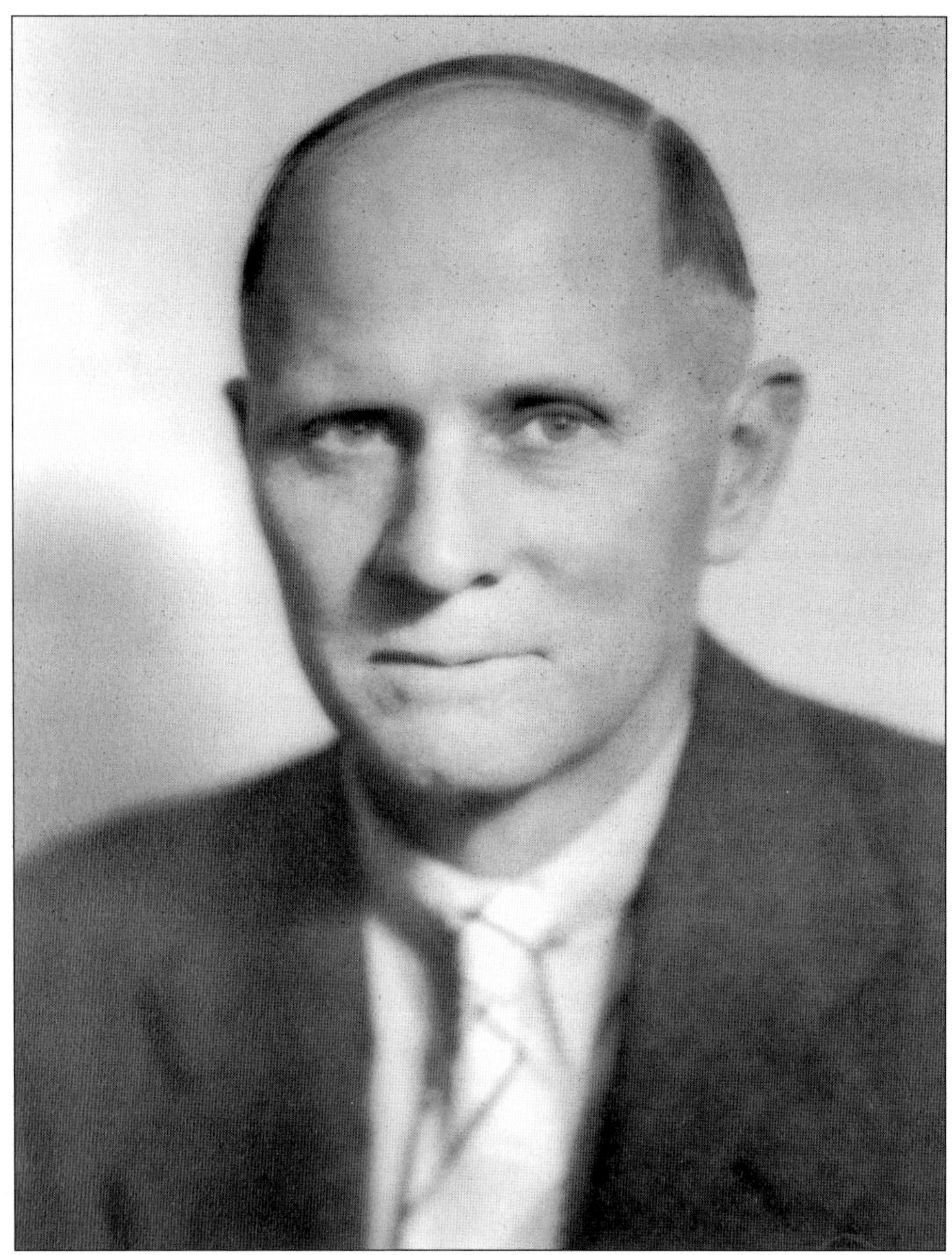

Russell R. Funk Sr., D.D.S, opened a dental practice in Lemoore around 1914. He married Edith Sophi Schlickeiser on December 31, 1913. This photograph was taken around 1941. Funk's first dental office in Lemoore was the corner office on the upper floor of the Volkman Building on the southeast corner of Fox and C Streets. His second office was located at 158 C Street, just east of the Seventh Day Adventist Church. Funk was born on January 5, 1884, in Kelly, Kansas, where he was a teacher before becoming a dentist. He came to Lemoore after playing professional minor league baseball, first in the Midwest and later in the "Outlaw League," which became the Pacific Coast League. He retired from dentistry in 1949, when his son Russ, also a dentist, took over his practice. (Courtesy of the Sarah A. Mooney Museum.)

Five

ENTERTAINMENT

There was more to Lemoore in the early years than just hard work, saloons, and church. Residents joined together for family visits, formed clubs and fraternal organizations, and took part in a whole host of social events. Horse races were popular with the men. There was a racetrack where the golf course is today. Traveling troupes often came to town. The opera house on D Street hosted a variety of entertainment acts, while it was also an ideal place for dinners and dances. According to J. L. Brown in his 1941 book *The Story of Kings County*, "Many of the early settlers of the Lemoore district were cultured people, and Lemoore attained a reputation for musical and literary accomplishments unmatched by many pioneer towns. There was an early literary society that had a long and noteworthy existence." Parades with floats and bands were frequent entertainment as they traveled parallel to the tracks on Front Street, a route that was sometimes very dusty. In the early 20th century, families took advantage of a skating rink, and the Lemoore Theatre showed double features from the late 1920s until the mid-1960s.

Sporting events were enjoyable and taken very seriously by many locals. The city, schools, and many organizations fielded a variety of teams. Lemoore baseball and softball teams took on other local teams as well as teams from other areas of the valley. Occasionally a traveling team would be on the roster. Lemoore High School was a rallying site for teams, and amateur sports enthusiasts were welcome. A boxing ring was set up behind Terra's Clothing on D Street during the 1930s.

Over the years, several Lemoore residents have become prominent and well known throughout the nation and the world. George Truckell, a Lemoore High School sports standout, played on the first San Francisco 49ers team. Tommie Smith took his track ambitions to the Mexican Olympics and won gold. He also stirred up controversy when he raised his fist in the Black Power salute while receiving his medal. Lorenzo Neal, who played for several NFL teams, became one of the top blockers ever to play professional football. Neal spent five seasons with the San Diego Chargers and is currently a free agent. Steve Perry became famous as the lead singer of the group Journey.

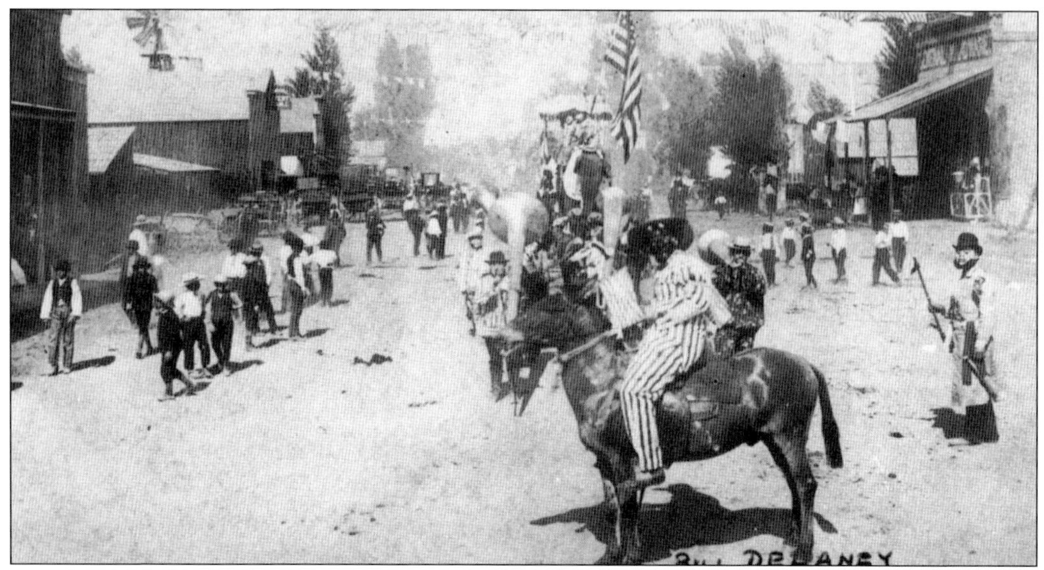

The Calithumpians brought up the rear of a parade in 1885. The Calithumpians often followed regular parades, providing fun-loving "doo-da." (Courtesy of the Sarah A. Mooney Museum.)

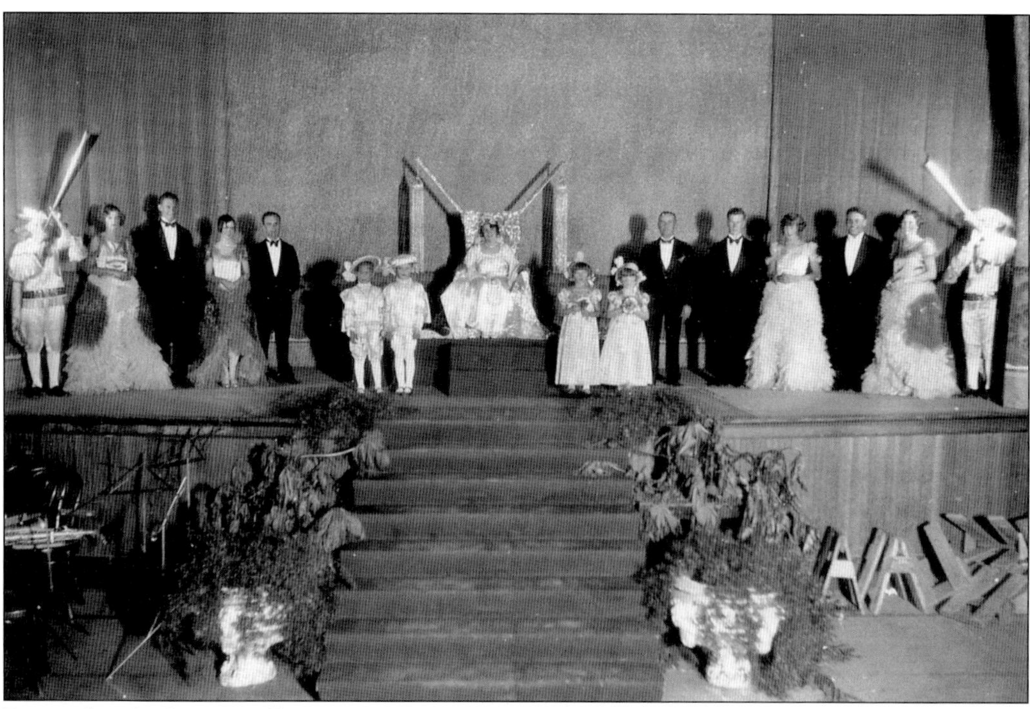

Pictured is the Lemoore Fair coronation ceremony in 1928. The queen is Mary Avila, and the trumpeters are James Burke and Bill Harp. The attendants and escorts are Carol Cobb Clawson, Juel Burke Pereira, Oliver Pereira, Alvin Sanborn, Lois Henley Plank, and Albert Nichols. The pages are Burton Lowe and George Cobb, and the flower girls are Mary Stevens and Dorothy Graham. (Courtesy of the Sarah A. Mooney Museum.)

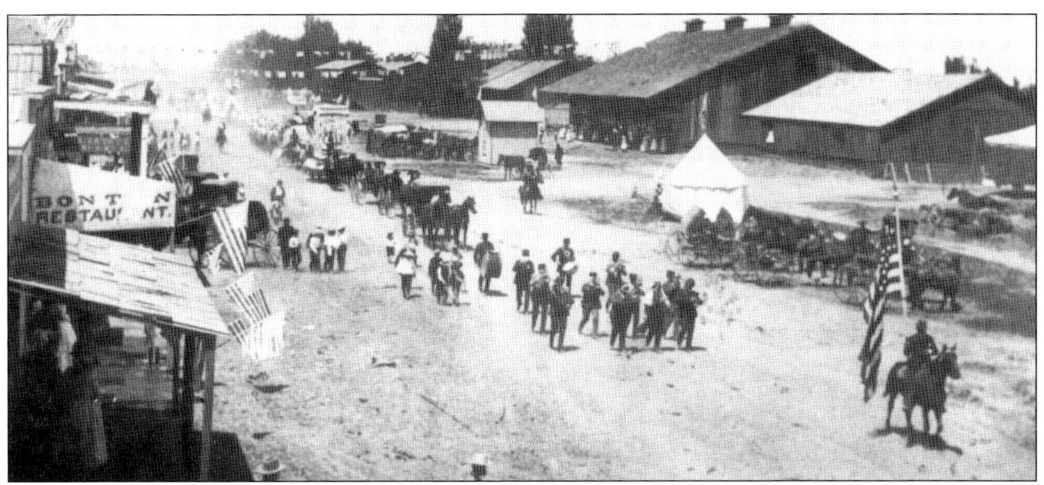

John Wesley Esrey was the grand marshal of the Fourth of July parade on Front Street in 1882. An 11-piece marching band follows the flag bearer. (Courtesy of the Sarah A. Mooney Museum.)

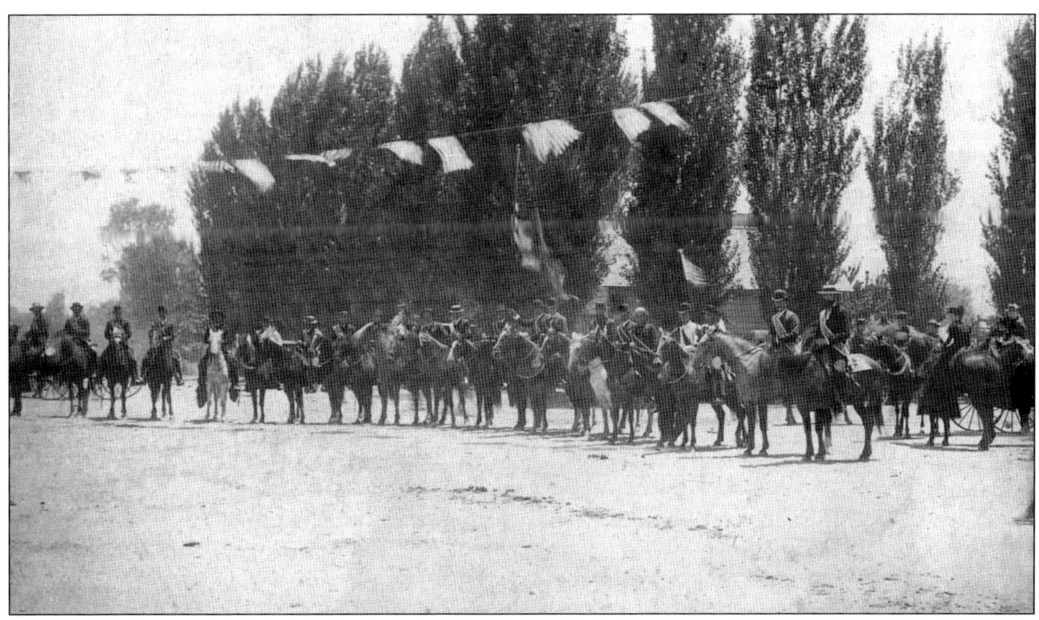

Horsemen line up for the Fourth of July parade in 1898. Lemoore residents have always loved their parades. (Courtesy of the Sarah A. Mooney Museum.)

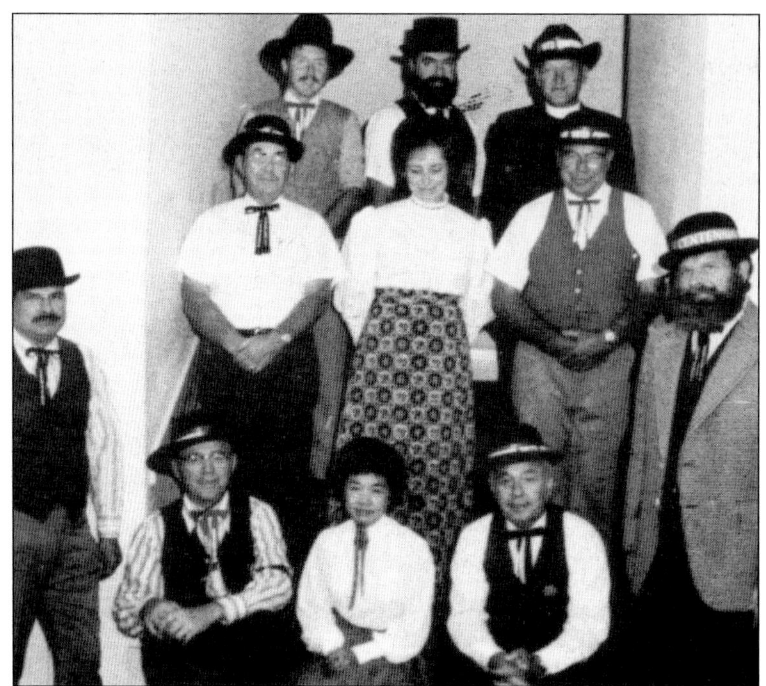

The Lemoore Centennial Committee put on a year of activities for the city's 100th birthday in 1973. The main festivities were intensified during a week in May that year. The committee consisted of, from left to right, (first row) Juan Almanza, Gerald Bendale, Virginia Lee, Keith Lowe, and Dale Cowan; (second row) Ted Armstrong, Marge Lowe, and Harold Hotchkiss; (third row) Ron Allvin, Jim Forte, and Mel Addington. (Courtesy of the Sarah A. Mooney Museum.)

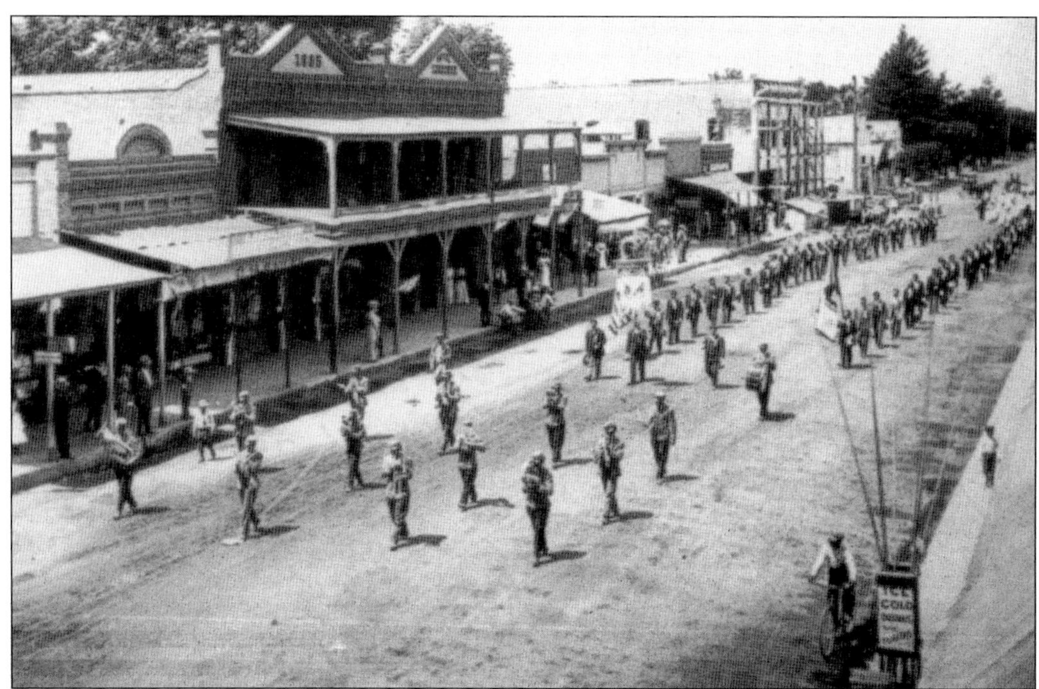

Lemoore was famous for its parades in the early days and still is today. This is the Our Lady of Fatima parade and shows a view of D Street looking west. (Courtesy of Jack Stone.)

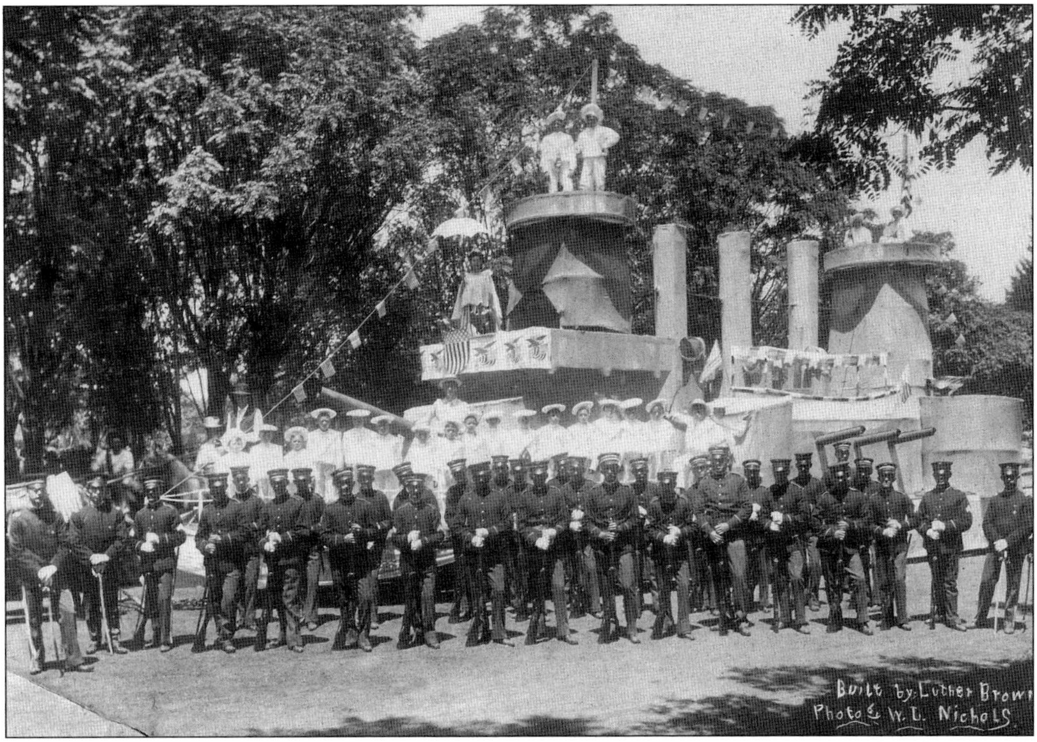

This float was built by Luther Brown for the Fourth of July celebration in 1908. The photograph was taken by W. L. Nichols. (Courtesy of the Sarah A. Mooney Museum.)

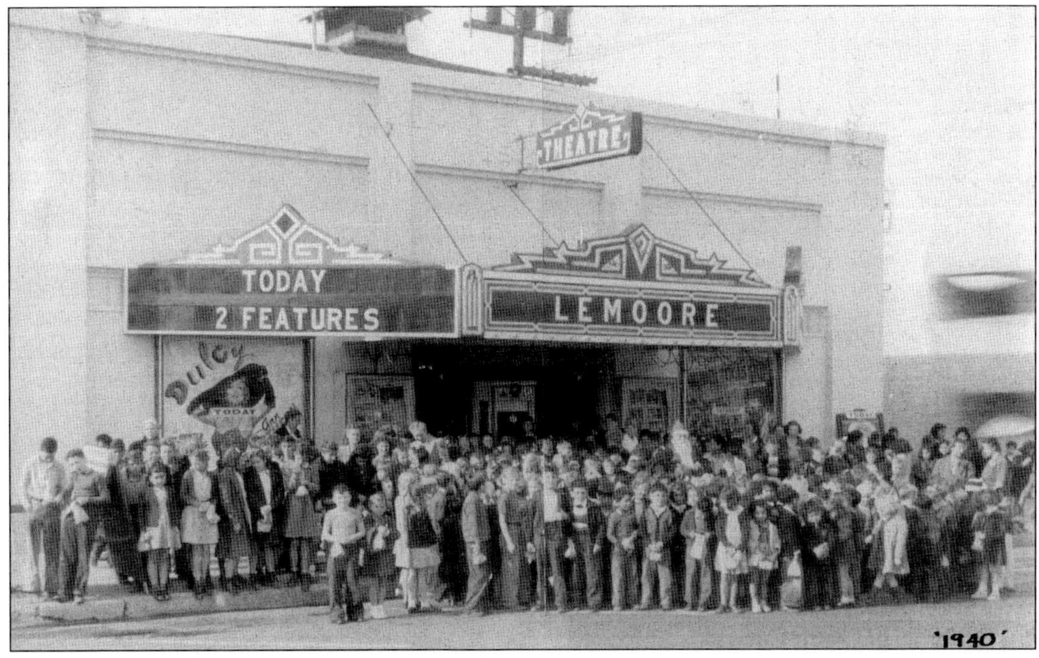

A crowd gathers in front of the Lemoore Theatre in 1940. Each Christmas season during the 1940s the theater presented a free family viewing of a film as a holiday treat. (Courtesy of the Sarah A. Mooney Museum.)

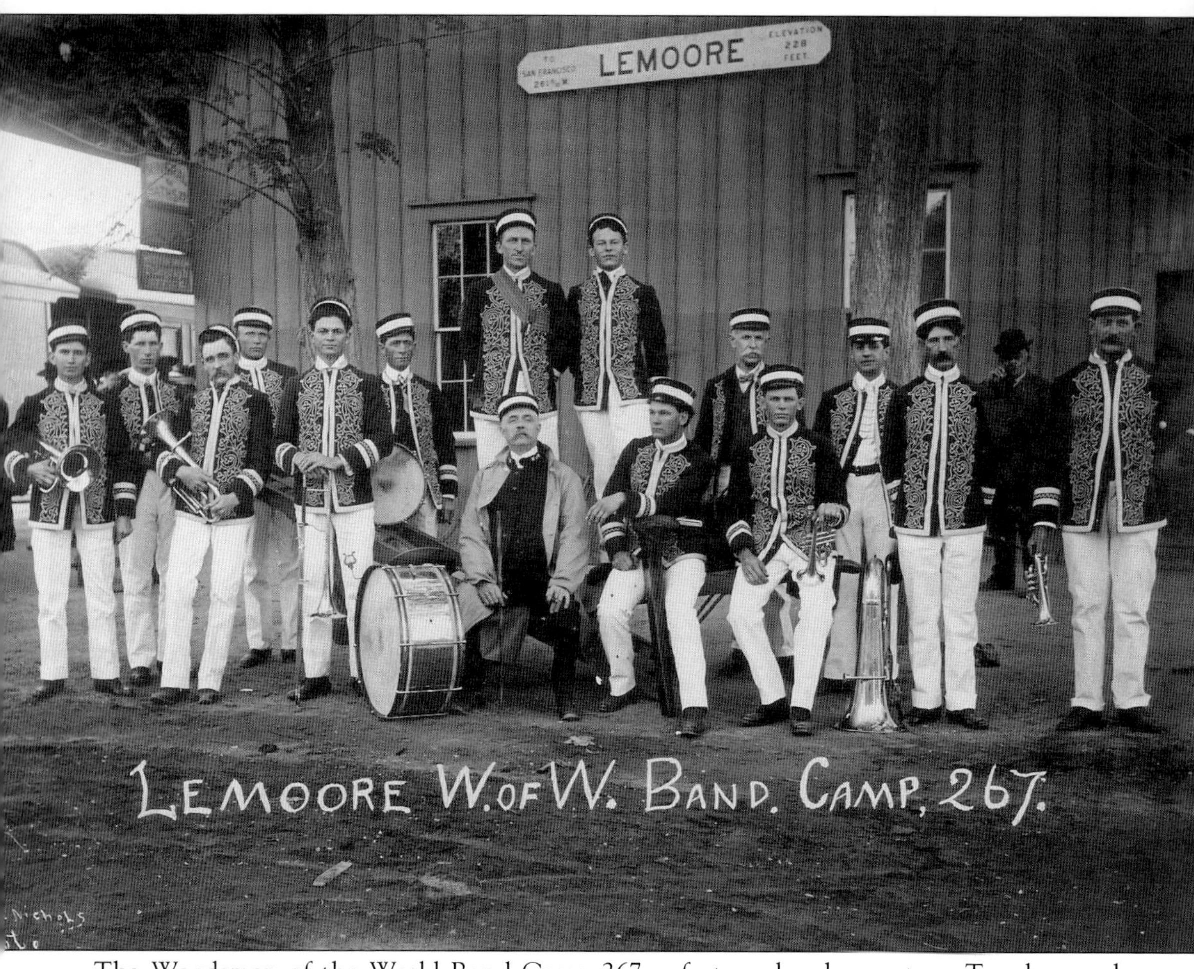

The Woodsmen of the World Band Camp 267, a fraternal order, met on Tuesdays and Saturdays in Lemoore. They were known for being willing to play any night of the week when asked. This photograph was taken at the Lemoore Train Depot. (Courtesy of the Sarah A. Mooney Museum.)

Six

Historical Homes and Buildings

Lemoore has many wonderful historical buildings. Perhaps the earliest building in the outlying area was the adobe constructed by Dan Rhoads for his family in 1856. Early pioneers and travelers knew it as a welcome chance to rest, visit, and maybe get a meal.

Dr. William Peter Bryon, a Lemoore native, established his medical practice in 1905 and built a house in 1910 at 42 Heinlen Street, which still stands today. Mary Smith established a licensed maternity home at 62 Champion Street after coming to Lemoore in 1888.

Early structures like the Mooney store, the Lucerne Hotel, the Odd Fellows building, and the Antlers Hotel still grace Lemoore's downtown along D Street. The Oak Rooms Hotel, built in 1894 on Front Street, was a hotel and saloon. It still stands and now houses a small gift shop. A historic "Can't Bust Em Overalls" billboard mural remains on the east-facing wall of the hotel. One of the most celebrated of Lemoore's historical buildings is the Sarah A. Mooney Museum, built in 1893. Donated to the city by descendants of the Mooney family, it now houses a display depicting what a middle-class home in Lemoore would have looked like in the late 1880s and early 1900s. It also houses historical photographs and records. Adjacent to the museum is the Meyer house, built by Ernest and Anna Meyers in 1898 on their ranch to the east of Eighteenth Avenue. Later it was moved to 17770 Hanford-Armona Road. The home's facade is historically accurate. Lemoore High School's main building is a source of community pride. Built in the early 1920s, its mission-style architecture was restored, and the interior was remodeled to meet the needs of 21st-century students. City hall at Fox and C Streets has its original 1924 structure almost completely intact, while the United Service Organization (USO) building, just west of city hall on C Street, has been remodeled and is now used as Lemoore's Civic Auditorium. Surrounding Lemoore City Park are many historical homes, including that of Dr. William Byron.

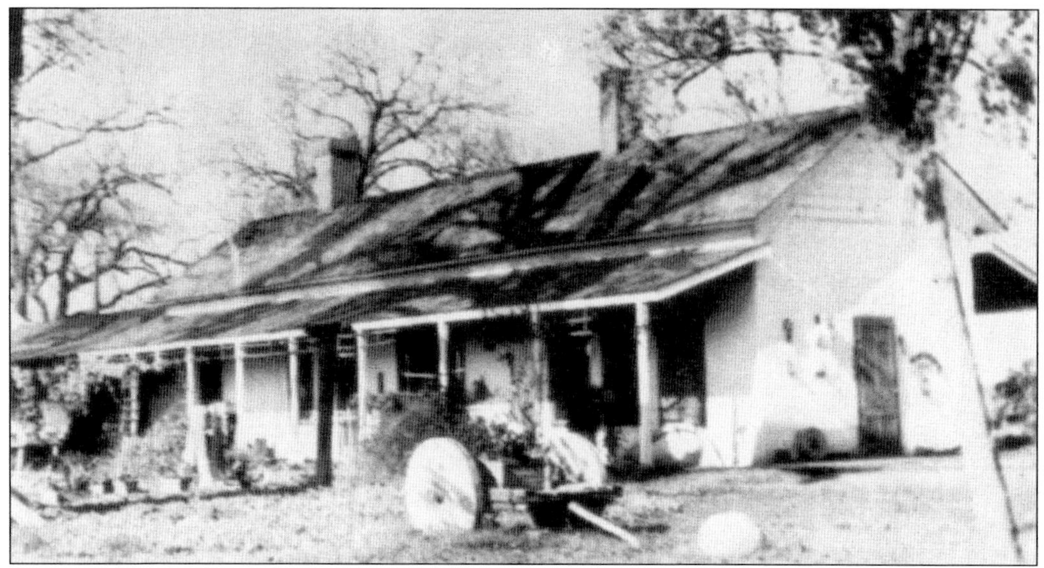

This adobe ranch house was built by Daniel Rhoads in 1856. Rhoads came to California in 1846 from Gilroy by overland wagon train. The restored adobe stands today and is the second-oldest adobe house in the San Joaquin Valley. (Courtesy of www.esarey.us/reunion/Jesse1800.htm.)

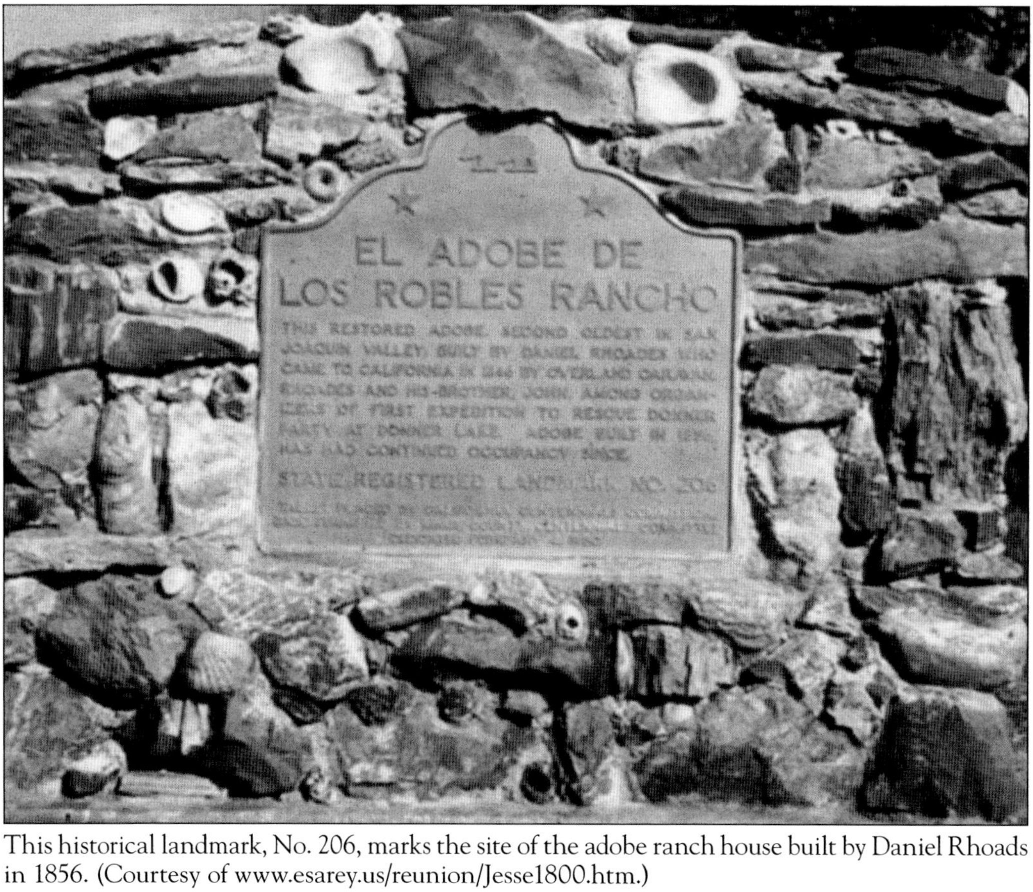

This historical landmark, No. 206, marks the site of the adobe ranch house built by Daniel Rhoads in 1856. (Courtesy of www.esarey.us/reunion/Jesse1800.htm.)

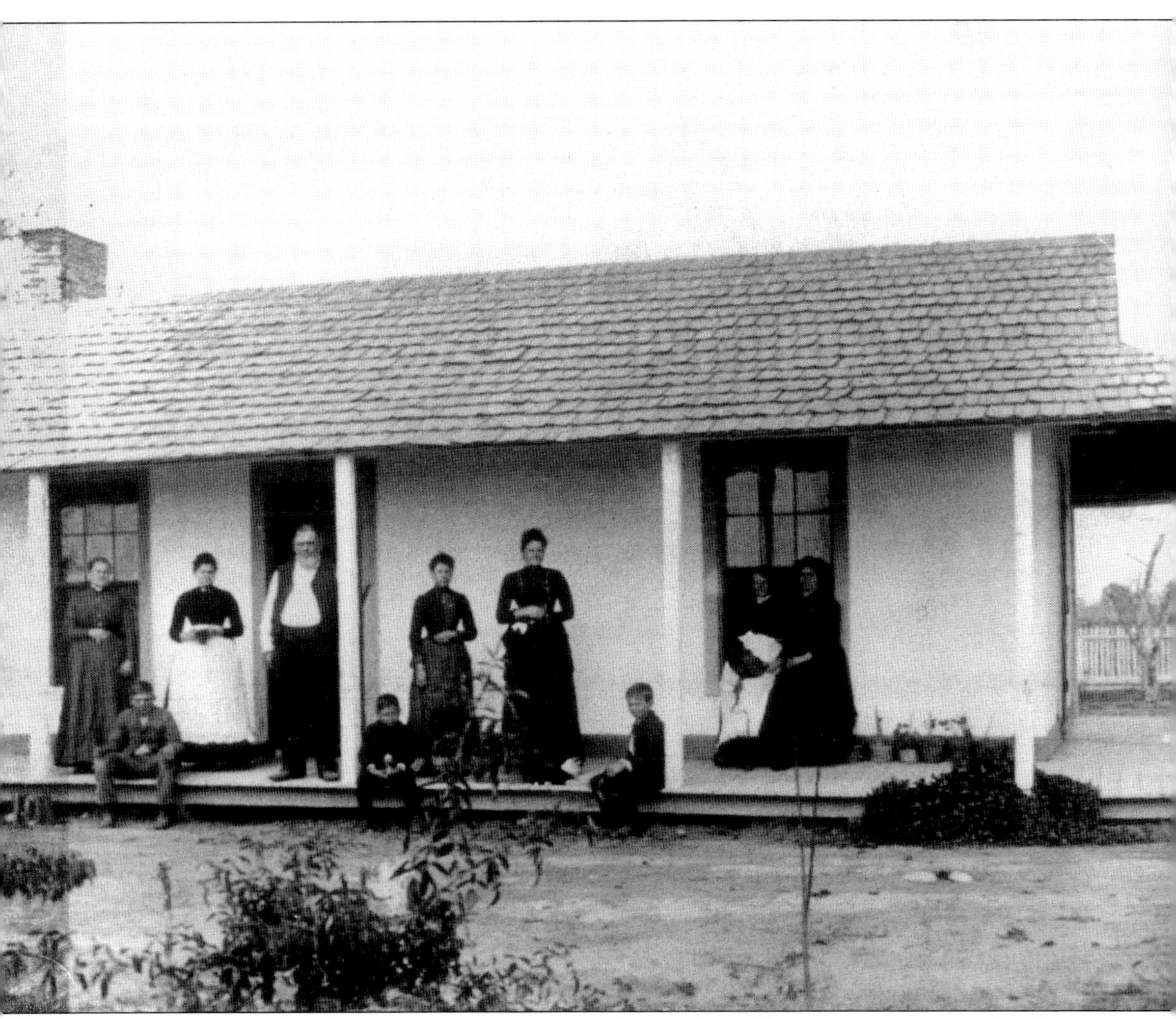

Jonathan and Justin Esrey were brothers who arrived from the gold mining region in 1857. They settled northeast of today's intersection of Highway 41 and Lacey Boulevard, north of Lemoore. This photograph was taken in about 1885. Justin Esrey is not shown. From left to right are Sarah Ann Winsett Esrey (Jonathan's wife), George Esrey (son), Nan Esrey Schooler (daughter), Jonathan Esrey, Justin Esrey (son), Kate Esrey Follett (daughter), Hattie Hatch Esrey, and Robert J. Esrey. The two women at far right are unidentified. The house remained standing until the 1920s. (Courtesy of the Sarah A. Mooney Museum.)

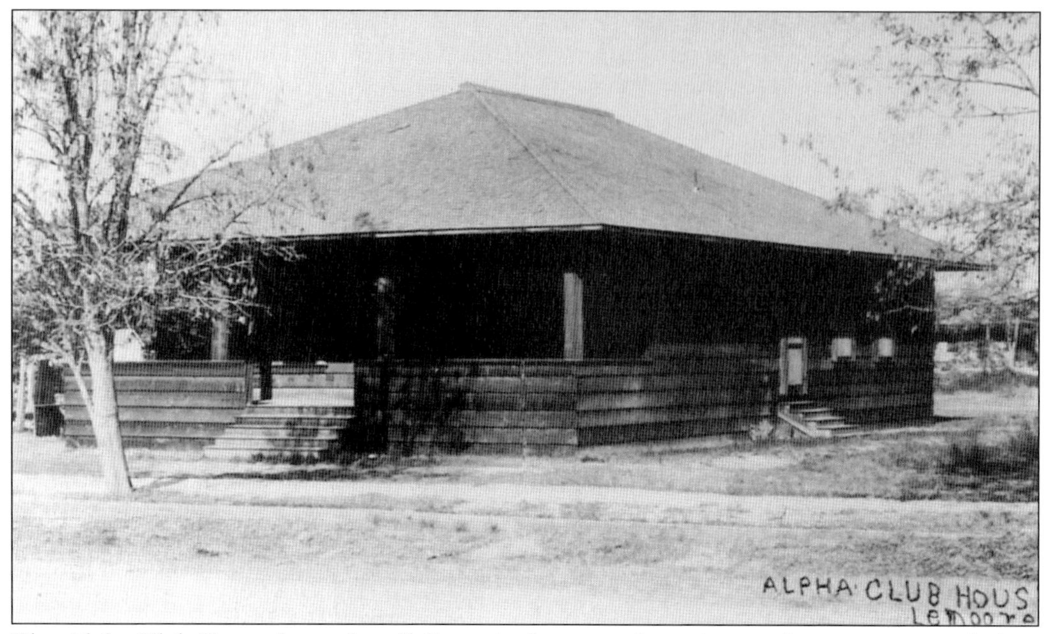

The Alpha Club House, located on B Street in Lemoore, hosted many fun activities, including church breakfasts and Boy Scout meetings. (Courtesy of St. Peter's Catholic Church.)

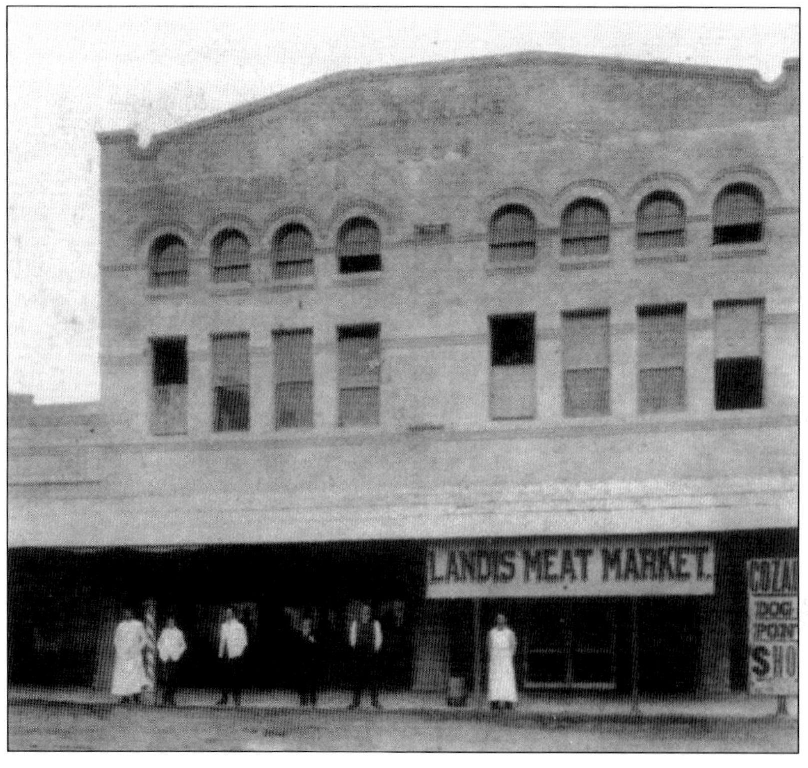

The Lemoore Opera House, located above the Landis Meat Market on Heinlen Street, held many events and productions until it was destroyed by fire in 1927. (Courtesy of the Sarah A. Mooney Museum.)

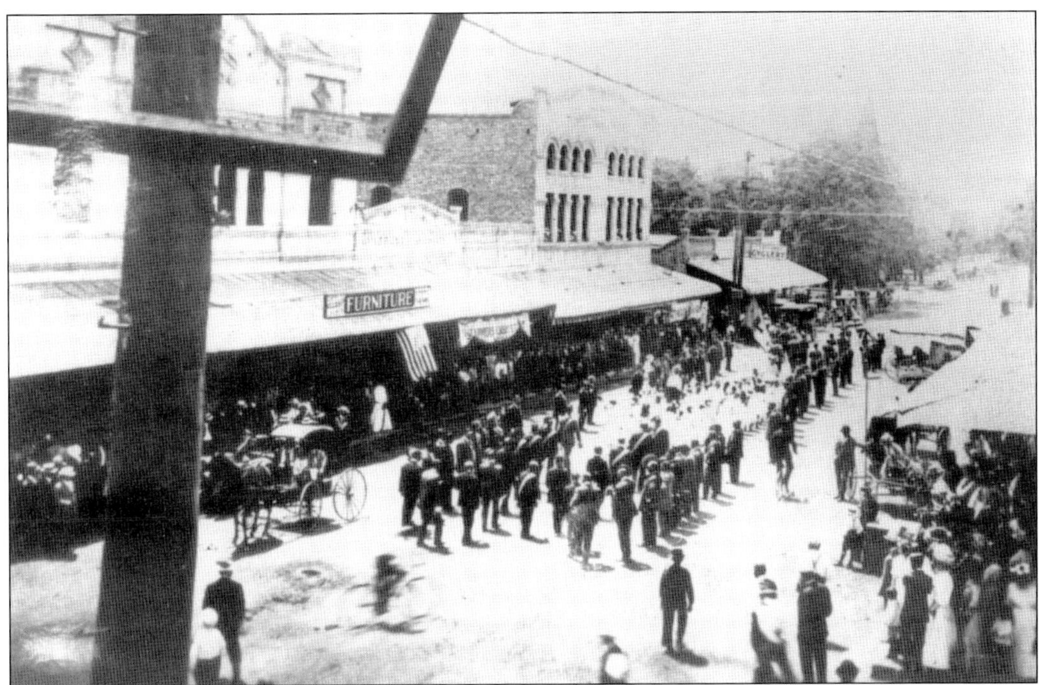

The Lemoore Opera House was built in 1904 on the west side of Heinlen Street, south of D Street. It is the two-story building in the center of the photograph. (Courtesy of Jack Stone.)

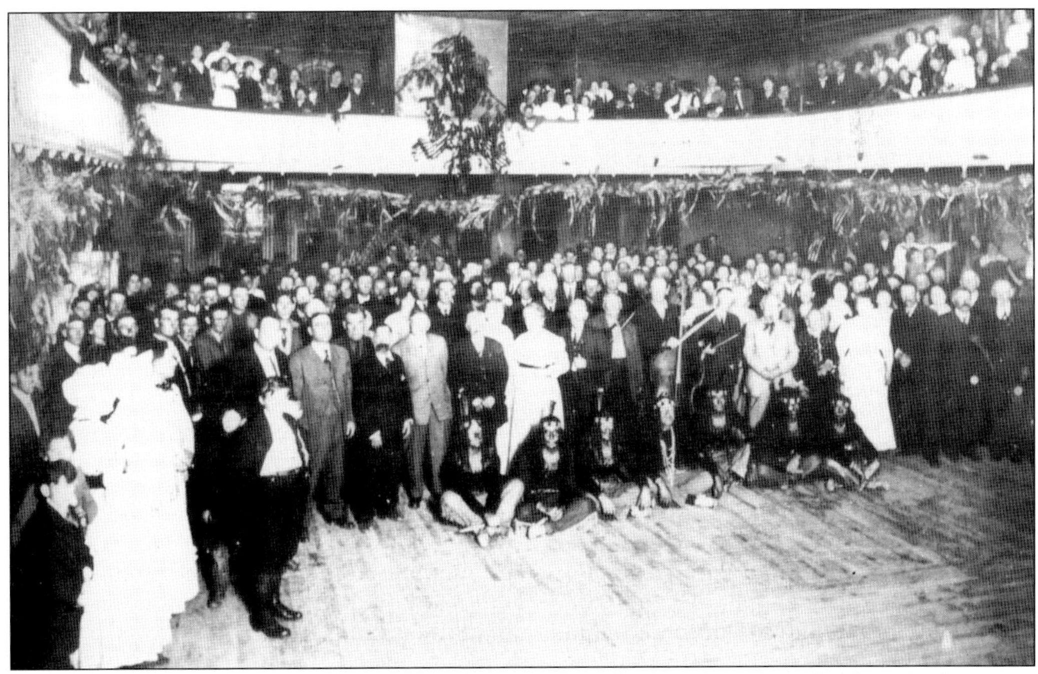

All kinds of events, including dances, graduations, and receptions, were held at the Lemoore Opera House. (Courtesy of Kings County Museum.)

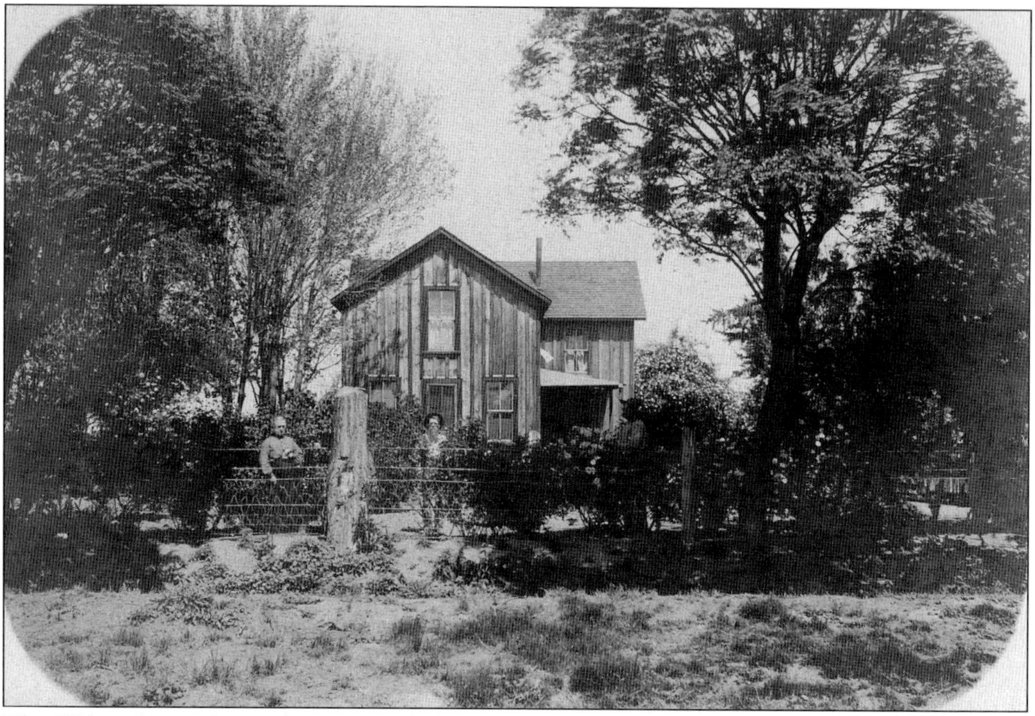

The Wilson home, located at 307 Bush Street in 1915, was one of the early houses in Lemoore. The Lemoore Methodist Church is now located on this site. (Courtesy of the Sarah A. Mooney Museum.)

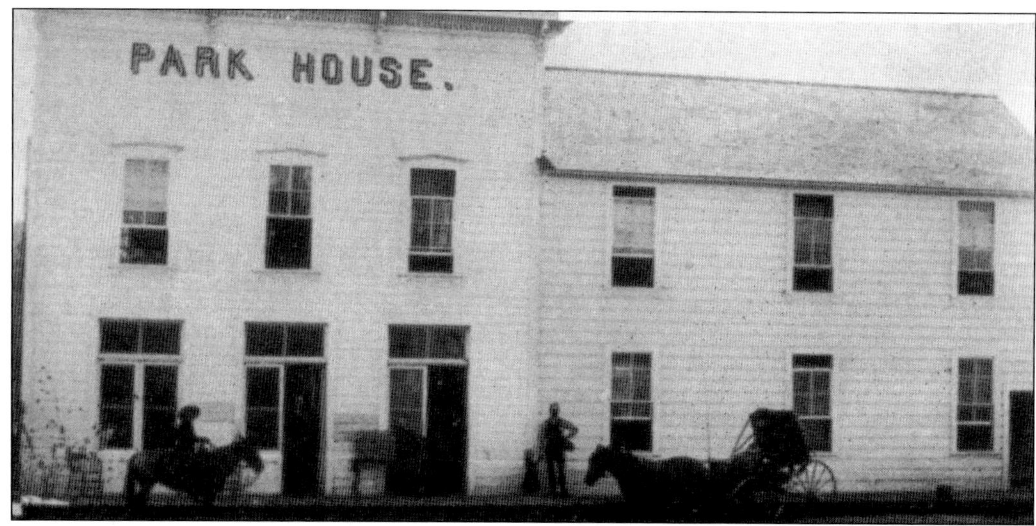

The Park House Hotel at Heinlen and Front Streets was the first Lemoore hotel. (Courtesy of Kings County Museum.)

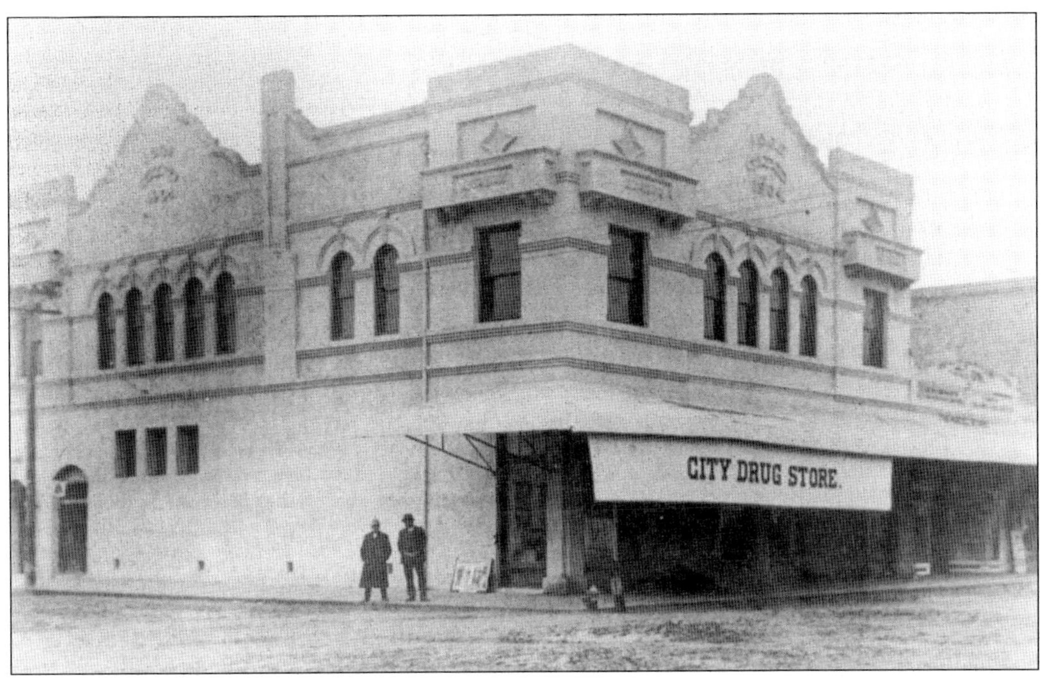

The International Order of Odd Fellows building still stands at the corner of Heinlen and D Streets today. It was built in 1904 and was home to the City Drug Store and then Leoni's Drug Store until 2009. (Courtesy of the Sarah A. Mooney Museum.)

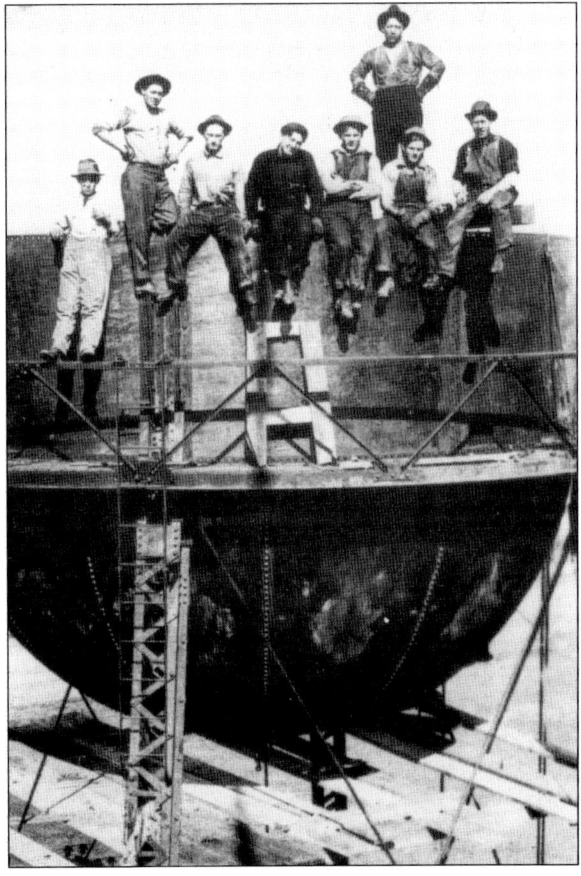

Early Lemoore residents sit atop the water tower in Lemoore. This tower was demolished in 1991. (Courtesy of Jack Stone.)

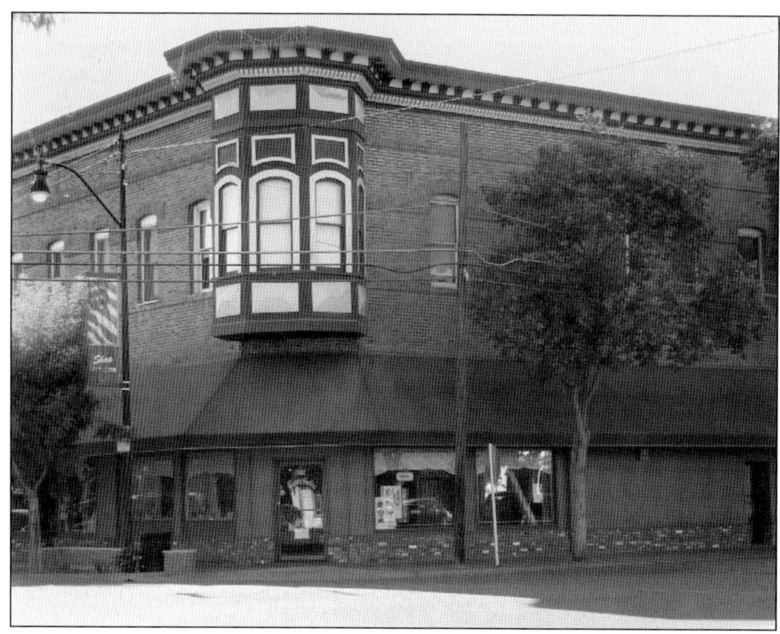

The Antlers Hotel, built in 1908 in downtown Lemoore, was renovated a few years ago to a historically authentic condition. The ground floor contains shops, and the second floor now provides studio and one-bedroom apartments to senior-aged tenants. The hotel received the 2008 Preservation Design Award from the California Renovation Project. (Photograph by Cynthia J. Wright.)

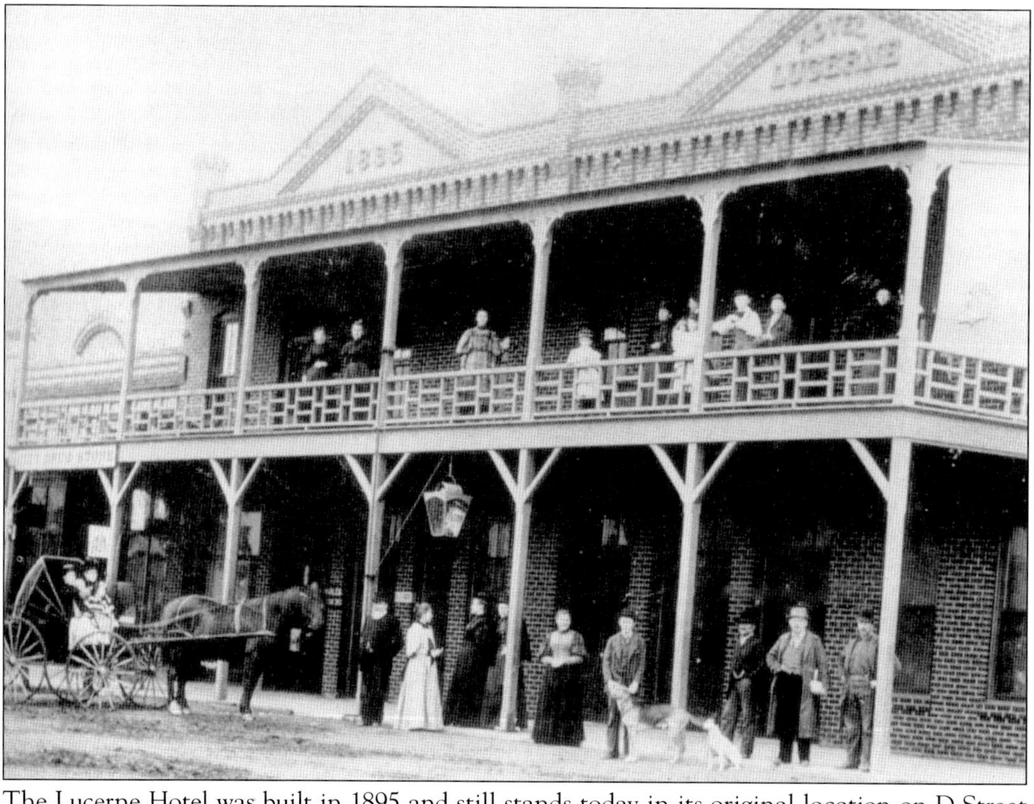

The Lucerne Hotel was built in 1895 and still stands today in its original location on D Street between Fox and Heinlen Streets. (Courtesy of the Sarah A. Mooney Museum.)

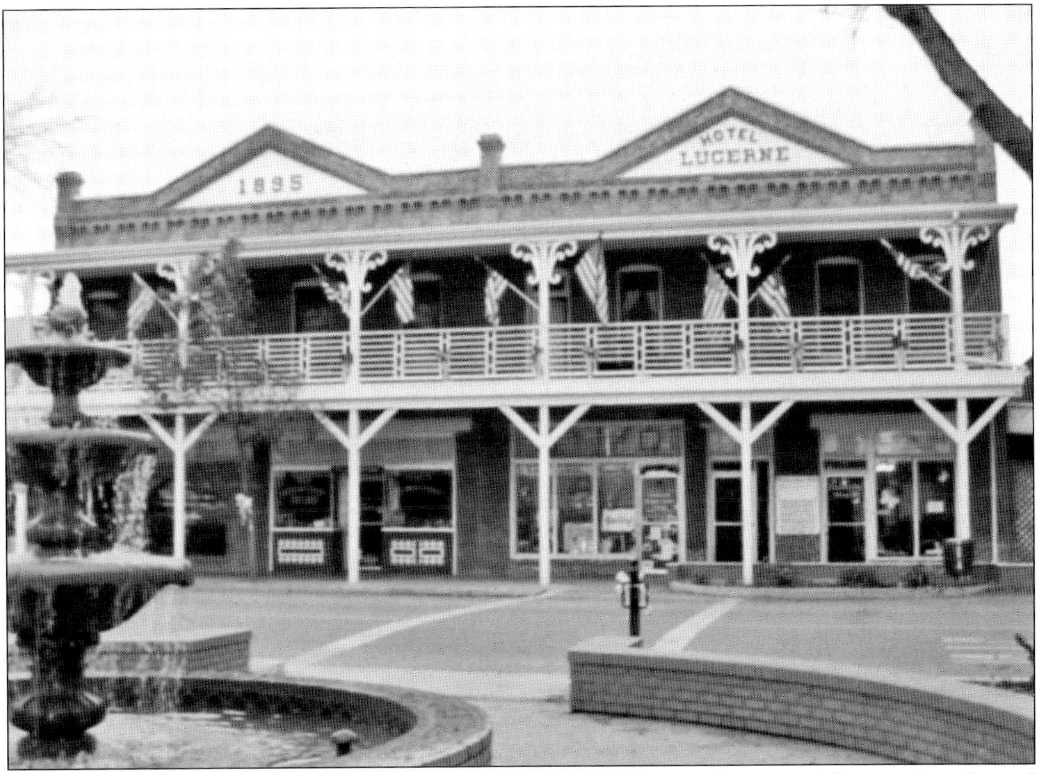

The Lucerne Hotel, as it looks today, contains commercial units on the ground floor and residential housing on the top floor. (Courtesy of the City of Lemoore.)

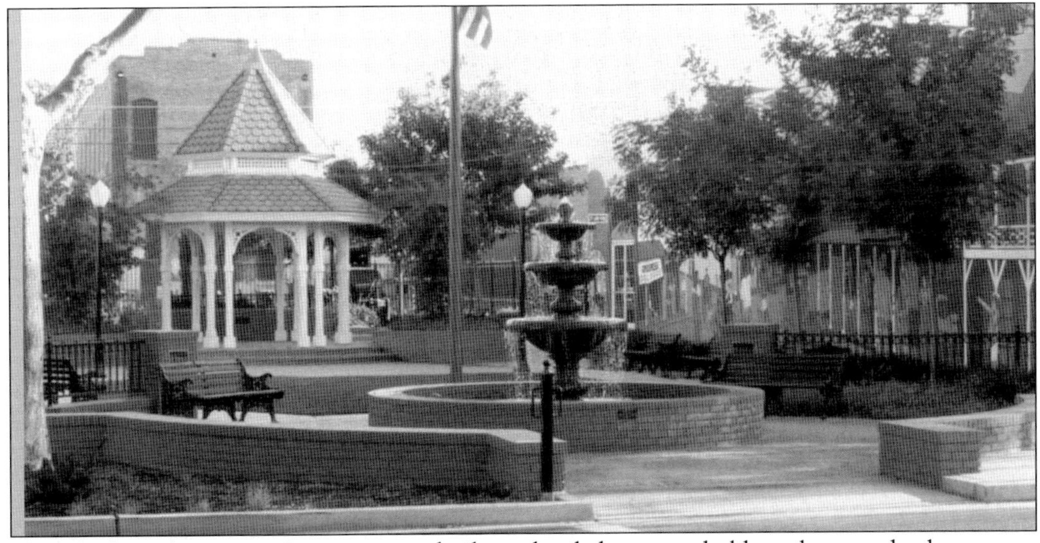

Plaza Park in downtown Lemoore was built on land that once held a saloon and other stores. With its fountain, gazebo, and colorful murals, it provides an oasis in the middle of the downtown stores. (Courtesy of the City of Lemoore.)

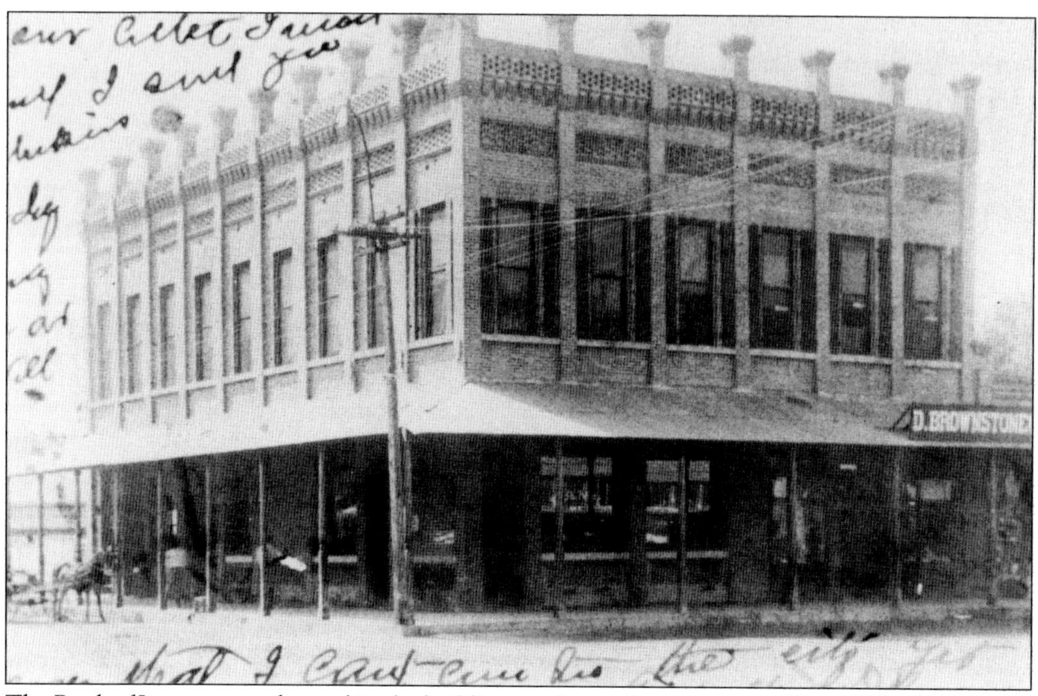

The Bank of Lemoore was housed in the building on the southwest corner of D and Heinlen Streets. Wells Fargo Bank is now located on this corner. (Courtesy of the Sarah A. Mooney Museum.)

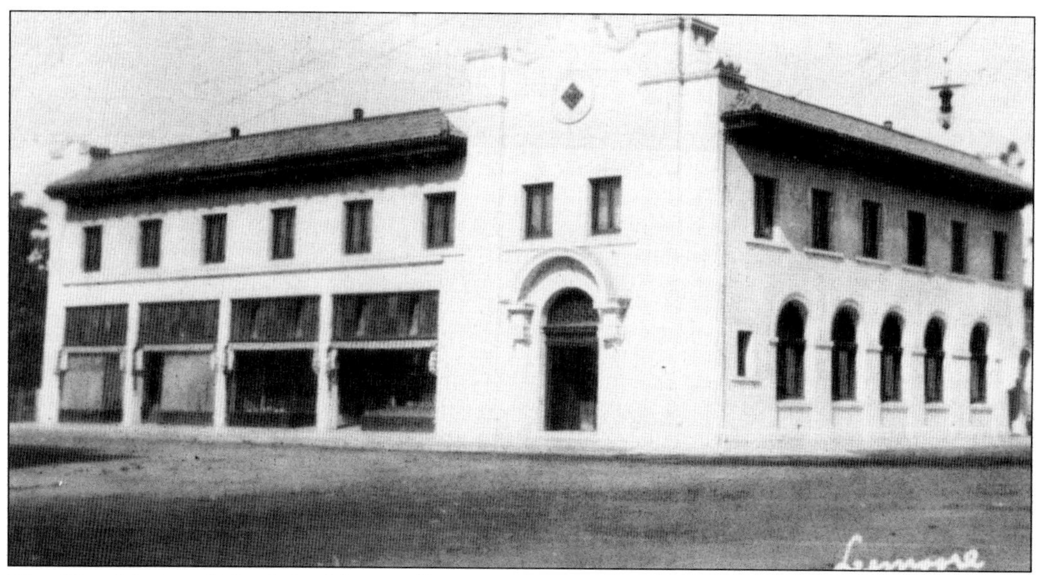

The First National Bank building still sits at the corner of D and Fox Streets in downtown Lemoore. It currently houses a series of shops. The Lemoore Branch Library was located in this building between 1920 and 1960. (Courtesy of the Sarah A. Mooney Museum.)

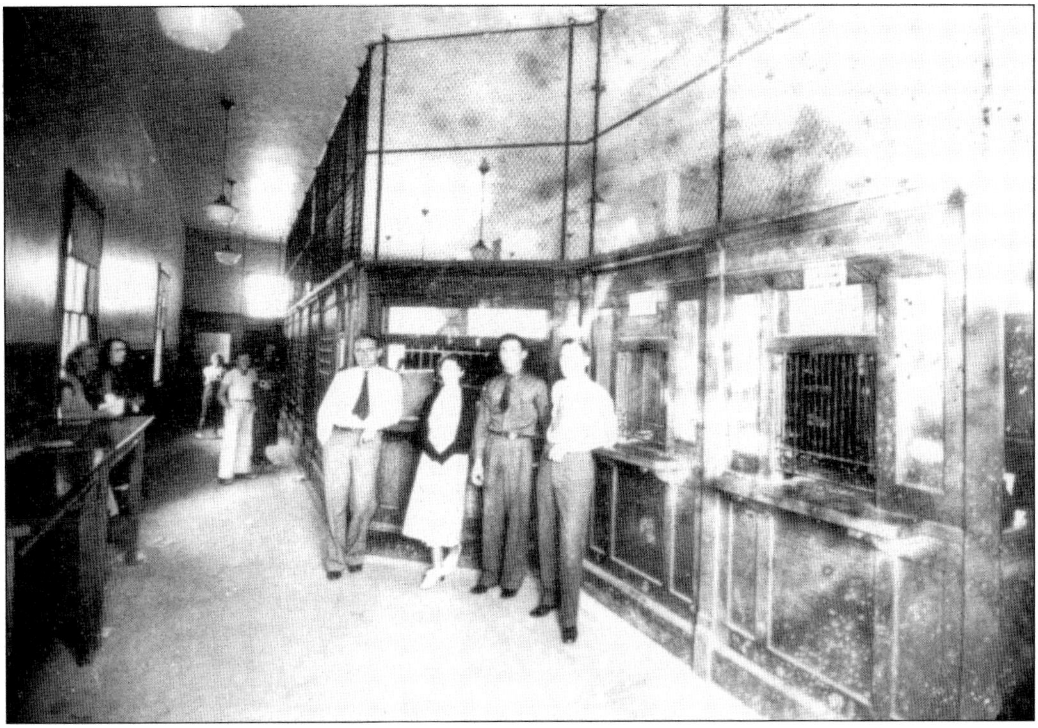

Employees stand inside the Lemoore Post Office, which was located in the 200 block of West D Street. (Courtesy of the Sarah A. Mooney Museum.)

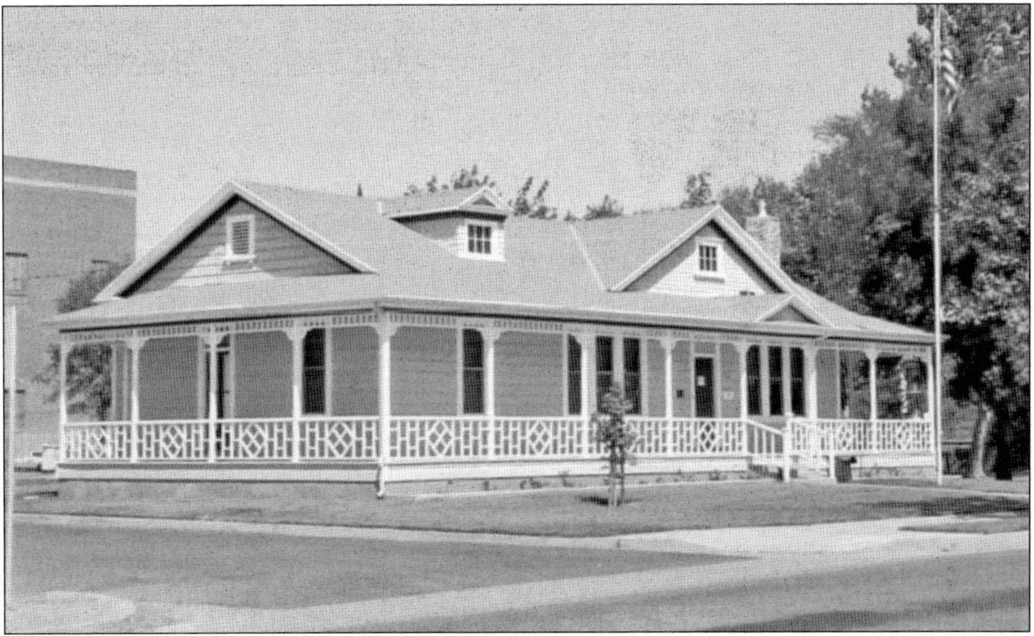

Ernest and Anna Meyers built the Meyers house in 1898 on his ranch to the east of Eighteenth Avenue. Later it was relocated to 17770 Hanford-Armona Road. It was then moved to D Street next to the Sarah A. Mooney Museum and is now a transitional home for teenage girls needing a place to live. (Courtesy of the City of Lemoore.)

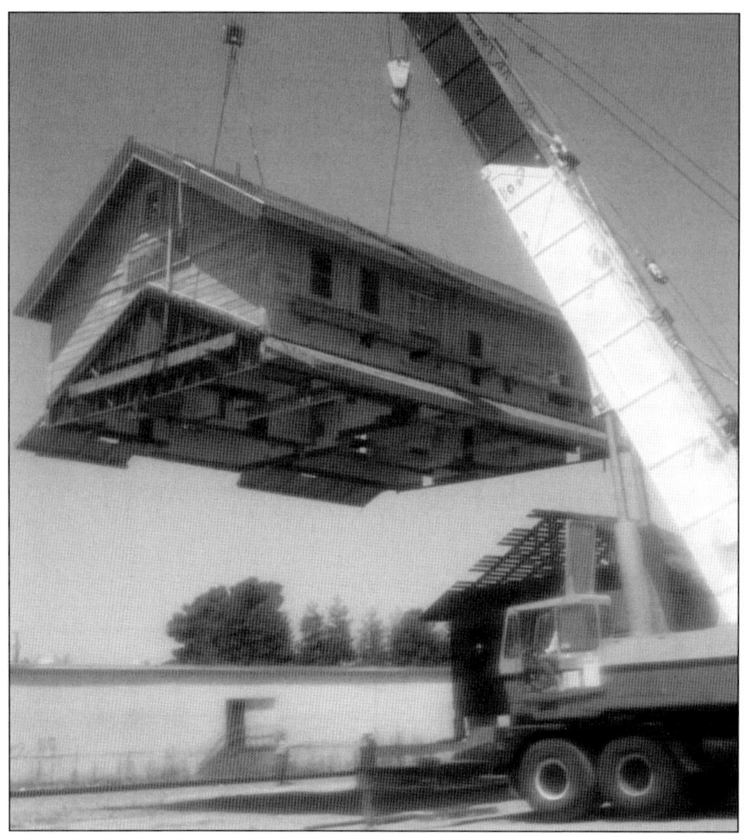

The Lemoore train depot is located at 300 E Street. It is a Southern Pacific Combination Model 22 Depot that was originally located in Strathmore. It was purchased by the City of Lemoore in 2003 to replace the exact same depot model that was originally on this Lemoore site, but was torn down in the 1960s. It now is the home of the Lemoore District Chamber of Commerce as well as several rental office spaces and a freight room for meetings and events. (Photograph by Judy Cox-Finney.)

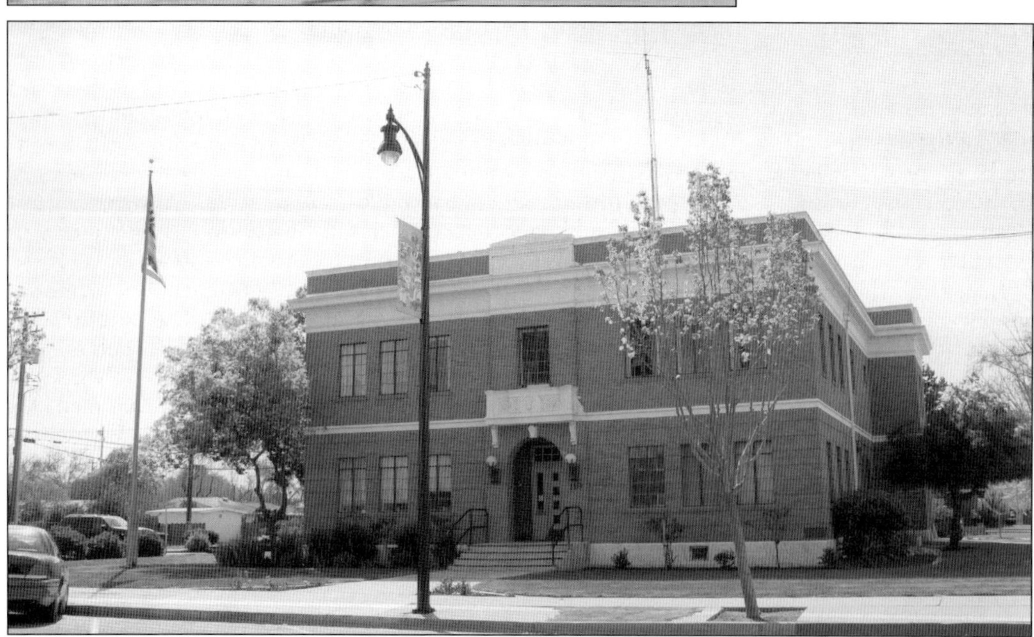

Lemoore City Hall, at 119 Fox Street, was built in 1924. It originally housed the city clerks' office, the Lemoore Volunteer Fire Department, the police department, and two small jail cells. Today it is home to city administrative offices. (Courtesy of the City of Lemoore.)

Seven

Schools and Churches

Education and worship have been high on the list of necessities for Lemoore residents. Even before Lemoore was founded, parents sent their children to the Rhoads adobe where Amanda Rhoads taught classes. In 1866, the Lake School was constructed on Lacey Boulevard; it was the first in what would become Kings County and continued in operation until 1920.

After Lemoore was officially created, an elementary school was built, probably in 1873, on Lemoore Avenue, half a block north of Bush Street. By 1882, a new school was built at Bush and Follett Streets. It was an impressive two-story structure complete with a bell tower. Lemoore High School held its first classes in 1901 in the Heinlen Hall on Front (E) Street with 25 freshmen students. Two years later, classes were taught in a brand new school building at Fox and B Streets. In 1926, a smaller version of the present high school was built on Eighteenth Avenue, south of Bush Street. The Lake School served double duty as a church for the Methodist community in the early years. It was also the record office for the Lower Kings River Ditch Company in 1873.

Lemoore's First Methodist Church was built in 1878 at Hill and D Streets. The Lemoore Presbyterians had their church constructed by 1889 at Heinlen and B Streets. The Seventh Day Adventist's first church was established in 1875 at C and Follett Streets. The Tachi-Yokuts did not have a church on their Rancheria until the mid-20th century, but that did not stop them from converting as a group to the Catholic religion in 1879. St. Peter's Catholic Church was ready for parishioners at Bush and Follett Streets in 1912. Lemoore Catholics still celebrate Portuguese festa, which is a festival honoring service to the poor. Baptists organized in 1884 and were located at C and Heinlen Streets. More than educational and spiritual organizations, the churches and schools played a vital role in helping residents socialize.

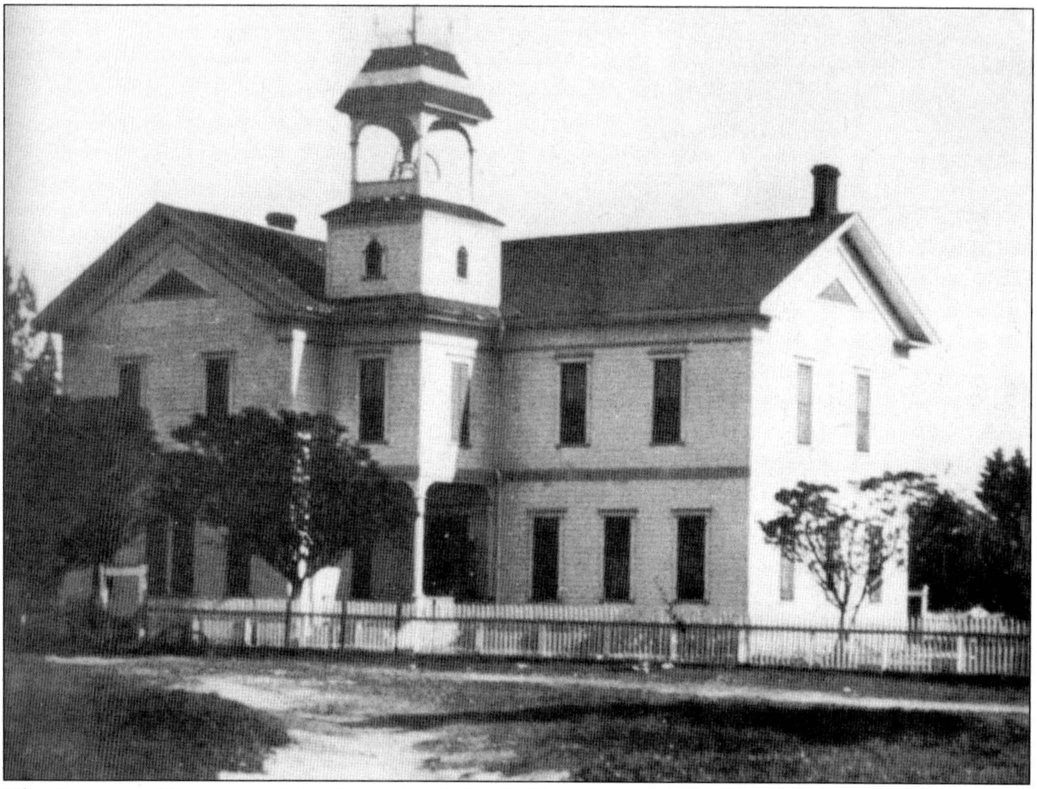

The Lemoore Grammar School was built in 1882 and was located at the northwest corner of Bush and Follett Streets. (Courtesy of the Sarah A. Mooney Museum.)

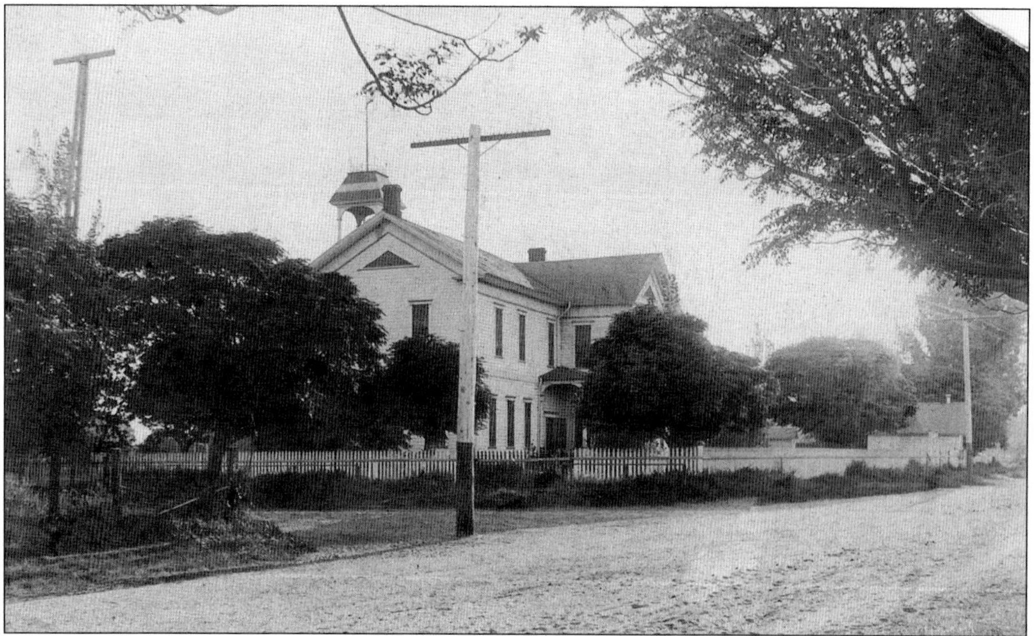

This photograph shows another view of Lemoore Grammar School at Bush and Follett Streets. (Courtesy of St. Peter's Catholic Church.)

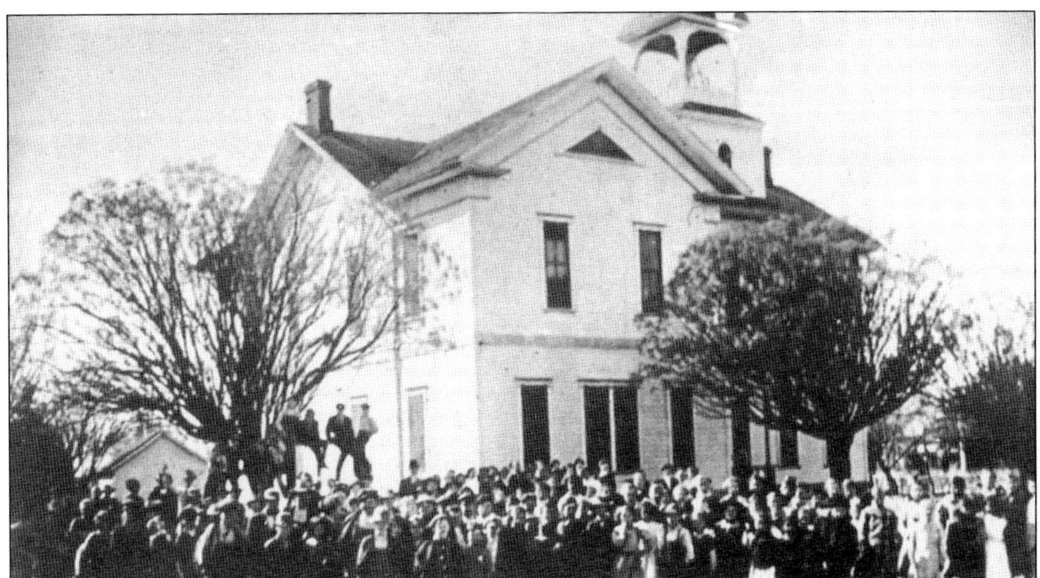

Lemoore Grammar School came to be known as Lemoore Elementary School by the early 1900s. Students and staff congregate around the Lemoore Elementary School on the corner of Bush and Follett Streets in about 1911. (Courtesy of St. Peter's Catholic Church.)

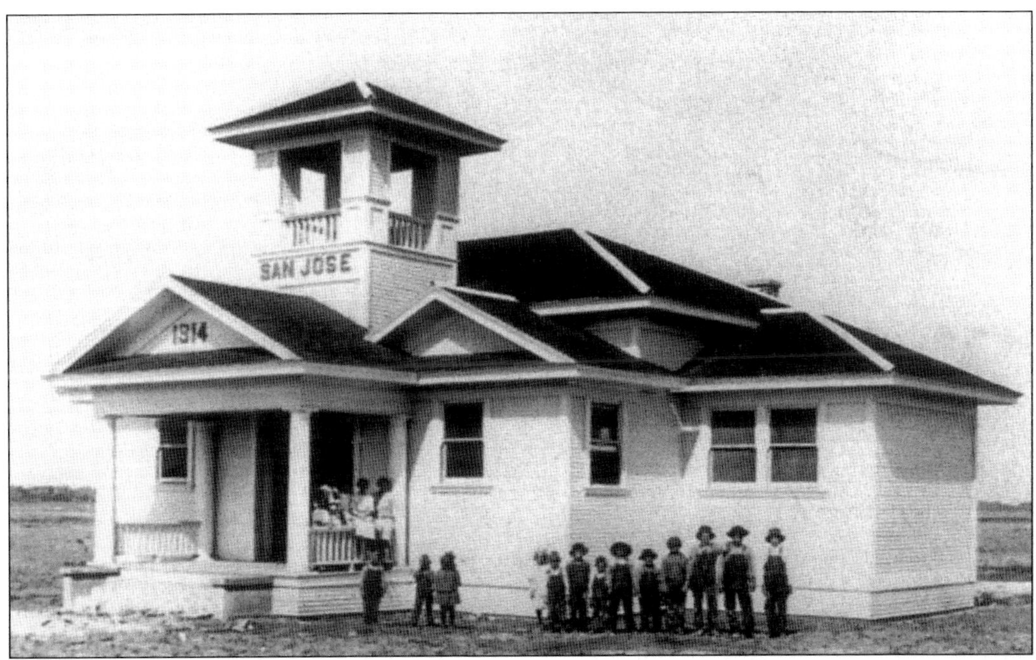

The San Jose School was built in 1913 between the north and south fork of the Kings River on the northwest corner of Twenty-fourth and Fairfax Avenues, about 4 miles from the Island School. A portion of the North Fork School District was annexed to the Island District in 1922, and after a second unionization vote was taken, the San Jose District became part of the Island District in 1958. (Courtesy of the Sarah A. Mooney Museum.)

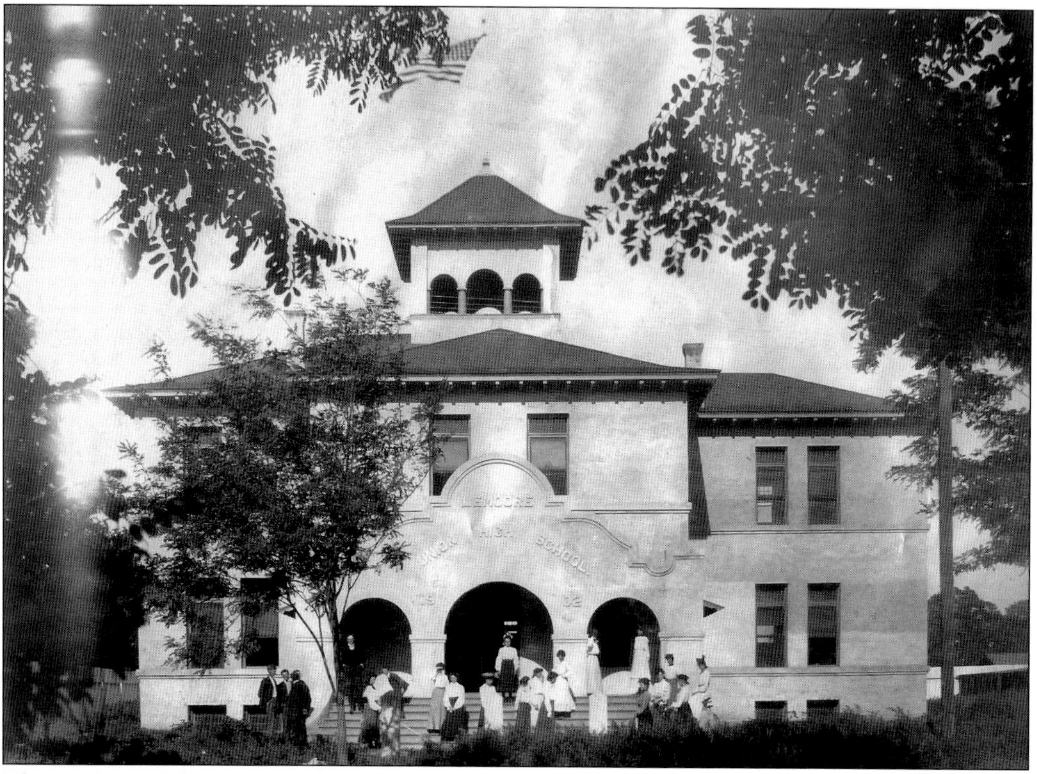

This picture of the Lemoore High School was taken in 1904. This building, on the southwest corner of C and Fox Streets, where Lemoore City Hall stands today, served as the high school from 1902 to 1925. (Courtesy of the Sarah A. Mooney Museum.)

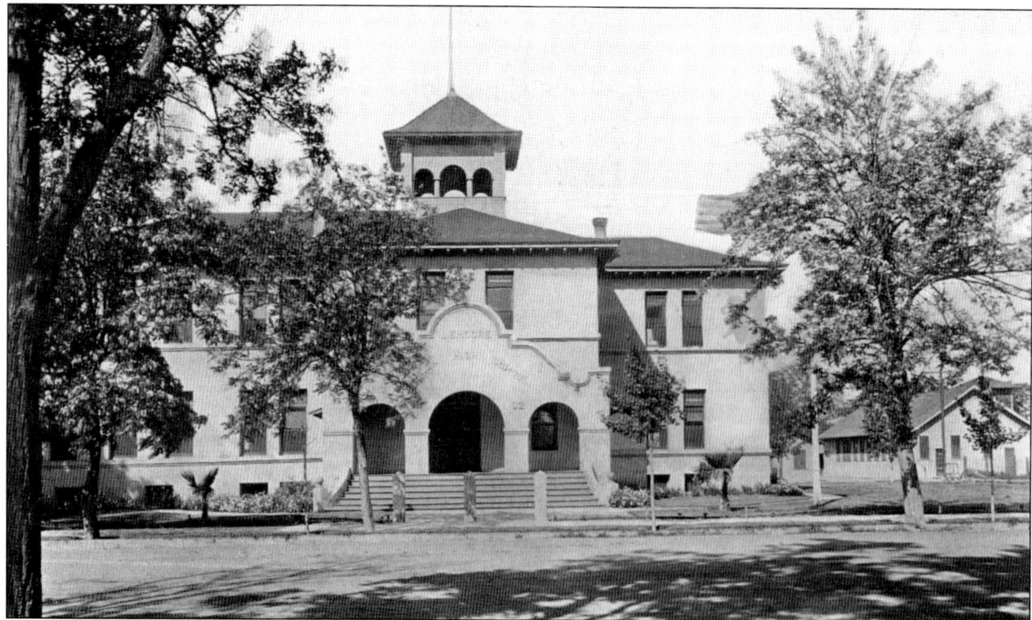

This photograph shows another view of Lemoore High School taken around the same time period. (Courtesy of the Sarah A. Mooney Museum.)

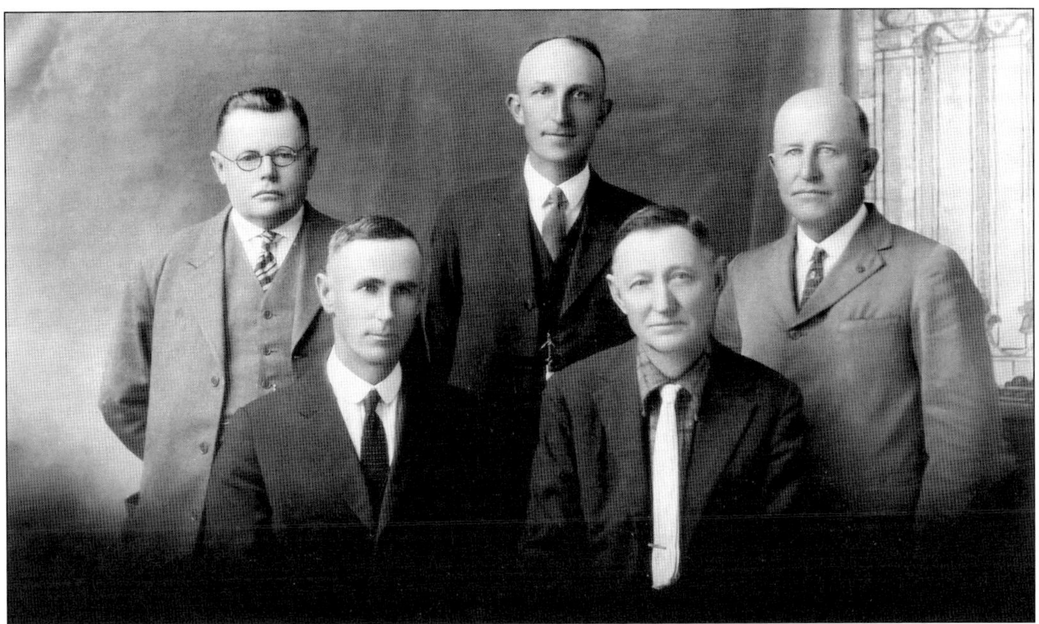

The 1922 Lemoore High School board poses for a picture. This was the board responsible for acquiring land, choosing plans, and supervising the construction of the new high school. Shown from left to right are (first row) R. E. Shore and John Kurtz; (second row) John Brothers, Farley Auble, and Ford Sorrick. (Courtesy of the Sarah A. Mooney Museum.)

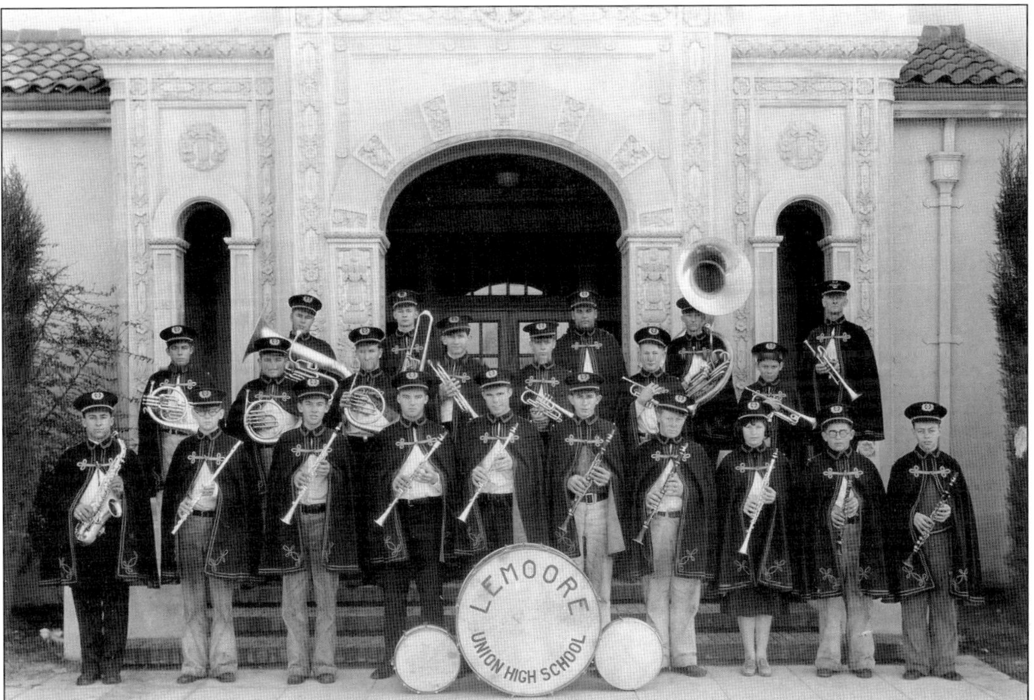

The Lemoore High School band poses in front of the school that was built in 1925. The current high school is in the same historical building, though it has been renovated and expanded since it was first constructed. (Courtesy of the Sarah A. Mooney Museum.)

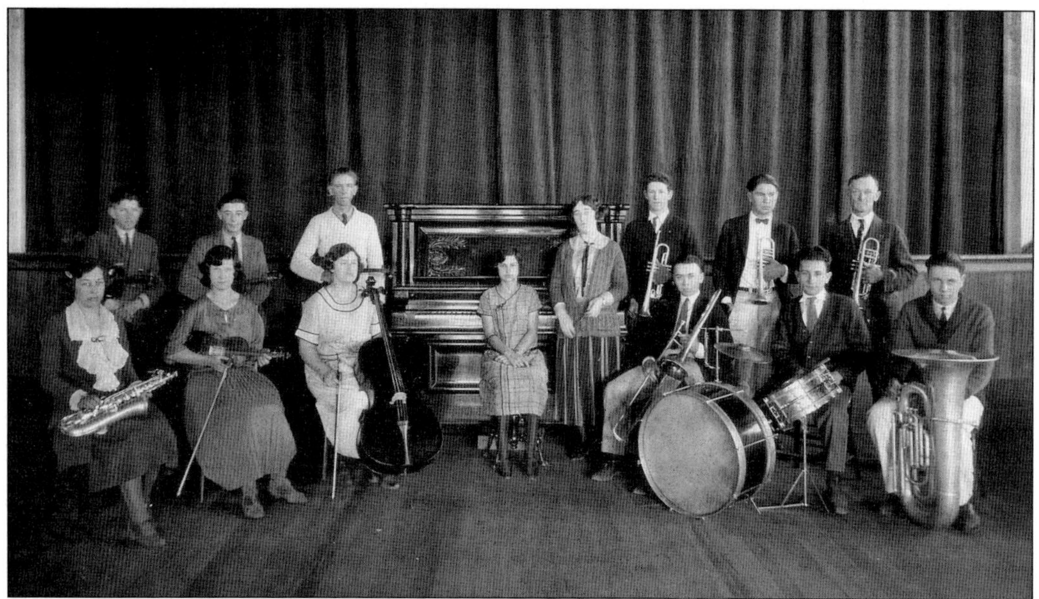

Members of the 1925 Lemoore High School orchestra are, from left to right, (first row) Loleta Graff, Gladys Meyer (Meser), Maurine Smith (McGlanahan), Marianne Moyer (Jacobus), Tommy Bettencourt, Patsy Bucaria, and Lorenzo Carrasco; (second row) Robert Summer, Iby Pierotti, Lyman Latham, Miss Benton (teacher), Shore, Elmer Miller, and Leroy Spencer (teacher). (Courtesy of the Sarah A. Mooney Museum.)

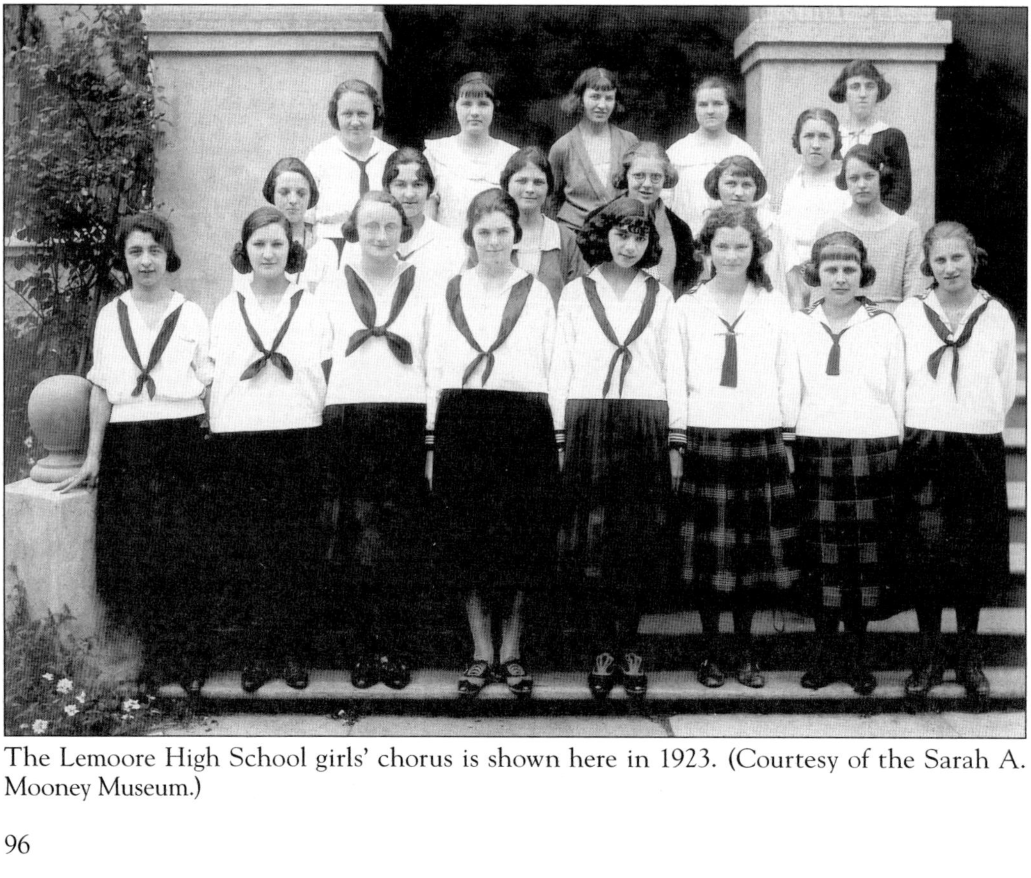

The Lemoore High School girls' chorus is shown here in 1923. (Courtesy of the Sarah A. Mooney Museum.)

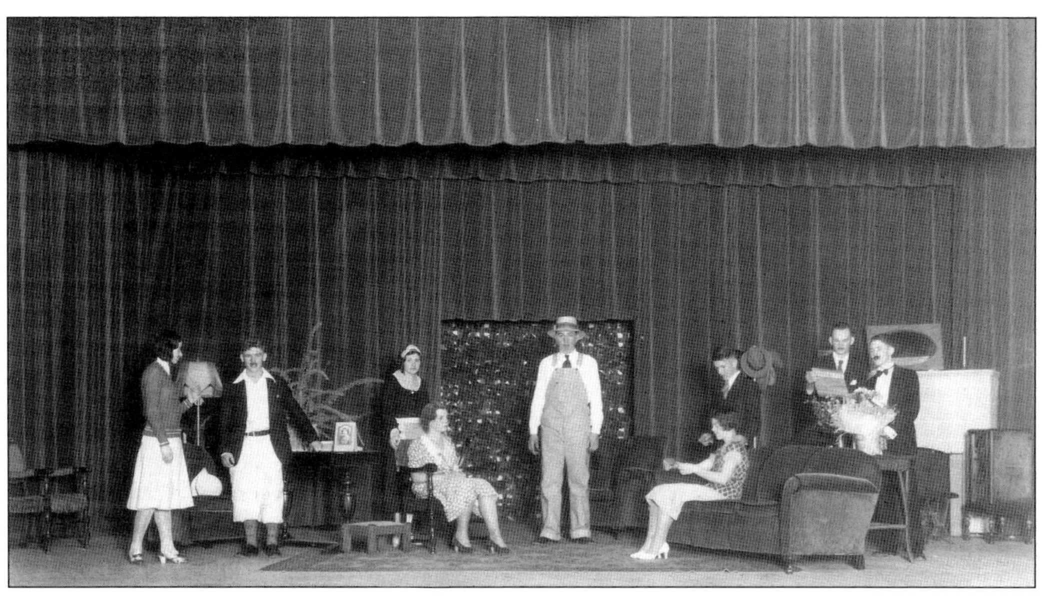

Plays at Lemoore High School were popular entertainment in the 1920s. The same props and sets were reused for many productions. (Courtesy of the Sarah A. Mooney Museum.)

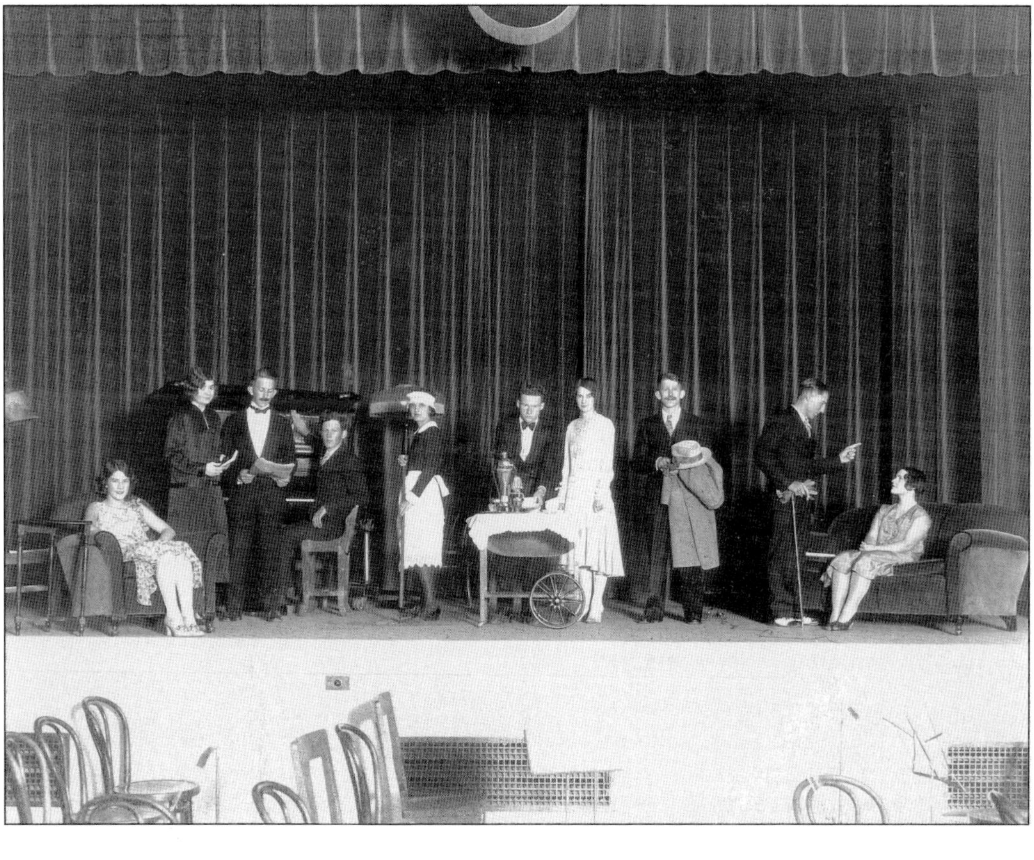

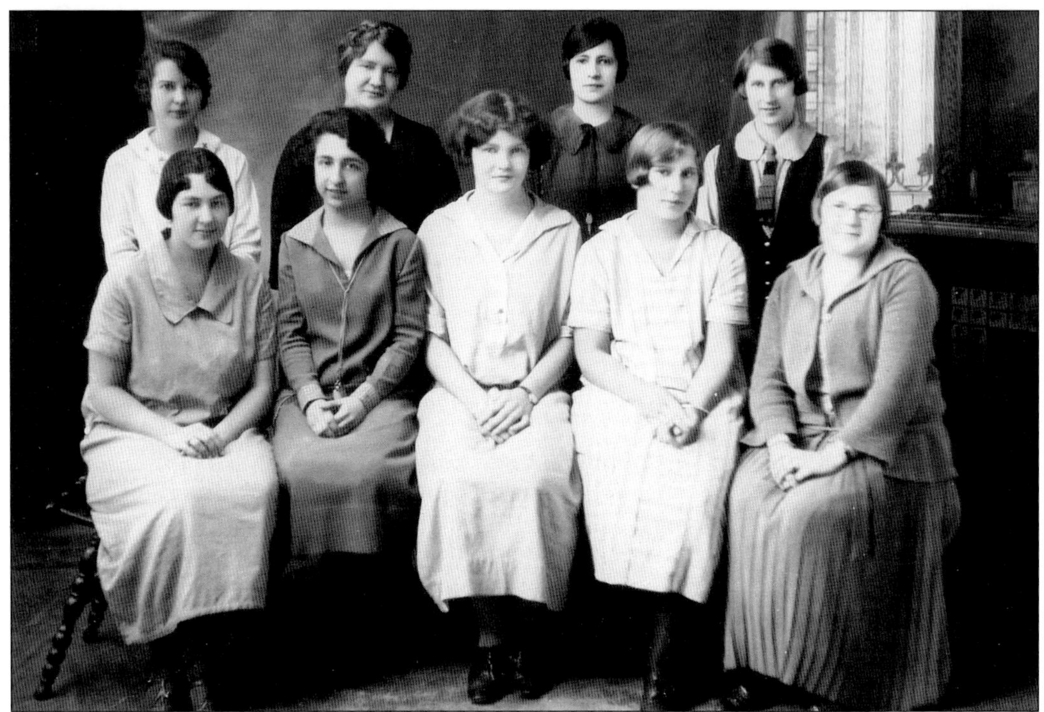

An early Lemoore High School girls' class poses for a picture. From left to right are (first row) Josephine Bucaria and four unidentified; (second row) Nadine E., Marie Pratt (teacher), Alice Lewis, and Ethel Blakeley. (Courtesy of the Sarah A. Mooney Museum.)

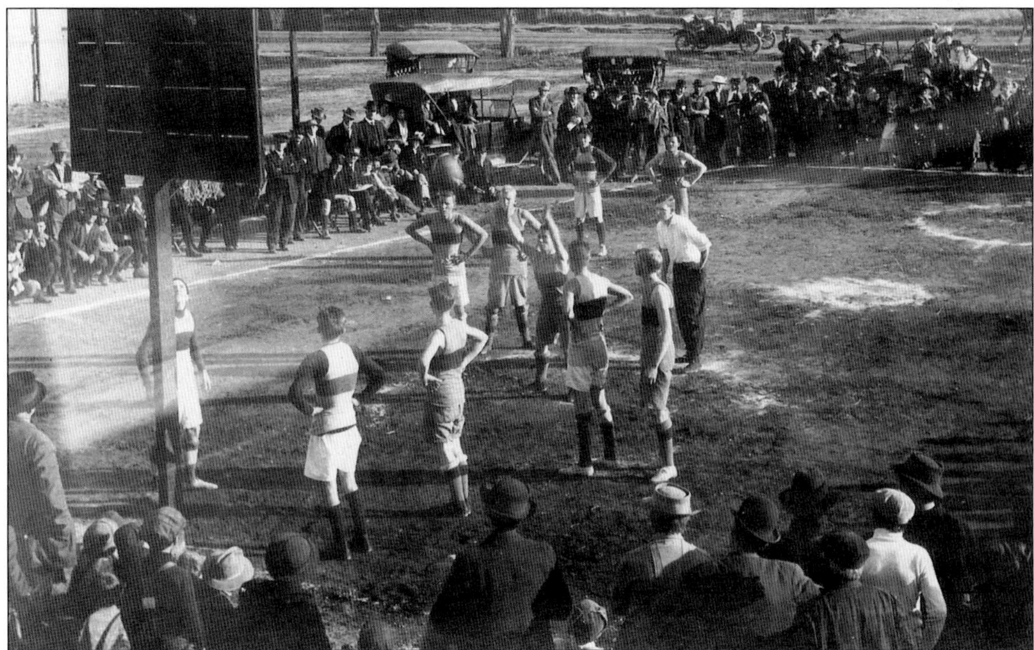

The 1915 Lemoore High School boys' basketball team consisted of George Dockstader, Cecil Evans, Paul Bauer, McKinley Johnson, Howard Hubbard, George Poole, Gene Tharp, and Clarence Willis. Dockstader is taking a free-throw shot. (Courtesy of the Sarah A. Mooney Museum.)

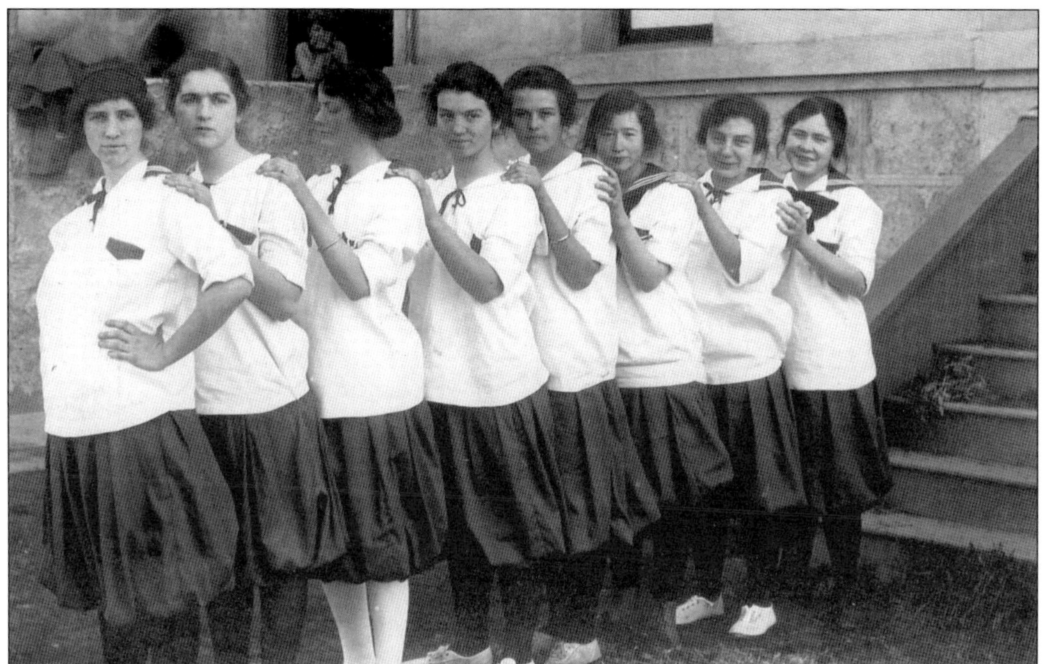

The 1915 Lemoore High School girl's basketball team included, from left to right, Clara Jennings, Jannie Bonfantini, Marie Hutton, Dela Brown, Marie Bailey, Evelyn Sanborn, Golda Gilcrease, and Mildred Lung. (Courtesy of the Sarah A. Mooney Museum.)

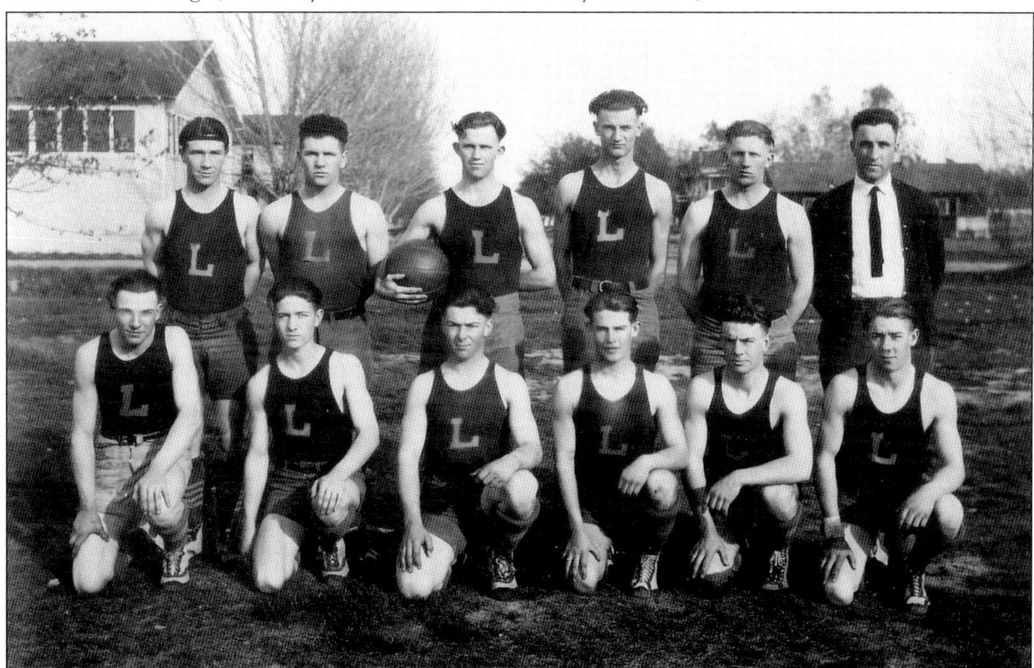

The 1923 Lemoore High School boys' basketball team consisted of, from left to right, (first row) Nathan Turner, Francis Littler, Robert Jones, Bernard Burton, John Dockstader, and Bert Brown; (second row) Louie Efird, Howard Littler, George Flaherty, Hugh Hancock, Lester Blakeley, and coach Howard Ross. (Courtesy of the Sarah A. Mooney Museum.)

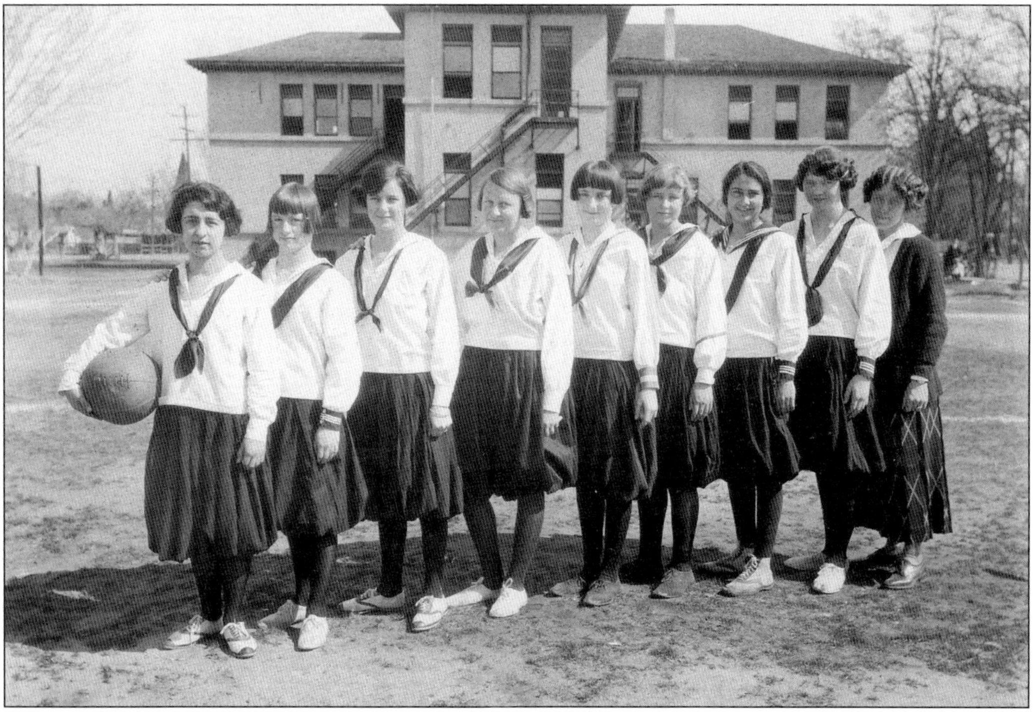

An early Lemoore High School girls' basketball team poses for a picture. (Courtesy of the Sarah A. Mooney Museum.)

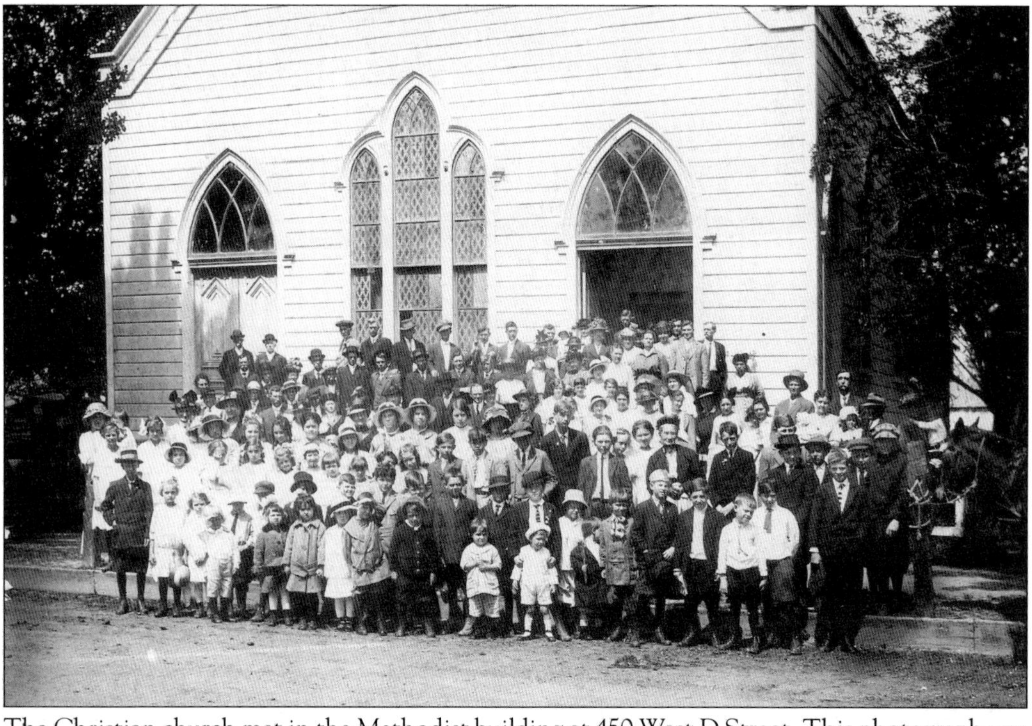

The Christian church met in the Methodist building at 450 West D Street. This photograph was taken in 1914. (Courtesy of the Sarah A. Mooney Museum.)

This shows Father Abrantes and Tom Bettencourt in about 1914. St. Peter's Catholic Church was built at Bush and Heinlen Streets in 1912. Mass is still held in the original building, but a new church is under construction in 2010 on Eighteenth (Lemoore) Avenue. (Courtesy of the Sarah A. Mooney Museum.)

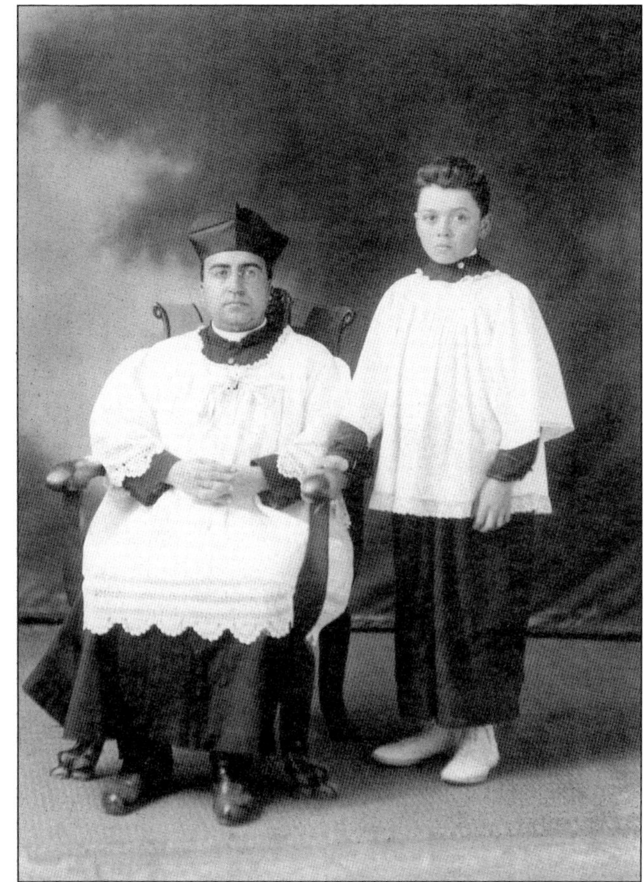

This is believed to be the earliest photograph of St. Peter's Catholic Church, taken in 1912 or 1913. (Courtesy of St. Peter's Catholic Church.)

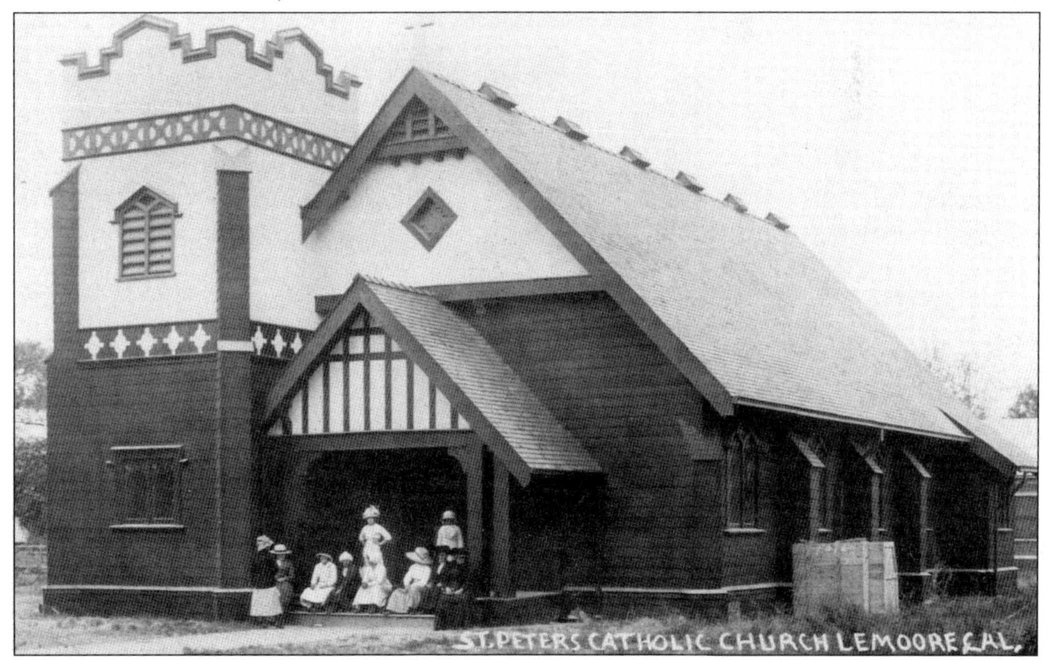

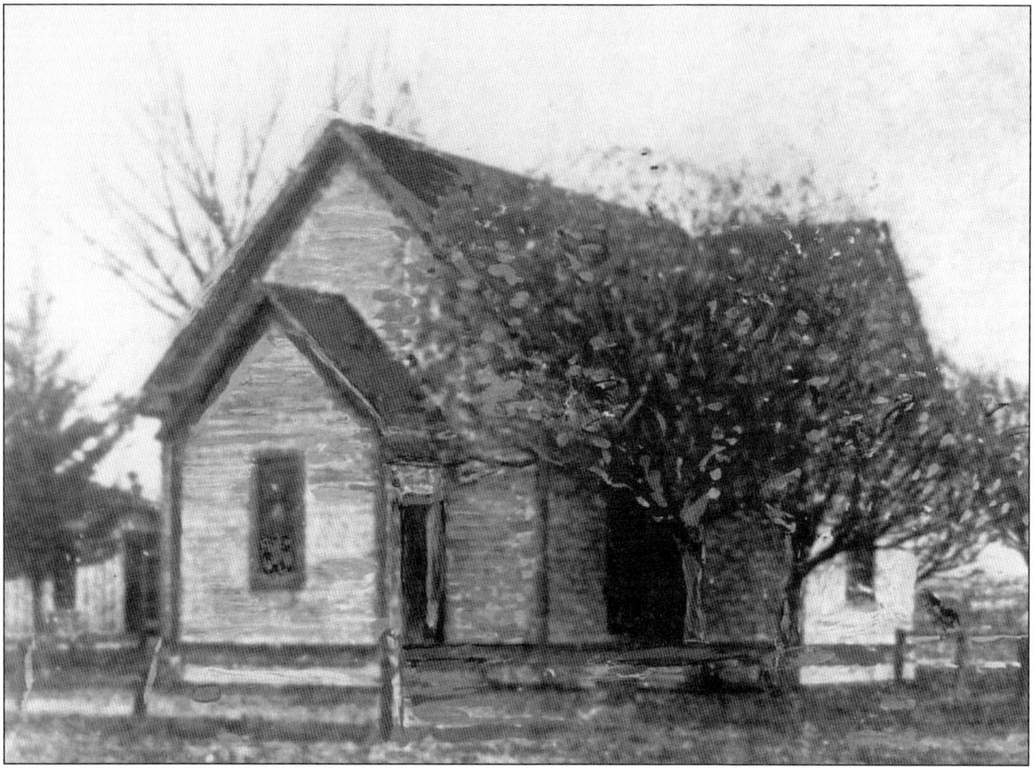

This is an early drawing of the first Presbyterian church in Lemoore, built in 1889 on the corner of B and Heinlen Streets, where the church is still located today. The Reverend N. W. Motheral held the first meeting to form the church on March 25, 1888. Motheral became the second pastor, as he was serving the Presbyterian church in Hanford when the Lemoore church was established. The first pastor of the Lemoore church was Rev. L. R. Bond. (Courtesy of the Lemoore Presbyterian Church.)

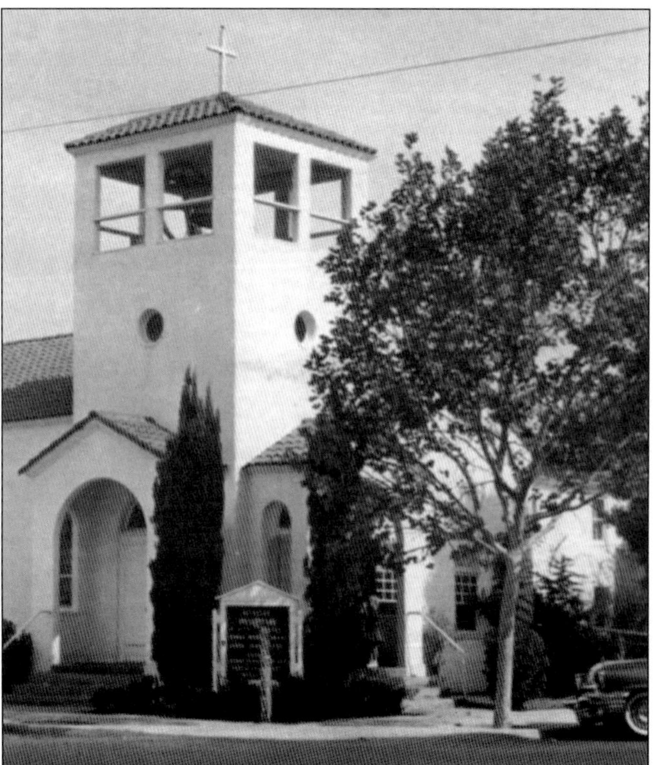

This photograph depicts the Lemoore Presbyterian Church on the corner of B and Heinlen Streets in the 1960s. (Courtesy of Jim Marvin.)

Eight

Police and Fire

Before incorporating as a city, Lemoore was served by county constables who helped keep the area as free from crime as possible. The city council was fast to recognize the need of a local police force and began the process of establishing one. The first Lemoore police chief took office in 1910. City council also worked up a detailed set of legal "do's and don'ts" for their fellow residents. Passed in 1913, the new ordinance governed everything from where one could hitch his or her horse to gambling, littering, and cursing.

The first police department was housed in part of the present city hall. Later it moved across the street and set up shop in what is currently the home of the Lemoore Planning Department and a truck barn for several of Lemoore's fire trucks. The police department moved to Fox Street and Cinnamon Drive, where it presently resides in its own building. Lemoore residents have always banded together to fight fires. Unfortunately, there are no records of Lemoore's earliest attempts to keep their town safe. The Lemoore Volunteer Fire Department (LVFD) was organized in 1920 after an earlier group, who had a 1917 Model T Ford fire truck, disbanded. The first chief of the reorganized group was Paul R. C. Winans, with R. R. Long completing his role as the department's head 1921. In 1923, a brand new La France truck was delivered to Lemoore. The LVFD emphasized training and the use of the latest technology. The local firefighters bragged about having the first fire pumper with pneumatic wheels in the state in the mid-1920s. Lemoore residents now take advantage of one of the lowest home insurance costs in the state as a result of this training and technology. LVFD members and their families have always supported community projects. The department even raised and decorated a community Christmas tree on the corner of Fox and D Streets in 1925, becoming an annual tradition in Lemoore. In 1980, they fully restored the original Model T fire engine with the help of inmates at Avenal Prison. Jack Stone had performed a partial restoration many years before. It is on display in front of city hall.

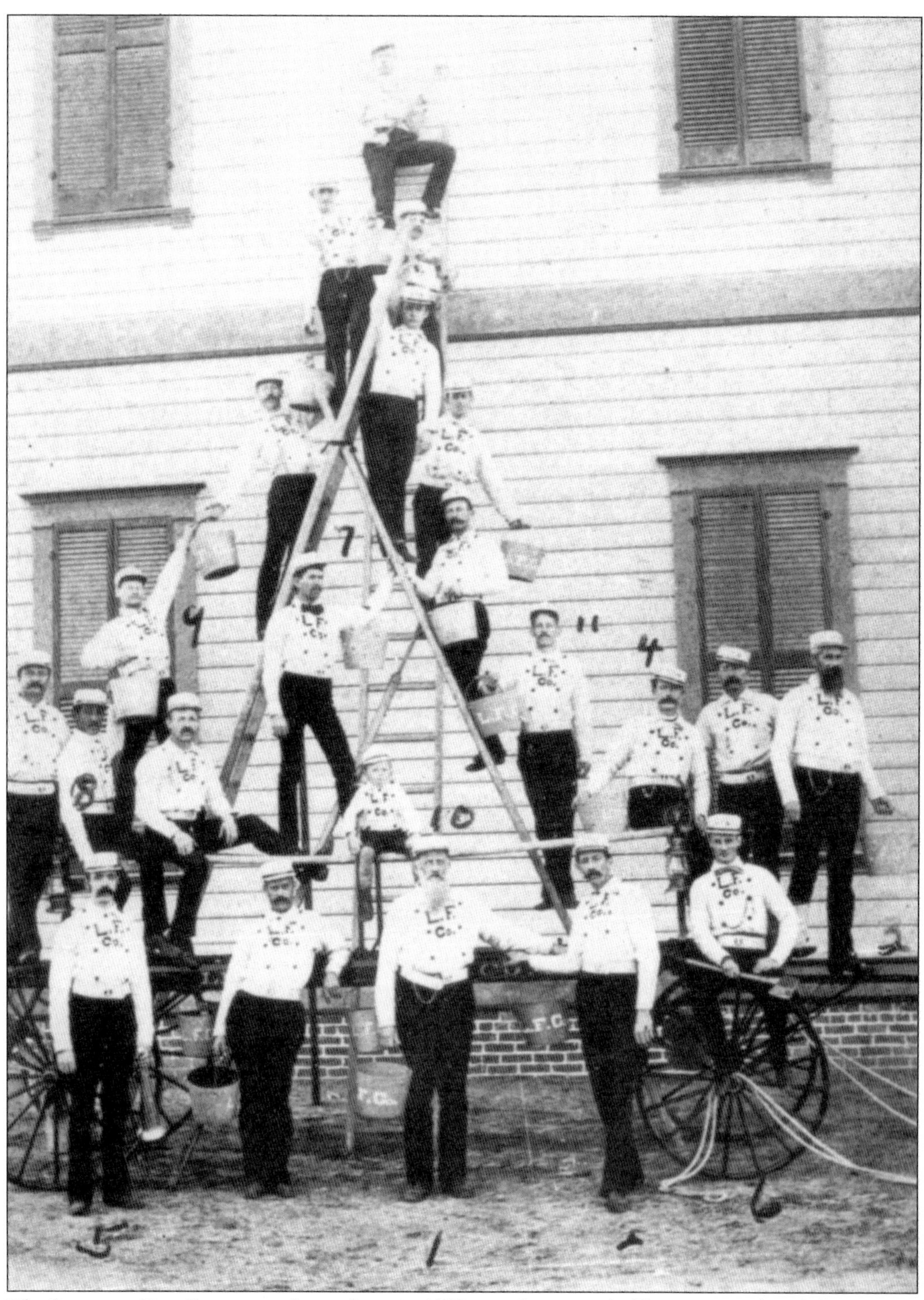

The Lemoore Fire Company, shown here in 1909 standing on a ladder cart, predated the present organization. (Courtesy of Kings County Museum.)

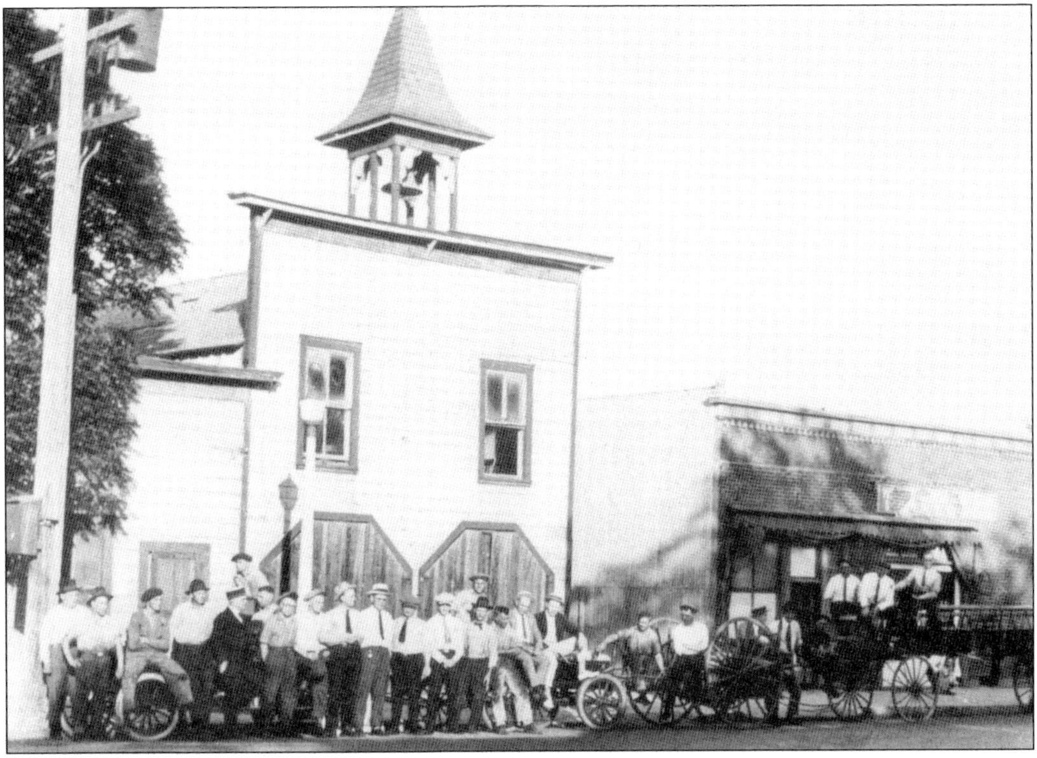

The Lemoore Volunteer Fire Department (LVFD) stands in front of the firehouse in 1921. The present LVFD was organized in 1920 and still serves Lemoore today. The firehouse was located on Fox Street, near D Street. (Courtesy of Kings County Museum.)

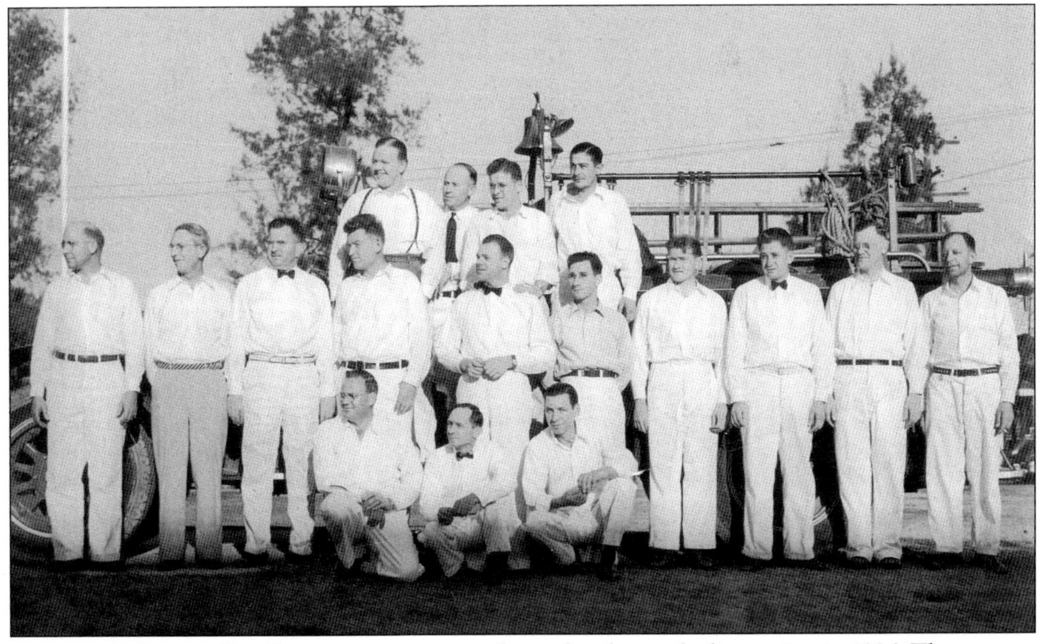

Lemoore Volunteer Fire Department personnel stand in front of a fire engine in 1936. The current LVFD consists of 35 volunteers. (Courtesy of Ted Schlosser and the LVFD.)

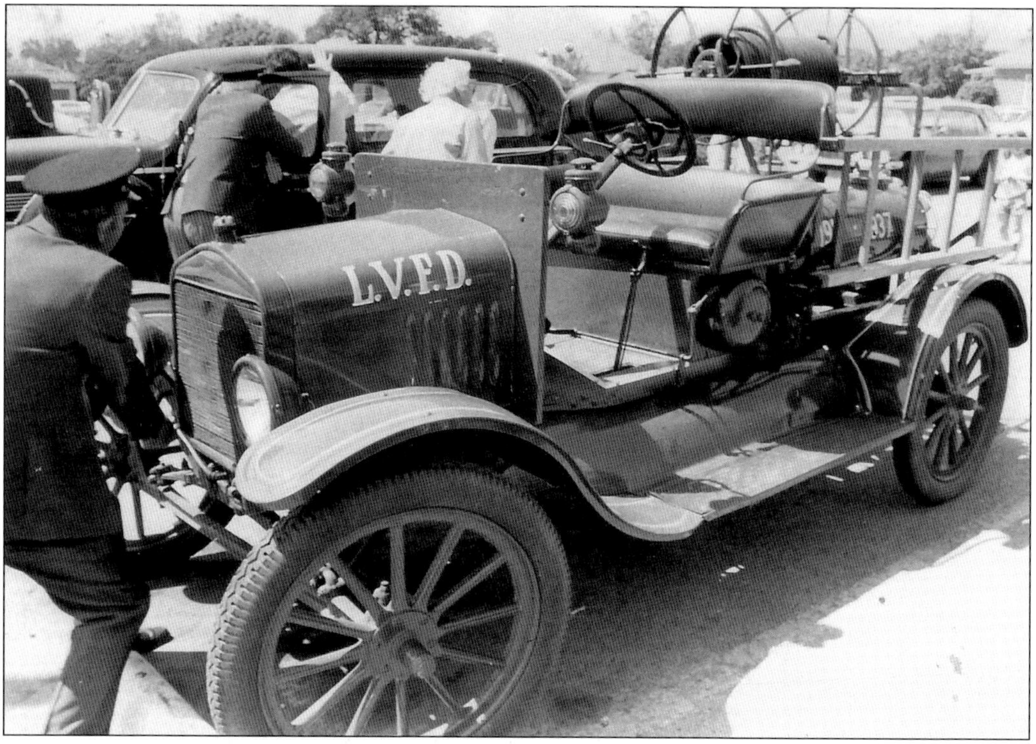

An old Lemoore Volunteer Fire Department Ford Model T chemical truck is being cranked by Art Borges in the late 1960s. Jack Stone and the California State Prison at Avenal inmates restored the Model T at different times. It is now on display in front of Lemoore City Hall. (Courtesy of Ted Schlosser and the LVFD.)

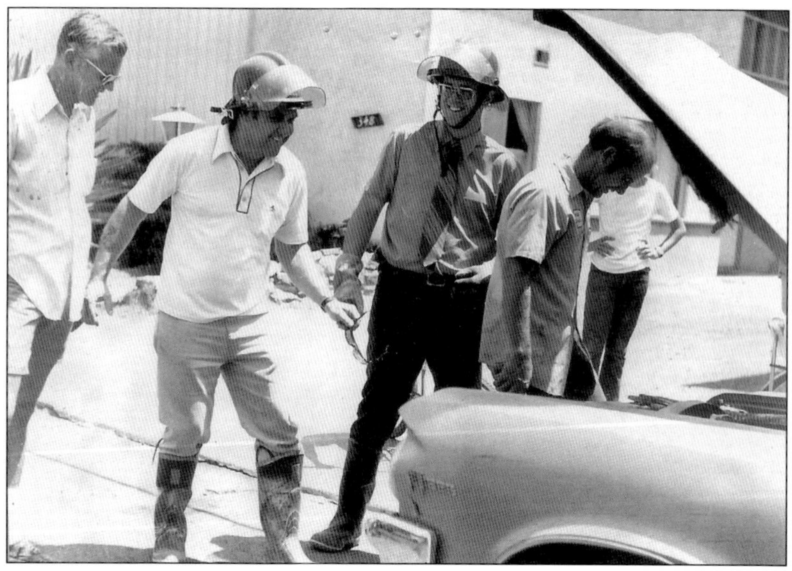

Members of the Lemoore Volunteer Fire Department ham it up in front of the first Lemoore firehouse in 1922, which was located on Fox Street, north of D Street, for 30 years. In 1924, it was moved to its current location on Fox Street near D Street. (Courtesy of Ted Schlosser and the LVFD.)

Henry Dickenson was the first chief of the Lemoore Police Department. He served from 1910 to 1943. (Courtesy of Lemoore Police Department.)

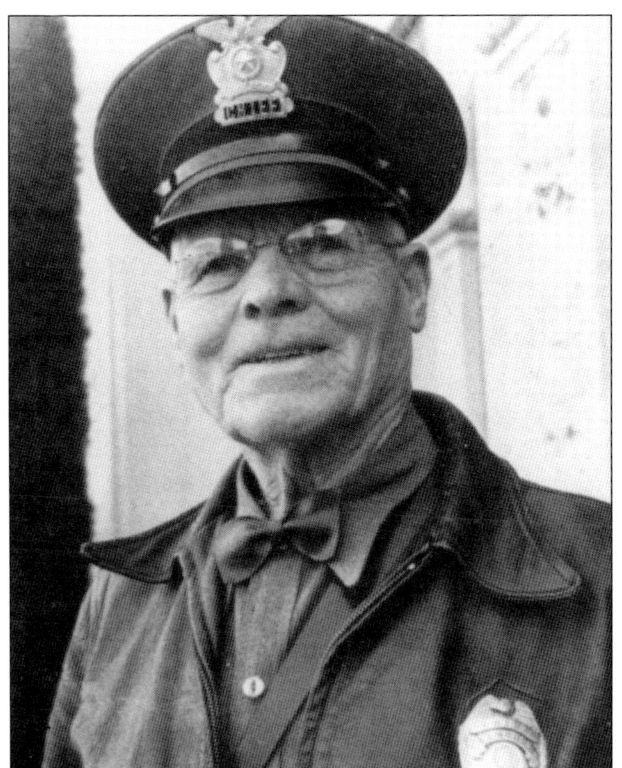

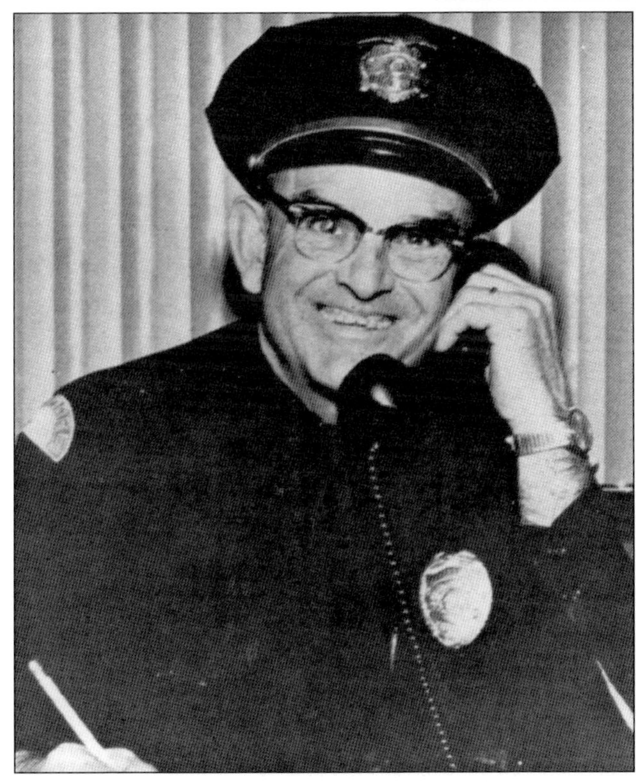

Bryan W. Short served as the Lemoore chief of police from 1943 to 1967. (Courtesy of Lemoore Police Department.)

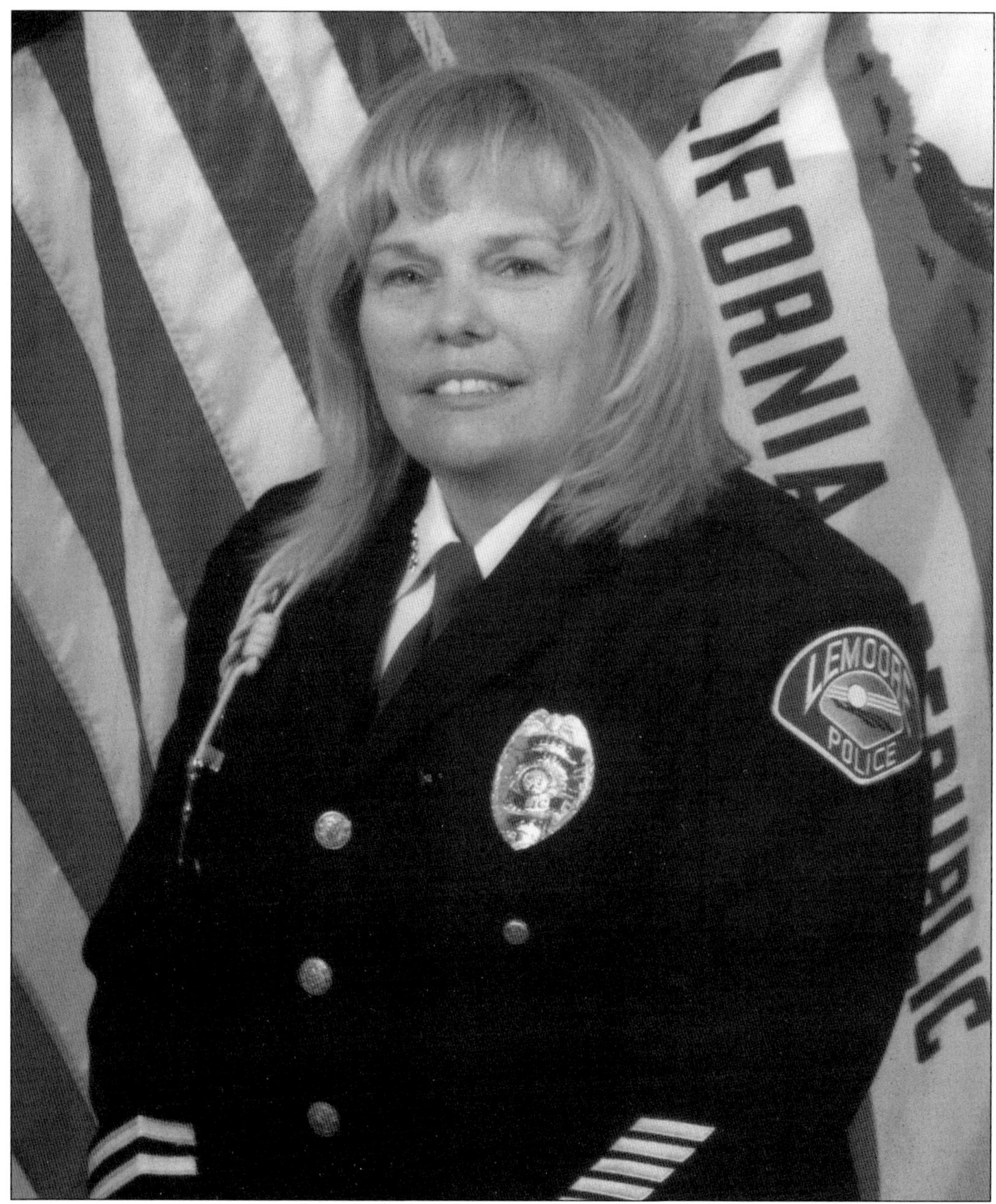

Kim Morrell served the Lemoore Police Department for 28 years. She was hired by the city in November 1981 and became Lemoore's first female chief of police. At one time she was one of only eight women police chiefs in California. Morrell retired in 2009. (Courtesy of Lemoore Police Department.)

Nine

The Military

Lemoore prides itself on being a town that supports its military and veterans. Many pioneers served with the nation before coming to Lemoore. Many other military service members came to the area when they were stationed at the Naval Air Station Lemoore (NASL) and chose to stay after their term of duty, making Lemoore their home. Local residents responded to the call for arms in World War I, with many homes proudly displaying their American flags and gold stars in their windows long after the war was over. Lemoore was a small town, but according to a special magazine tribute to World War I veterans, 10 young men who went to help fight the "war to end all wars" never returned. During the war, residents also helped their country by meeting to make bandages and care packages and buying Liberty Bonds. It was full throttle into World War II for Lemoore residents as well.

Adding to the local patriotism was a U.S. Army airfield, established in the early 1940s as a training facility just west of Lemoore. The soldiers were welcomed by Lemoore residents who often opened their homes to them, especially during holidays, to share dinner and a sense of family. The USO building was a big part of the excitement. Now the Lemoore Civic Auditorium on C Street, the USO was more than a place to go and dance on the weekends. It provided daily doses of support from local volunteers.

In the late 1950s, the 12th Naval District needed a new air base. Lemoore got the nod, and on July 8, 1961, the Naval Air Station Lemoore was commissioned. Construction began in 1958. The base, to the west of Lemoore, but not on the same land as the old army base, covers more than 18,000 square acres of land today. Local farmers lease some of the land, while the rest provides military training and support for five large carrier air groups and 18 fleet squadrons. Personnel from NASL took part in the Vietnam War and have played a critical role in America's commitment in both Iraq and Afghanistan. The air station is currently the West Coast home of the F-18 Super Hornet.

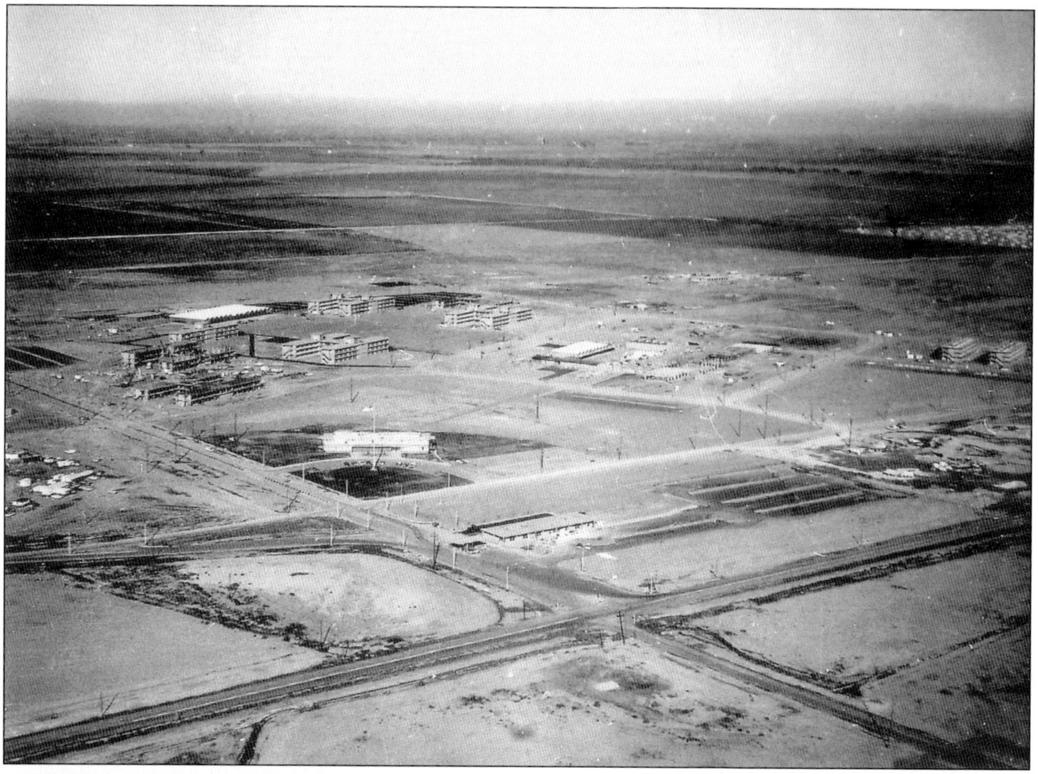

This is an aerial view of the Lemoore army airfield in 1941. (Courtesy of Jack Stone.)

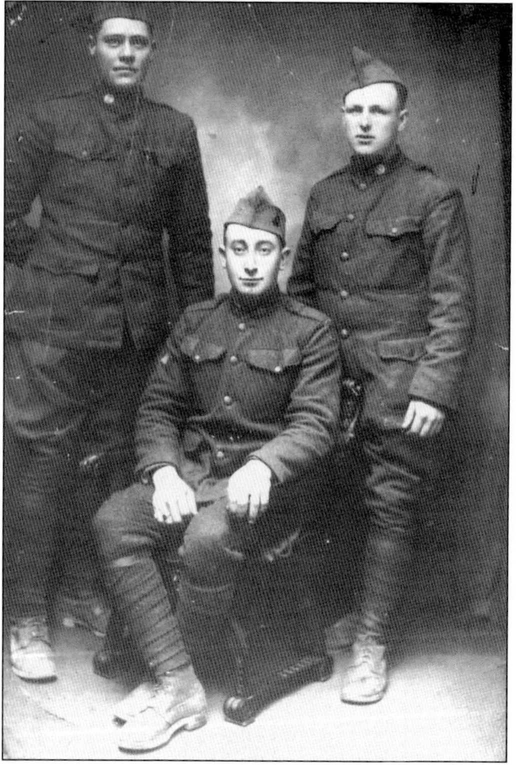

In 1917, A. F. Borges (center), of Lemoore, poses with two fellow members of the cavalry in France. The other two men are from Nebraska and Montana. (Courtesy of St. Peter's Catholic Church.)

Tony Bettencourt, 18 years old, is shown in his uniform during World War II. He lived on Laurel Street in Lemoore. A note on the photograph folio reads, "To dad, with all my love, Tony." (Courtesy of the Sarah A. Mooney Museum.)

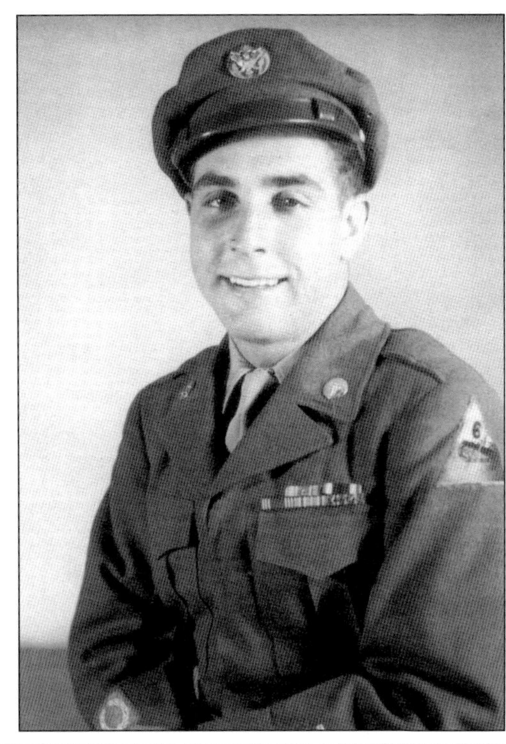

This aerial view of the Naval Air Station Lemoore shows the runways and surrounding agricultural fields. (Courtesy of U.S. Navy.)

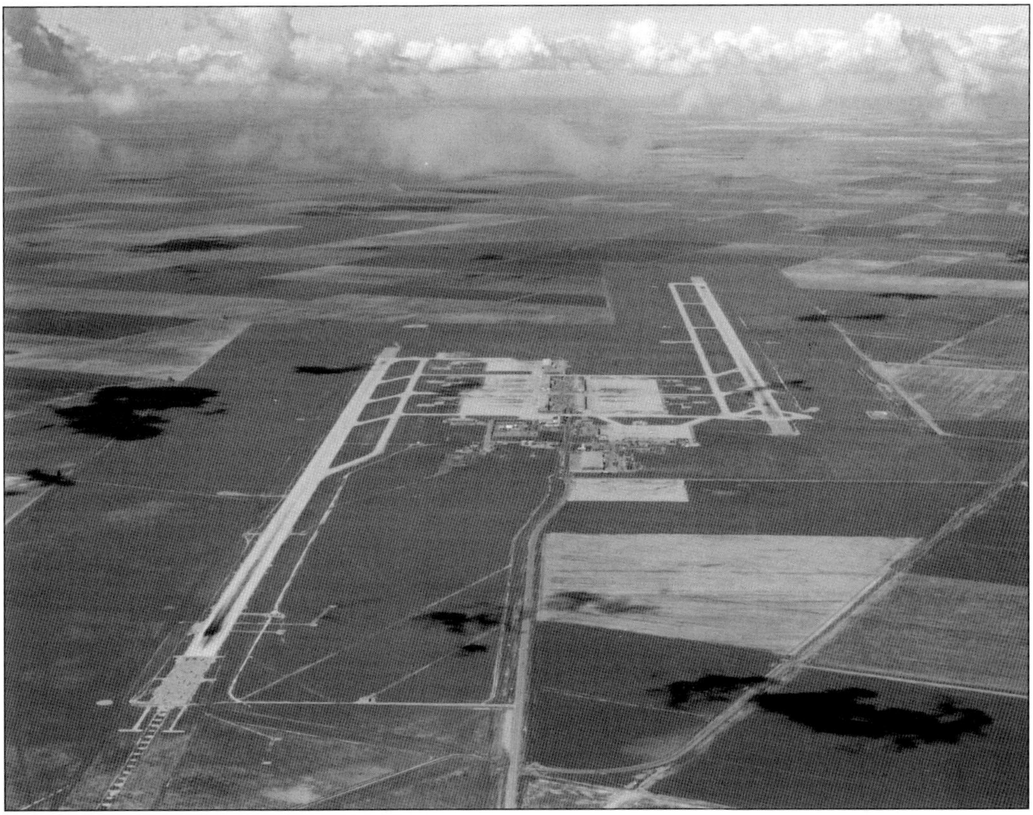

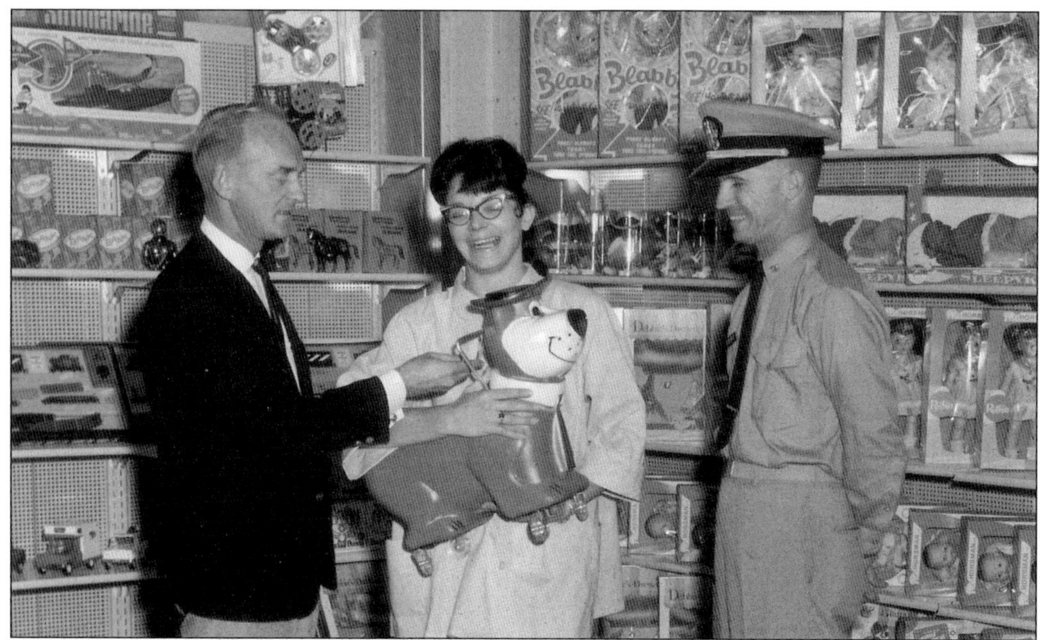

Pictured is the opening of the new NASL Navy Exchange Toyland in September 1963. Toyland was the toy section of the navy base's department store (NEX). From left to right are H. Wayne McClenaghan, merchandise manager; Judy Adams, saleswoman; and Lt. B. G. Sherman, Navy Exchange officer. (Courtesy of U.S. Navy.)

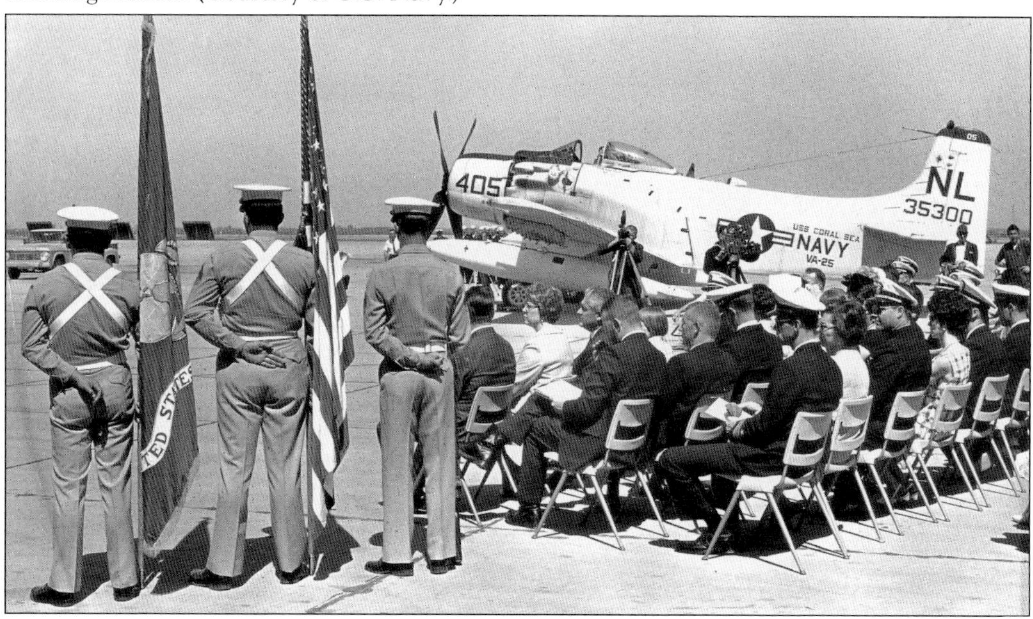

An A-1 Skyraider is honored during a ceremony at the Naval Air Station Lemoore on April 24, 1968. The event marked the retirement of the versatile and durable attack bomber from the U.S. Navy. McDonnell Douglas Corporation (then Douglas Aircraft Company) built 3,180 of the famous "Spads" between 1945 and 1957. A-1s were used extensively in the Korean War and served in air rescue and other support missions for the U.S. Air Force and South Vietnamese Air Force in Southeast Asia. (Courtesy of U.S. Navy.)

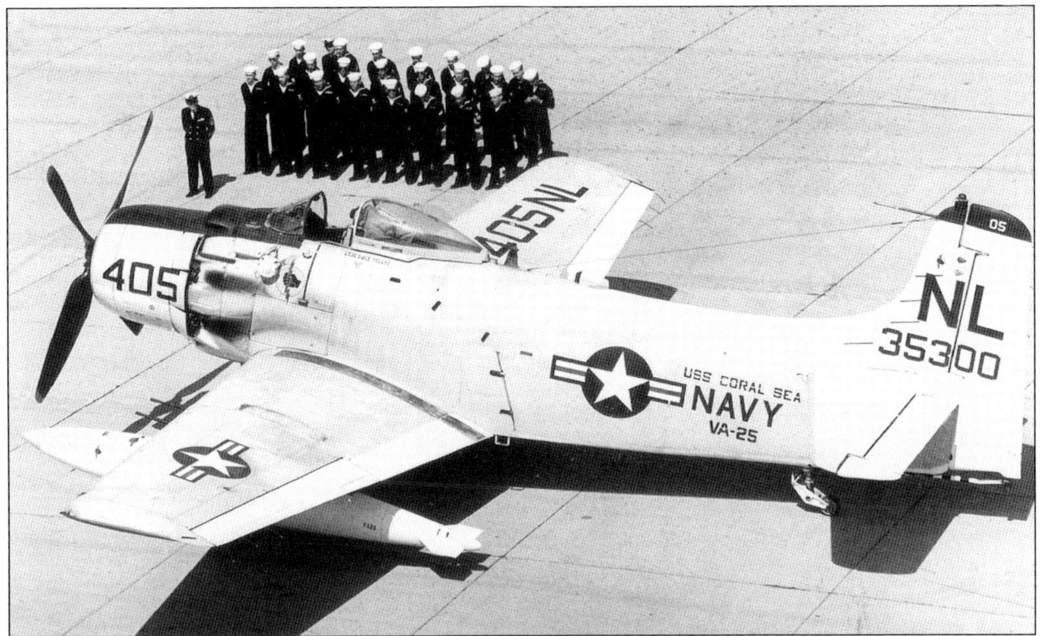

Retirement ceremonies were held for the Navy's A-1 Skyraider on April 10, 1968. The phaseout of the aircraft took place at the Naval Air Station Lemoore. Many distinguished guests were present for the ceremony. (Courtesy of U.S. Navy.)

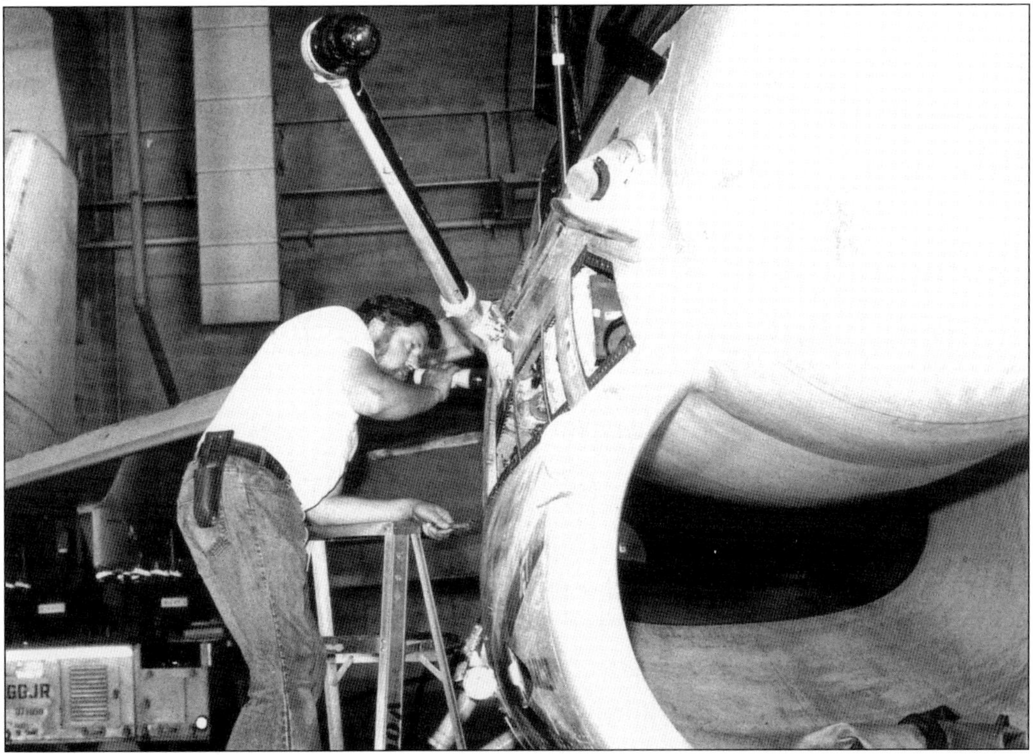

A navy airman works on a jet in the hangar at the Naval Air Station Lemoore. (Courtesy of U.S. Navy.)

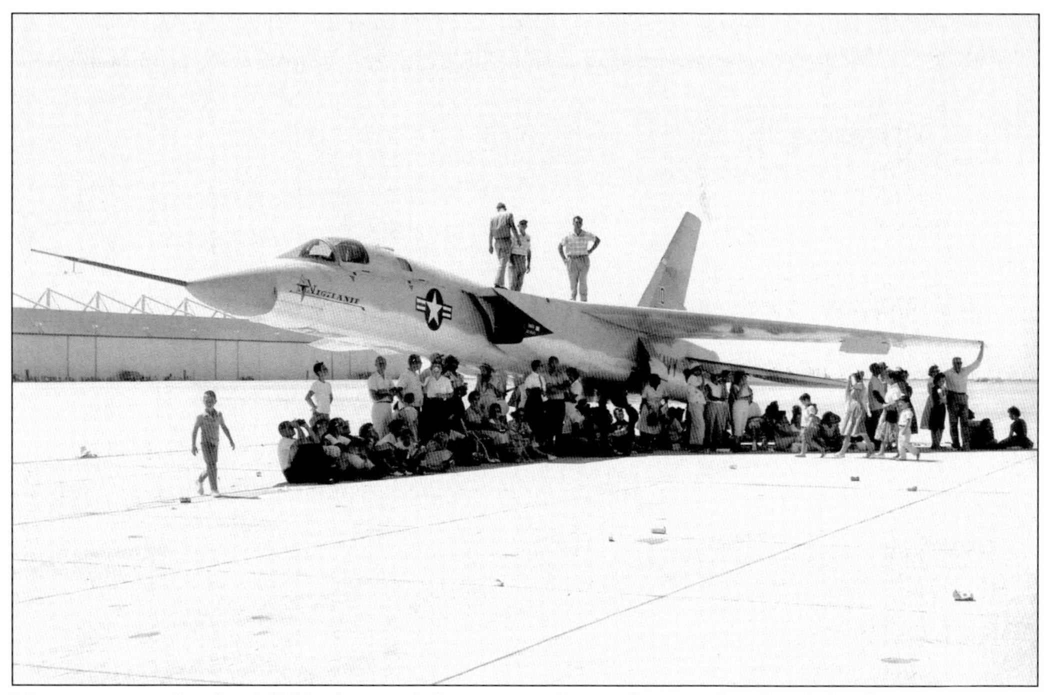

Visitors rest under the A3J Vigilante while viewing the air show at the Naval Air Station Lemoore in July 1961. (Courtesy of U.S. Navy.)

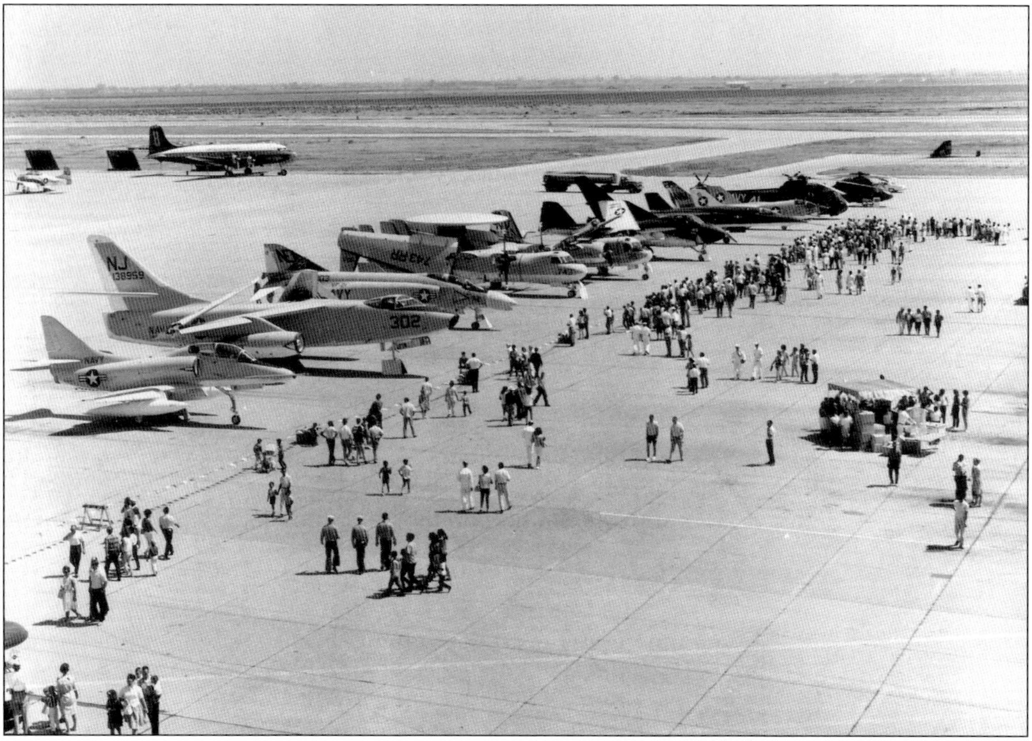

A complete lineup of static display aircraft was exhibited at the north end of the Hangar 2 ramp at the Naval Air Station Lemoore during an air show in July 1981. (Courtesy of U.S. Navy.)

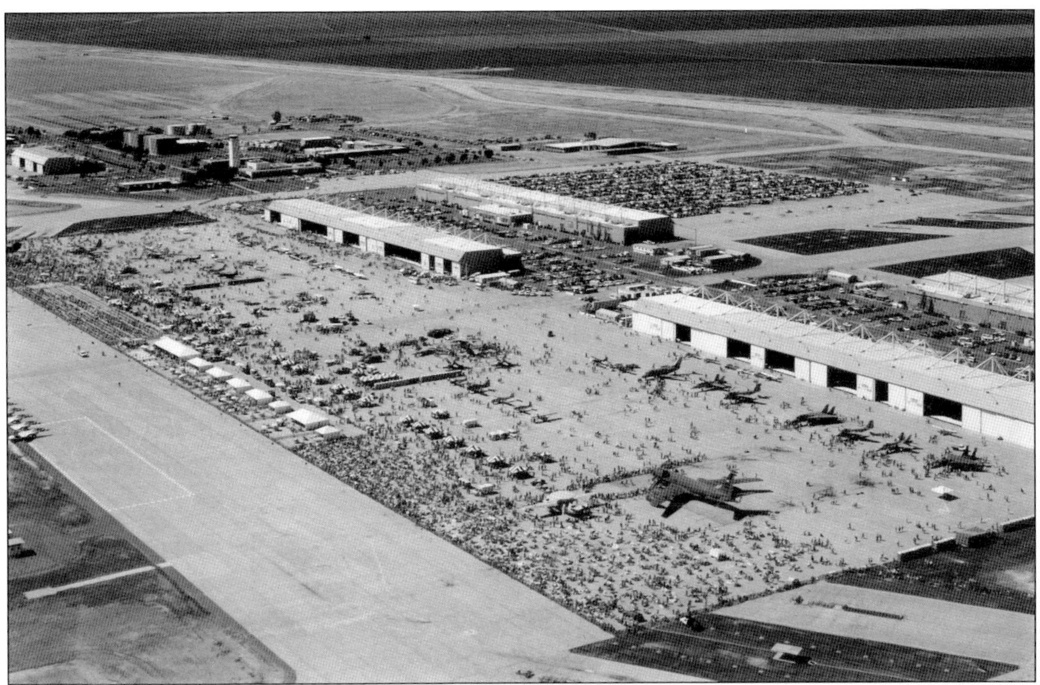

Aircraft and people pepper the airfield at the Naval Air Station Lemoore during the 1994 air show. (Courtesy of U.S. Navy.)

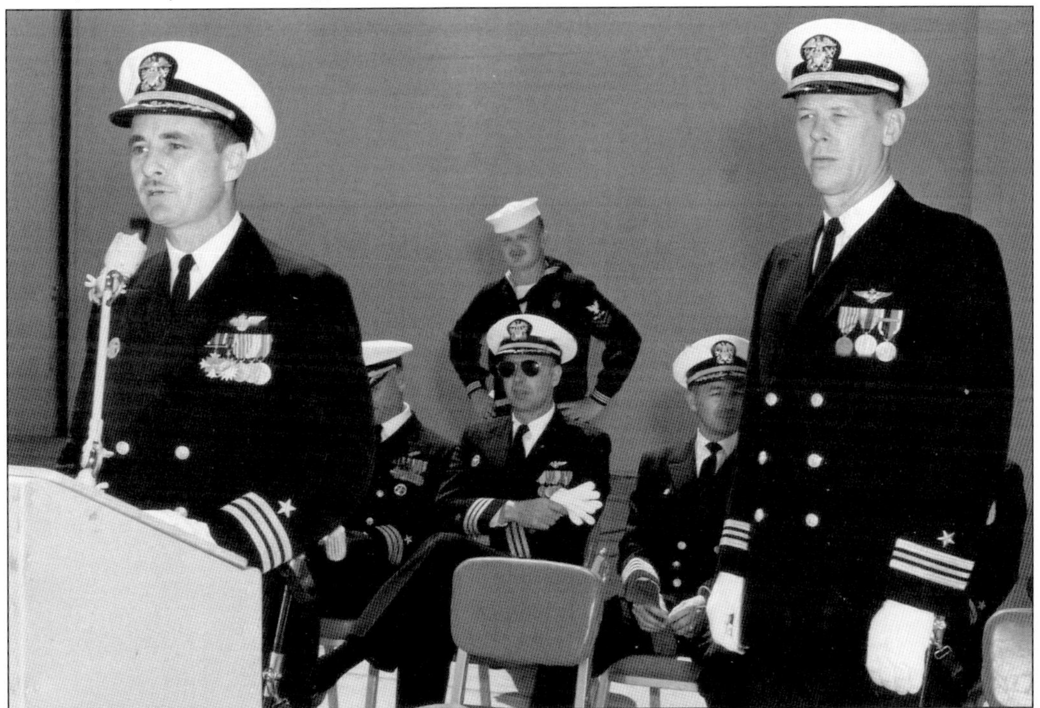

Cmdr. R. E. Schoultz reads his orders of transfer to the VA-93 squadron during change of command ceremonies on March 27, 1962, at the Naval Air Station Lemoore. Schoultz relieved Cmdr. J. W. Porter (right). (Courtesy of U.S. Navy.)

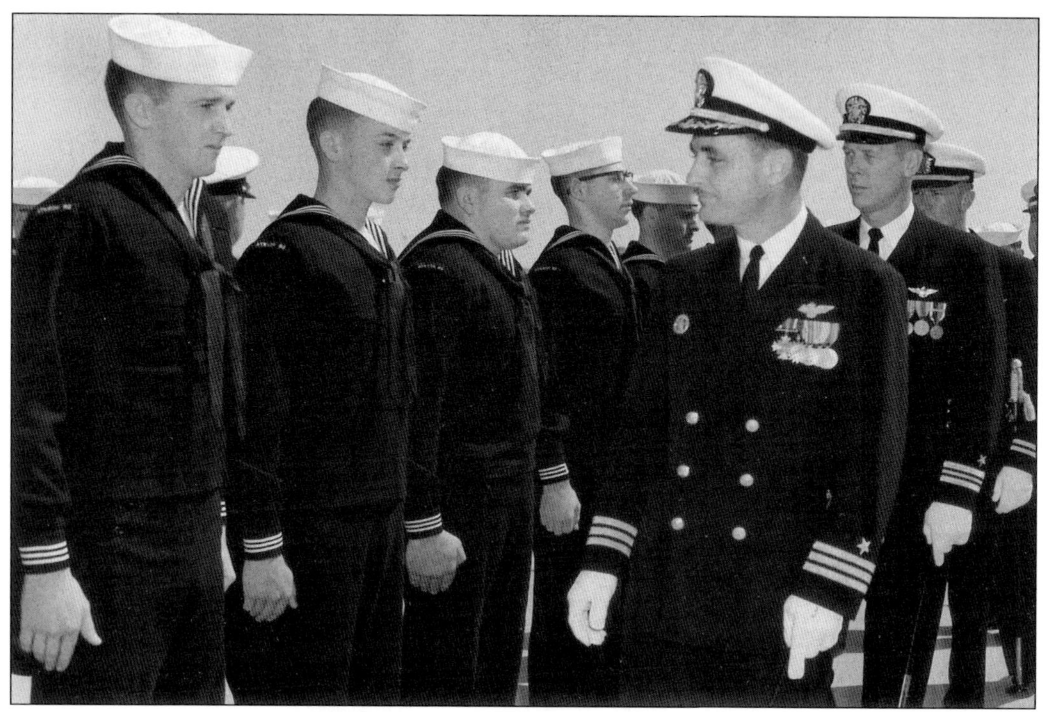

Cmdr. R. E. Schoultz, first on right of inspection team and the incoming commanding officer of VA-93, inspects the squadron during a change of command ceremony. Cmdr. J. W. Porter follows behind as they inspect the troops. (Courtesy of U.S. Navy.)

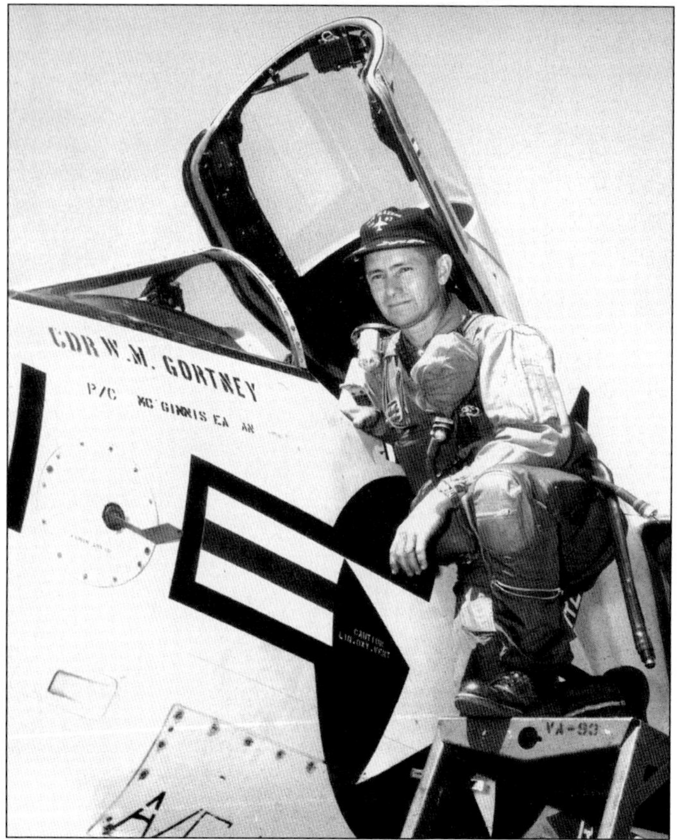

Cmdr. W. M. Gortney, commanding officer of VA-93, climbs into his aircraft in August 1963 at the Naval Air Station Lemoore. (Courtesy of U.S. Navy.)

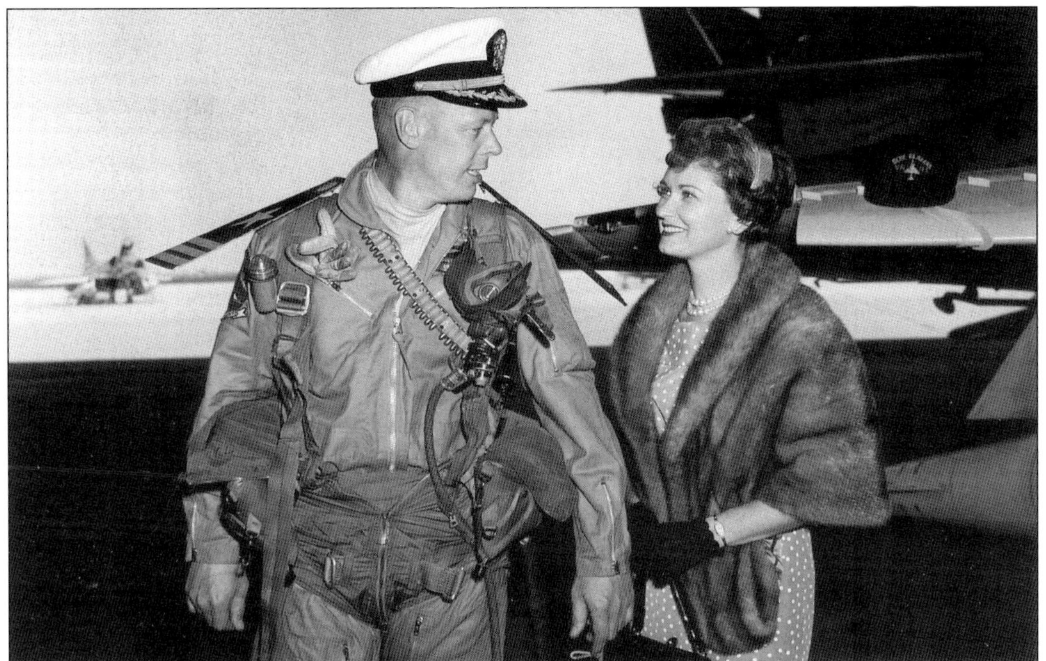

Lt. Cmdr. R. E. Schoultz, commanding officer of VA-93, was promoted to the rank of commander while on a routine trip to the Naval Air Station Lemoore on April 9, 1962. His wife surprised him with the promotion letter when he landed. (Courtesy of U.S. Navy.)

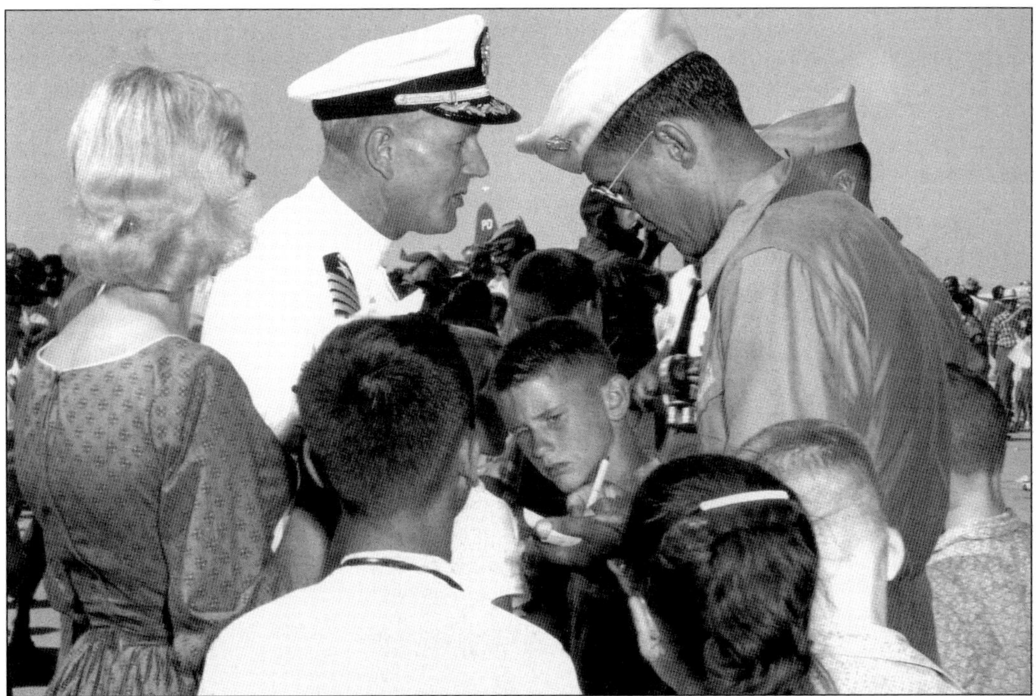

Capt. H. M. Avery, commanding officer of the Naval Air Station Lemoore, talks with Blue Angels leader Cmdr. Zeb Knott as he signs autographs for visitors at the Naval Air Station Lemoore commissioning. (Courtesy of U.S. Navy.)

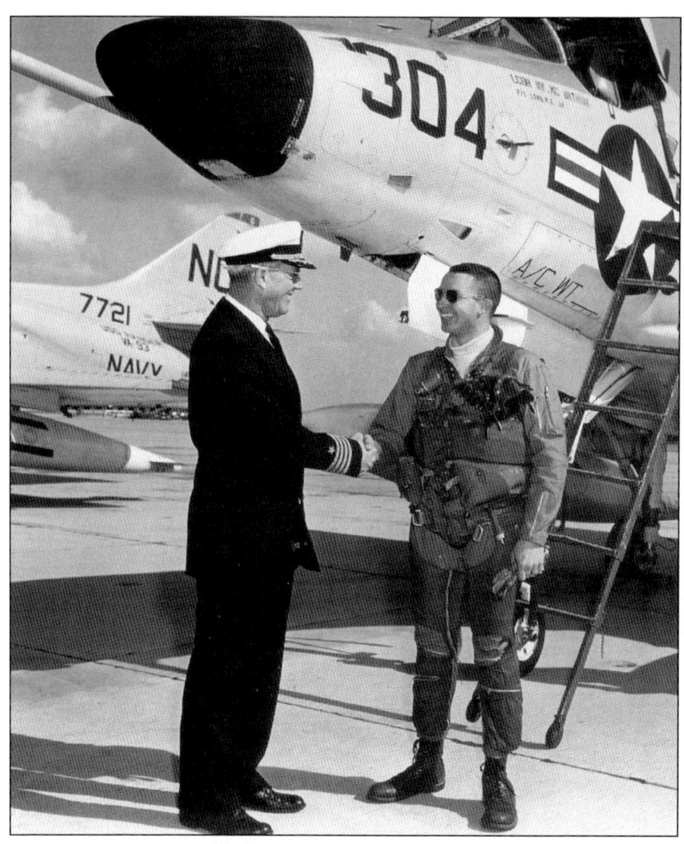

Capt. H. M. Avery welcomes VA-93 pilot Lt. R. E. Delmo upon his arrival at the Naval Air Station Lemoore. (Courtesy of U.S. Navy.)

Two squadrons fly in for a homecoming in February 1987. (Courtesy of U.S. Navy.)

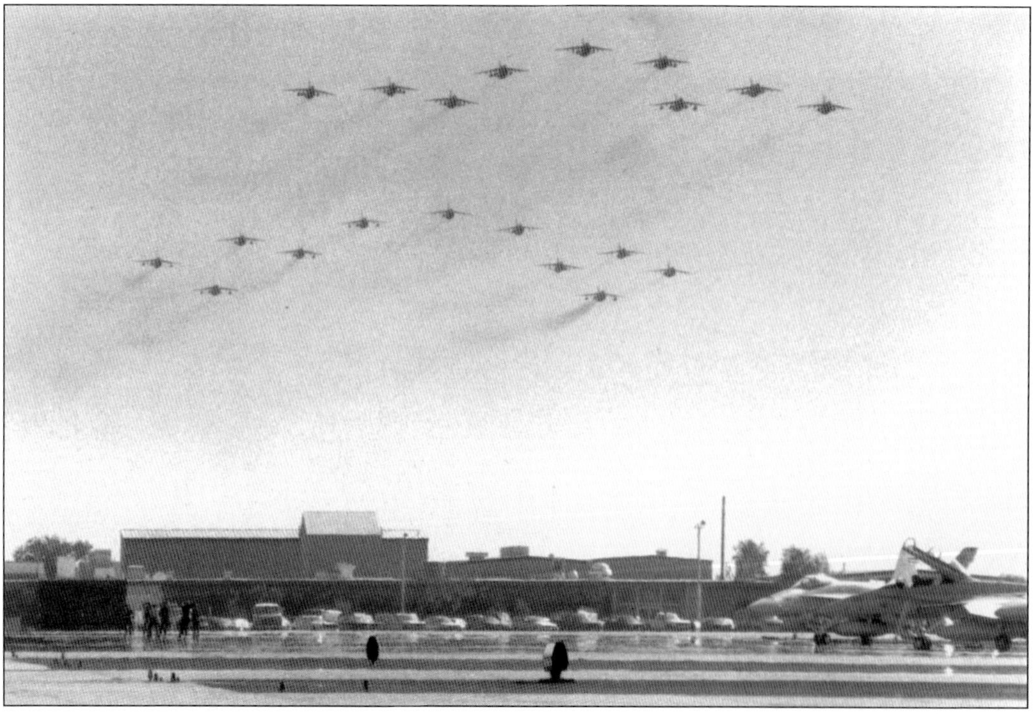

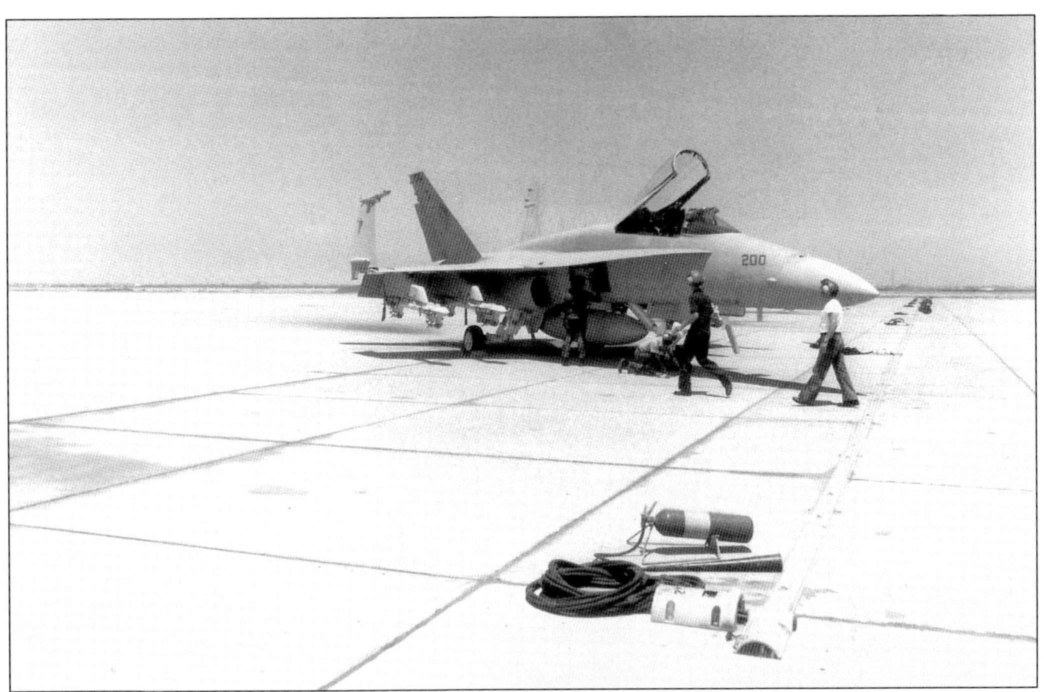

Navy airmen work on a jet on the airfield at the Naval Air Station Lemoore. (Courtesy of U.S. Navy.)

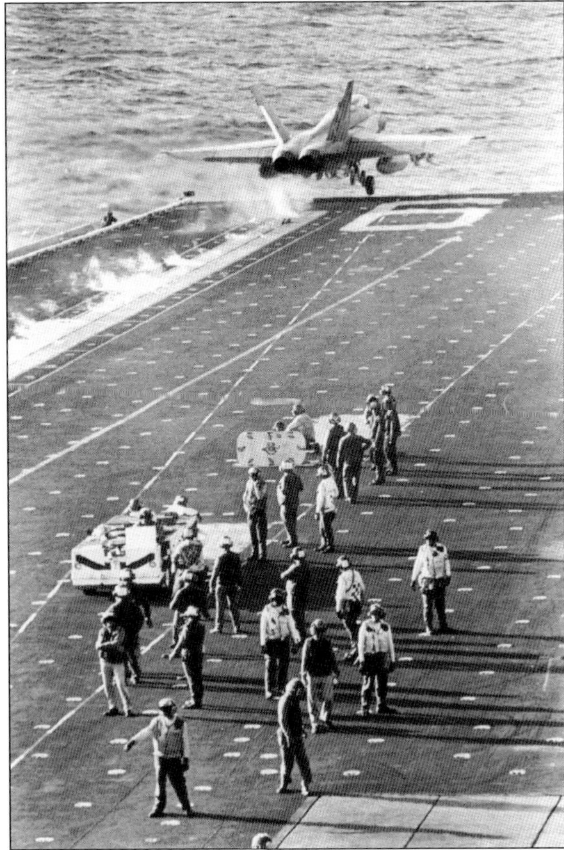

A jet is catapulted off an aircraft carrier. All squadrons from the Naval Air Station Lemoore regularly deploy onboard aircraft carriers for extended periods in defense of the nation. (Courtesy of U.S. Navy.)

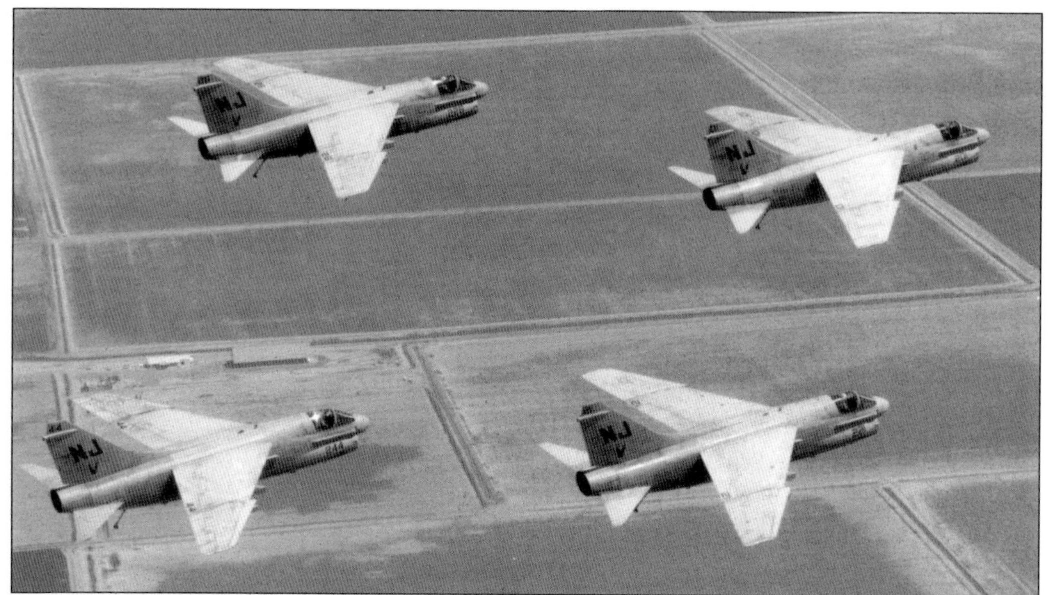

Jets fly over the agricultural fields that surround the Naval Air Station Lemoore. (Courtesy of U.S. Navy.)

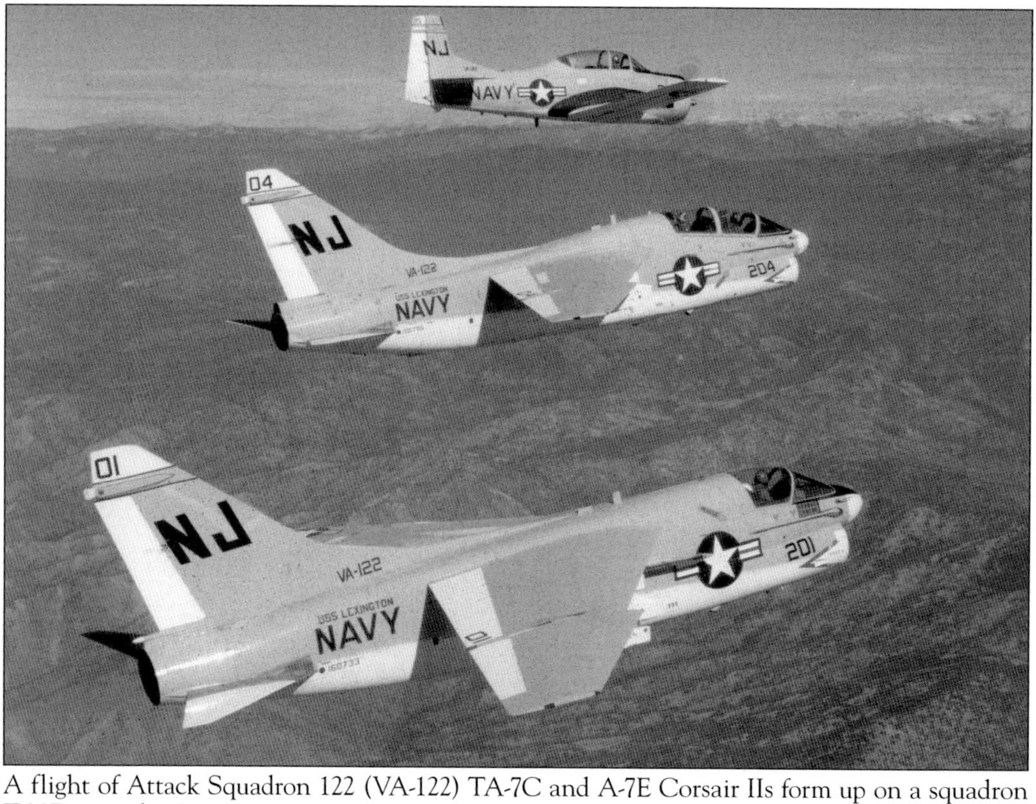

A flight of Attack Squadron 122 (VA-122) TA-7C and A-7E Corsair IIs form up on a squadron T-28B over the Sierra Nevada Mountains. Flying the T-28B Trojan is Lt. Bud King, while Lt. Cmdr. Will Trafton and Lt. Cmdr. Jeff Fredricks fly in the TA-7C Corsair II, with Lt. Cmdr. Glen Speaician flying the A-7E Corsair II. (Courtesy of U.S. Navy.)

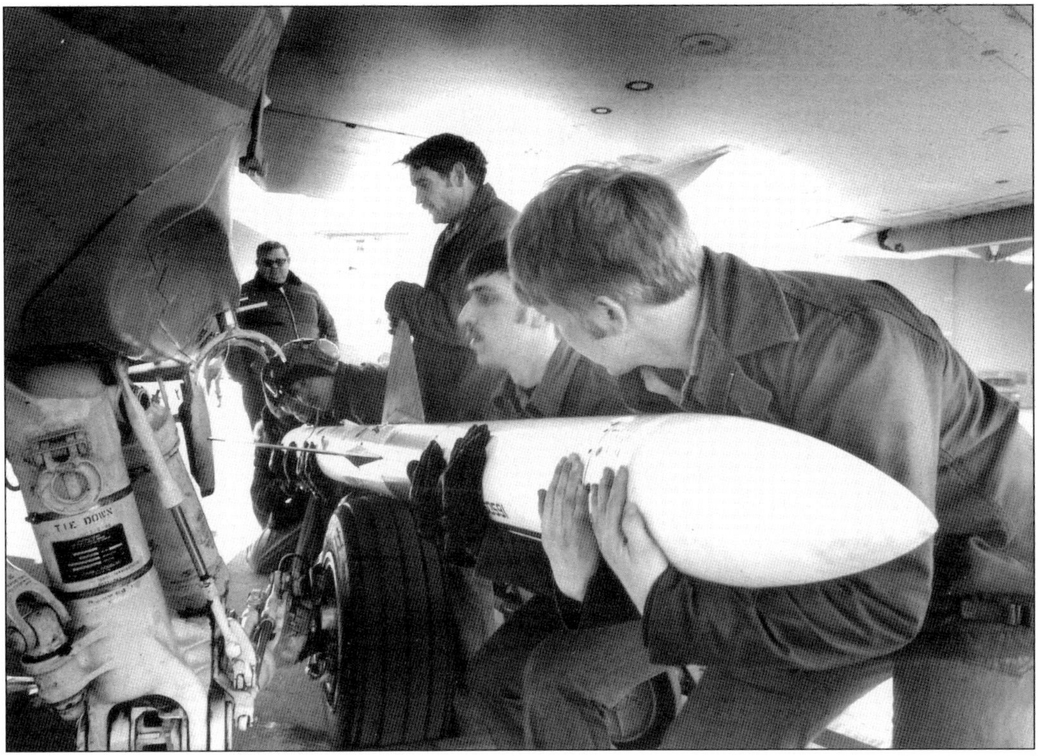

Sailors from the Naval Air Station Lemoore load ordinance on a navy aircraft. (Courtesy of U.S. Navy.)

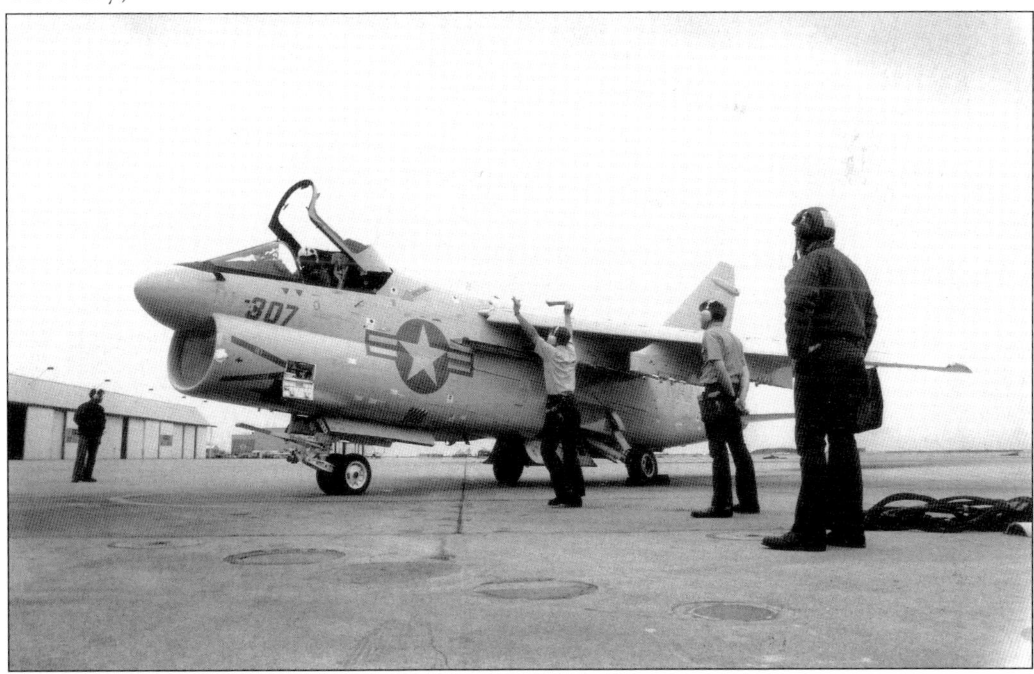

Navy airmen prepare an aircraft for flight on the Naval Air Station Lemoore airfield. (Courtesy of U.S. Navy.)

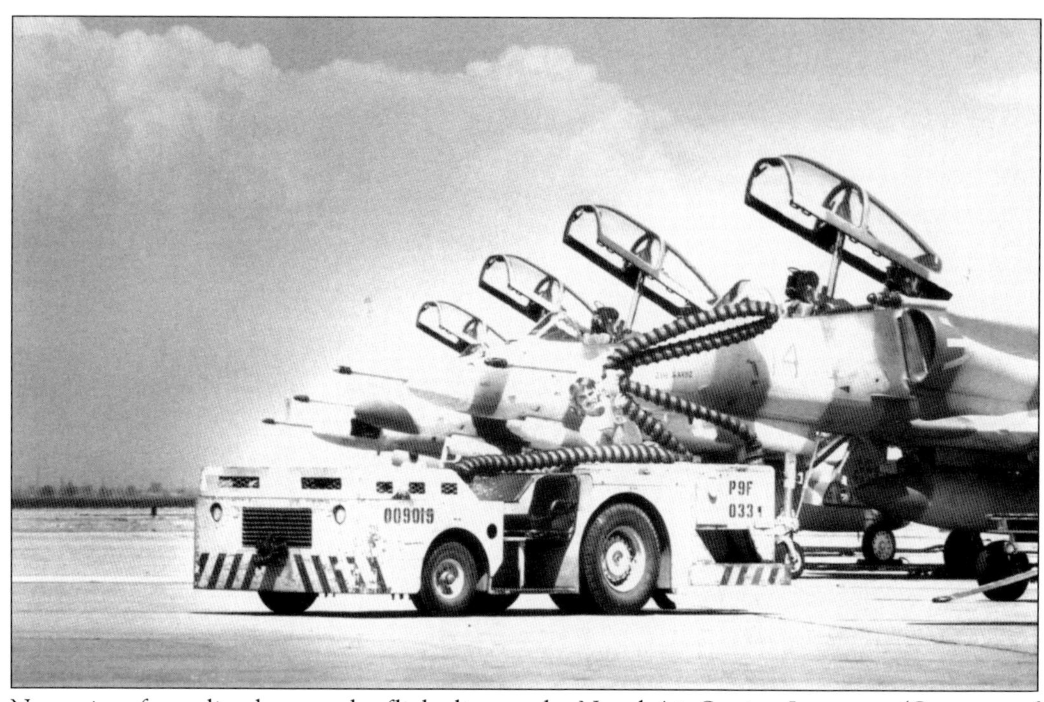

Navy aircraft are lined up on the flight line at the Naval Air Station Lemoore. (Courtesy of U.S. Navy.)

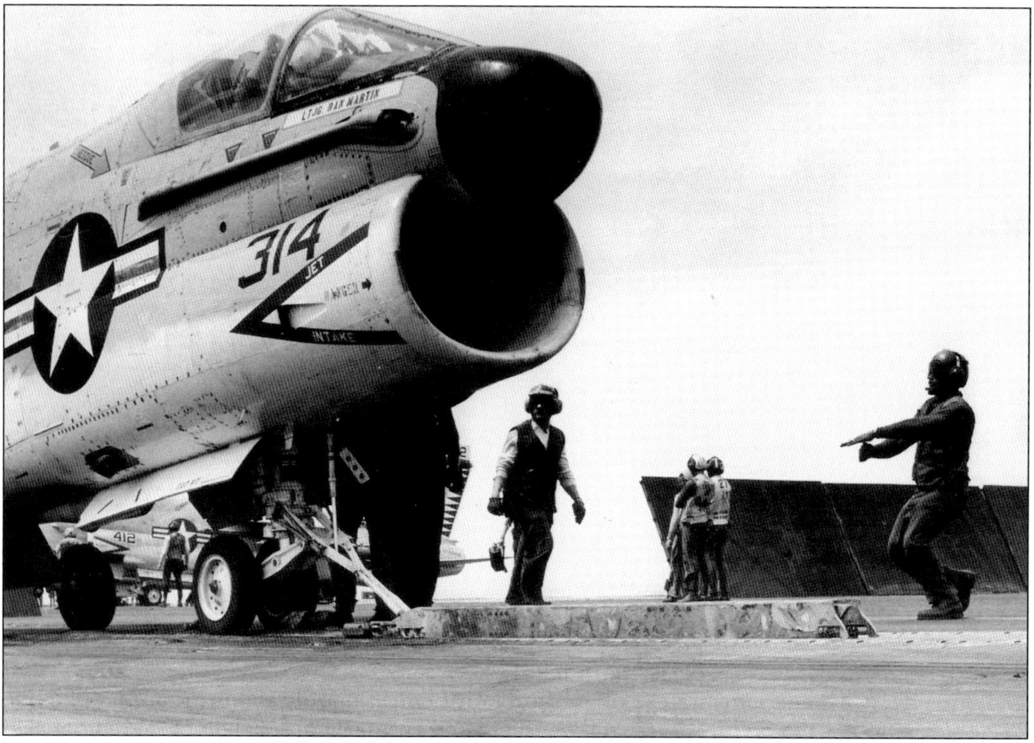

Navy airmen prepare an A-7 Corsair II aircraft from VA-97 for flight at the Naval Air Station Lemoore airfield in March 1987. (Courtesy of U.S. Navy.)

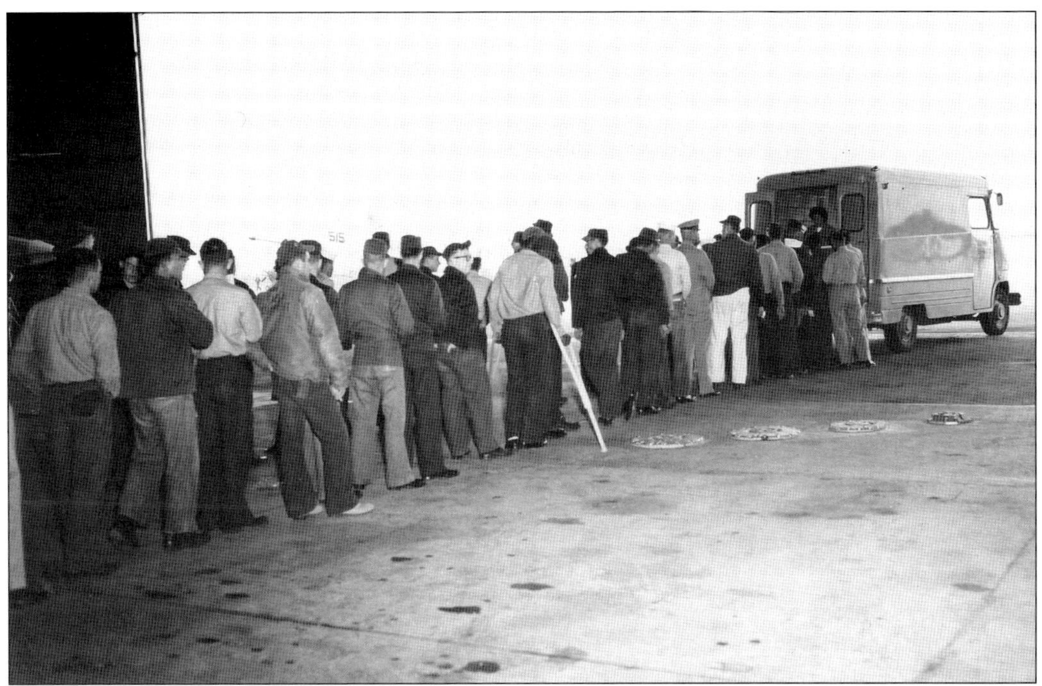

Sailors stand in line to get their paychecks cashed at the mobile bank at the Naval Air Station Lemoore in November 1967. (Courtesy of the Sarah A. Mooney Museum.)

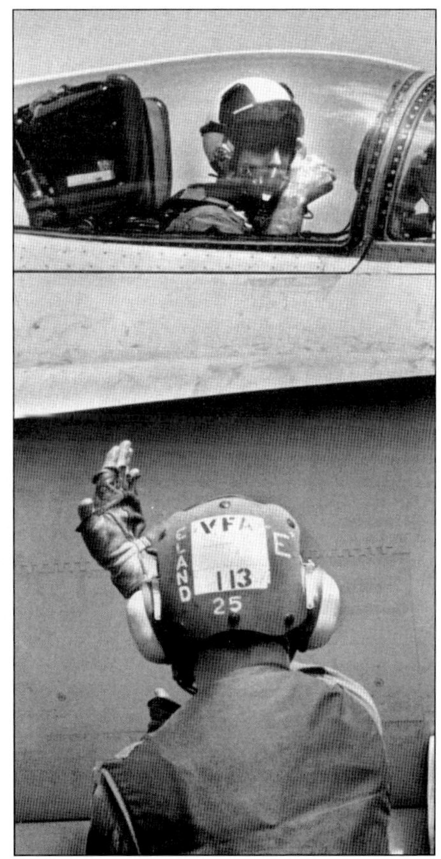

A pilot gives his plane captain the thumbs up as he prepares for takeoff. (Courtesy of U.S. Navy.)

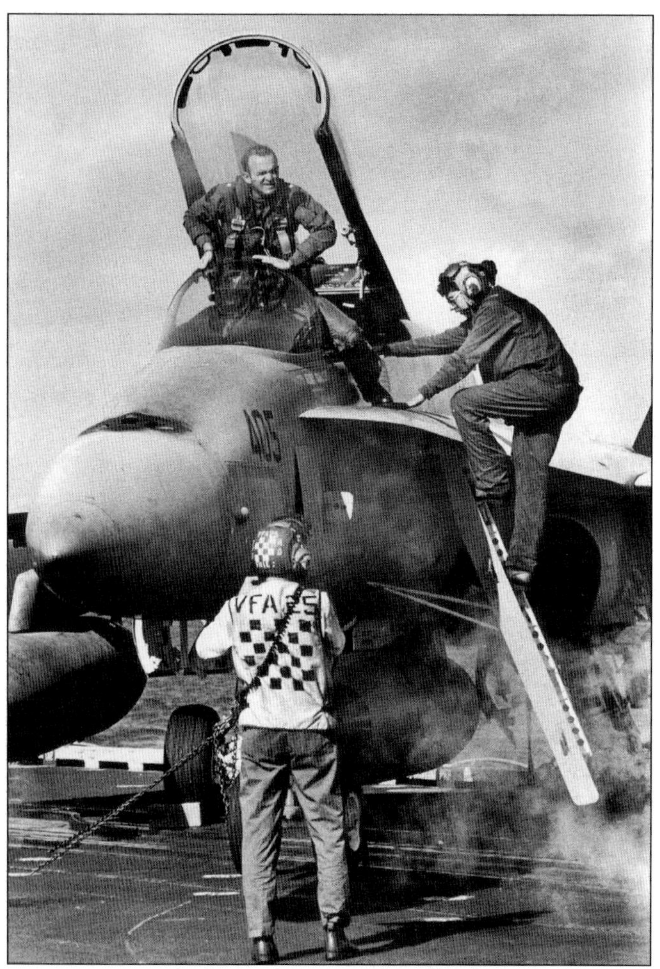

Cmdr. Jerry Arbiter, executive officer of VFA-25, climbs into his aircraft with the assistance of Aviation Mechanic Third Class (AD3) John Fries. The plane captain on the ground is Aviation Structural Mechanic/Hydraulics Airman (AMHAN) Scott Harmon. (Courtesy of U.S. Navy.)

Squadron VFA-25 spells out its designation on the airfield during a change of command ceremony. (Courtesy of U.S. Navy.)

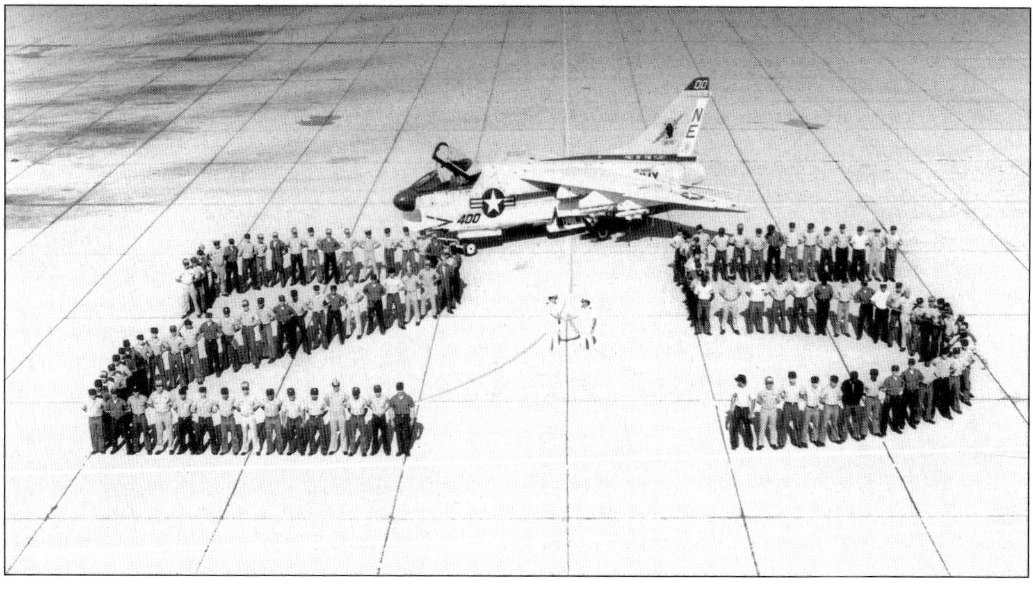

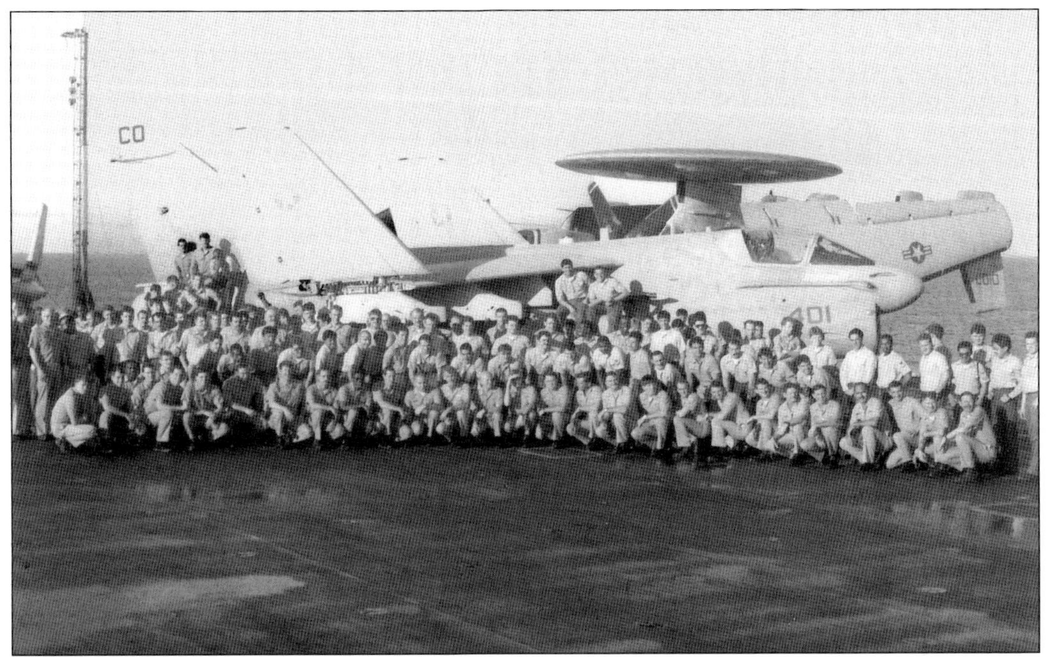

A squadron poses in front of its aircraft at the Naval Air Station Lemoore. (Courtesy of U.S. Navy.)

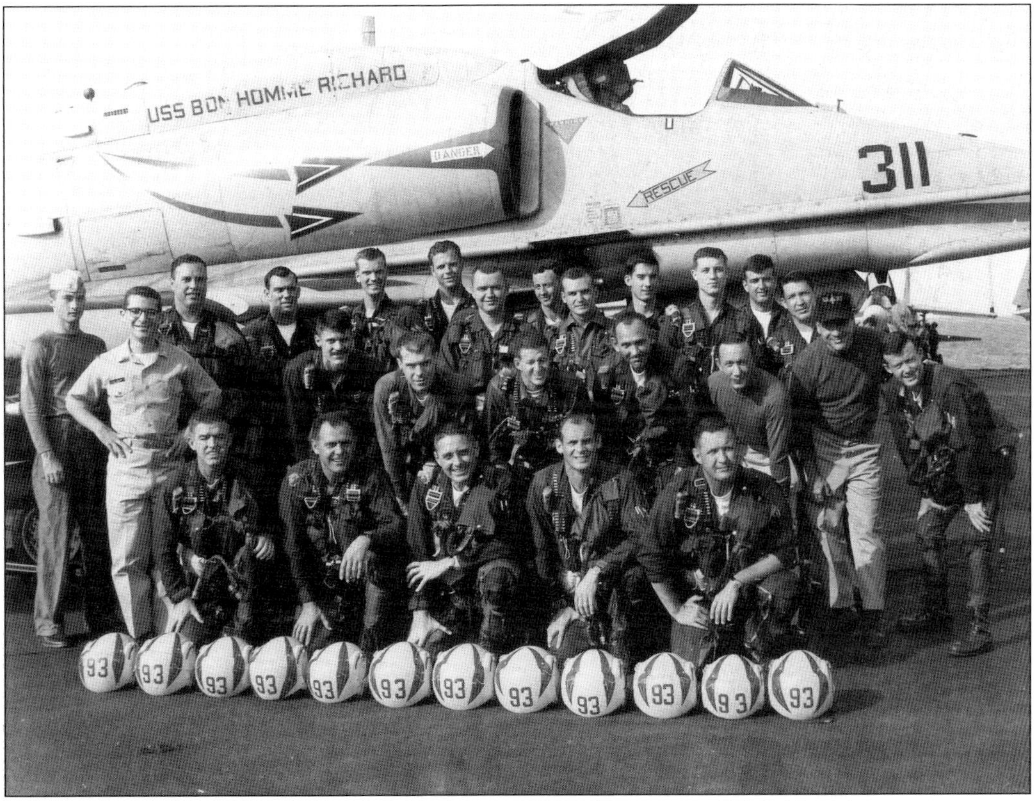

VA-93 aircrew men pose in front of squadron aircraft. (Courtesy of U.S. Navy.)

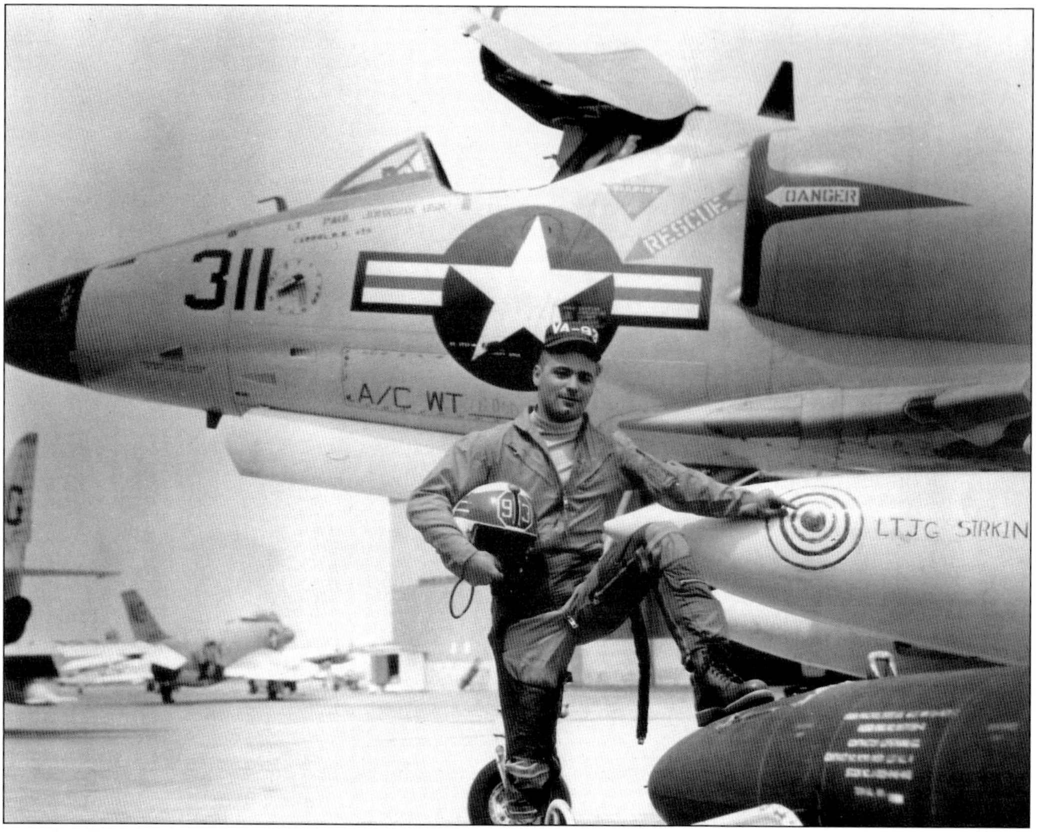

A pilot from VA-93 points out the bull's-eye on an aircraft drop tank in April 1961. The aircraft in the background is an A-4. (Courtesy of U.S. Navy.)

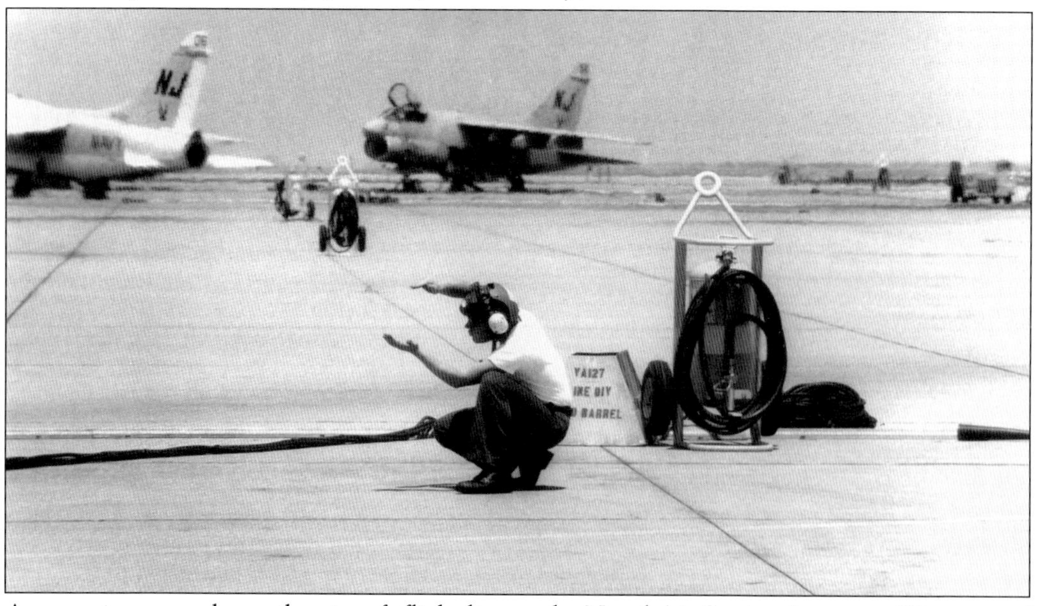

A navy airman works on the aircraft flight line at the Naval Air Station Lemoore. (Courtesy of U.S. Navy.)

BIBLIOGRAPHY

Brown, J. L. *The Story of Kings County California.* Lederer, Street, and Zeus Company, Inc., 1941.

———. *The Mussel Slough Tragedy.* 1958.

Brown, Robert R. *History of Kings County.* 1940.

Cummins, Marjorie W. *The Tachi-Yokuts Indians of the San Joaquin Valley.*

Emanuels, Stephen P. *The Rhoads-Esrey Letters.* Kings River Press, 1992.

Hanford Centennial Committee. *Hanford: A Pictorial History.* 1990.

Kaupke, Charles L. *Forty Years on the Kings River: 1917–1957.* Kings River Water Association, 1957.

Kings County Centennial Committee. *Kings County, A Pictorial History.* 1992.

Kings County Historical Society. *Kings County: A Short History.* 1987.

Lemoore Centennial Committee. *Lemoore Centennial: 1873–1973.* 1973.

Menefee, Eugene L., and Fred A Dodge. *History of Tulare and Kings Counties, California, with Biographical Sketches.* Los Angeles: Historic Record Company, 1913.

Pioneer Letters, typescript. Kings County Library, Hanford.

Preston, William L. *Vanishing Landscapes: Land and Life in the Tulare Basin.* University of California Press, 1981.

Small, K. E., and J. Larry Smith. *History of Tulare County, California and Kings County.* The S. J. Clark Publishing Company, 1926.

Smith, Wallace. *Garden of the Sun.* Lymanhouse, 1939.

William Hull Papers in the California State Archive, AC91-06-10. *Miscellaneous Working Papers*, Canals and Ditches. Late 1880s.

web.luhsd.k12.ca.us/staff/Foundation/hall_of_fame_inductees.htm

www.esarey.us/reunion/Jesse1800.htm

www.esarey.us/reunion/

www.lemoorechamberofcommerce.com/pdf/downtown_lemoore_historic_walking_tour_guide.pdf

www.lemoore.com/sammm.htm

www.lemoore.com/special/history/default.html

www.sjvls.org/cgi-bin/dig_b2/ki